[handwritten signatures]

LAW &
LAUGHTER

THIS BOOK MADE POSSIBLE BY:

CROWE & DUNLEVY

DURBIN, LARIMORE & BIALICK, P.C.

STIPE LAW FIRM

BANCFIRST

William G. Paul

Stratton Taylor Law Firm/
    Taylor, Burrage, Foster, Mallett, Downs & Ramsey

Michael Burrage & Sean Burrage

McKinney & Stringer, P.C.

Garvin A. Isaacs

John M. Harmon

Jack & Nell Gardner

Honorable Vicki Miles-LaGrange

OKLAHOMA *TRACKMAKER* SERIES

Law & Laughter

The Life of Lee West

BY BOB BURKE &
DAVID L. RUSSELL

FOREWORD BY HENRY BELLMON

SERIES EDITOR: KENNY A. FRANKS
ASSOCIATE EDITOR: GINI MOORE CAMPBELL

Printed in Canada.
ISBN 1-885596-28-6
Library of Congress Catalog Number 2002105058
Designed by Sandi Welch/2W Design Group

Unless otherwise noted, photographs are from the
Lee and Mary Ann West Collection.

OKLAHOMA HERITAGE ASSOCIATION
201 NORTHWEST FOURTEENTH STREET
OKLAHOMA CITY, OKLAHOMA 73103

contents

*f*OR*e*W*O*RD

by Henry Bellmon

IT IS A WELL KEPT SECRET that the first appointment that
devout Democrat Lee West received as a judge came from a
Republican governor—namely me. I have kept the secret as
best I could, but now that we are both semi-retired, I might as well
admit it. Confession is good for the soul, they say.

I decided to use this remarkable occasion—a judge and a lawyer
writing a book about Judge West—to explain just how he wound
up in this position.

You see, Lee lived in Ada, Oklahoma, and that is in the old
Third Congressional District, the area of Oklahoma called "Little
Dixie," where the folks are still peeved at the party of Abraham
Lincoln for the "recent war of Northern aggression." Back in the
1960s, it was pretty hard to even find a Republican there. I looked
and looked and looked. I did not look for qualifications—I just
looked for a Republican.

Well, failing to find one, it fell to me to select the least offensive
Democrat I could find. And, also, a man who is without peer as a
quail hunter. So, just in case anyone wonders how the star of this
book got started in the judge business, you can give me the blame
for that. Now that was for a state district judge position—a trial
judge in Pontotoc County.

Lee West was the law south of the South Canadian River. But
while I am at it, I will tell of another well kept secret. Some may
wonder how federal judges, who have tenure and the power of our
great Constitution behind them, get their august positions. Well, a

federal judge is simply a lawyer who knows a United States Senator. As a former member of the Senate, I cannot think of a better system.

But, as one who has convinced the good folks of this state to make himself a frequently elected public official, I think that maybe my instincts, whether influenced by the fraternity of quail hunters or not, were good when it came to Lee West. I think he might have been just the kind of judge our framers, many of whom were also quail hunters, had in mind when they created the Third Branch of government.

I can say without reservation that the founders of our Constitution showed unbelievable courage and foresight when they set up the federal judiciary and made it more or less independent of the electoral process. The problem was—and is—that in our society some questions arise that are simply too tough, too hot, too politically dangerous for the political branches—the elected officials—to deal with. And the federal judiciary, which is bound only by the Constitution and the law of the land, and not by the will of the voters at the next election, makes these tough decisions that elected officials have a difficult time making.

For this, I believe we can all be thankful and I further believe that we need to recognize always the vital role that the federal judicial system plays in our process. Without this system, we would not have a country of which we would be so proud.

Further, I do not believe that we would have the Oklahoma we have today, if it were not for Lee West. The reality is that governors, when they appoint trial judges, and United States senators, who nominate federal judges for life terms, take their jobs very seriously.

When I appointed Lee West district judge, there was no one with such qualifications. An outstanding lawyer, who despite his Reba McEntire accent, or Little Dixie dipthongs, possessed a Master of Laws degree from Harvard University. His judgment and good sense were as well known as his wit and affable nature. I knew that Lee West would try, as John Adams' Massachusetts'

Constitution demands, to make this a "government of laws and not of men." Lee would apply the law skillfully, but also fairly and equally to the litigants who came before him.

Time has repeatedly vindicated my choice.

HENRY BELLMON
Former Governor of Oklahoma and United States Senator

acknowledgments

L EE WEST HAS A WONDERFUL FAMILY—a fact we have known for years. But our appreciation for his wife, Mary Ann; his daughters, Kim and Jennifer; his sister Deloyce West Johnson; and niece, Sandra Mantooth, has grown during the process of gathering information for Lee's biography. They were gracious and more than cooperative by sharing memories and photographs.

Lee also has wonderful friends. They provided details of a funny story or a good bird hunt—glimpses into the heart and soul of Lee West. Among those who granted interviews or wrote of their friendship with Lee were President Jimmy Carter; Griffin Bell; Henry Bellmon; David Boren; Andrew "Andy" Coats; William "Bill" Paul; Robert Henry; Marian Opala; Stratton Taylor; Thomas Word, Jr.; Preston Trimble; Burck Bailey; Joe Packnett; Joe Stamper; Austin Deaton, Jr.; John Harmon; Jim Gassaway; Juliana Winters; Robert Middlekauff; Barney Ward; John Golden; Jack Cornelius; Bernie Ille; J.B. Beall; Robert E. Lee; Lee Jenkins; J. Duke Logan; Stephen Jones; and Parke Brinkley.

Debbie Neill, Eric Dabney, Stephanie Ayala, and Laura Saddison provided editorial assistance. Anna Hubbard was a great help with photographs. Lee's longtime administrative assistant, Wilma House, spent dozens of hours typing and editing the Judge's memoirs and recollections.

Thanks to our manuscript reviewers—George Nigh; Stratton Taylor; Thomas S. Word, Jr.; John Harmon; Tim Leonard; J. Duke

Logan; Steve Dow; Cindy Smith; Baxter Black; and Marcia and George Davis—our expert editors, Dr. Kenny Franks and Gini Moore Campbell—and book designer extraordinaire, Sandi Welch.

Finally, we are indebted to the Oklahoma Heritage Association, its president, Dr. Paul Lambert, and chairman of the board, Pat Henry, for their support in preserving great Oklahoma stories such as the saga of Lee West.

In addition to the contributors listed on the half-title page, donations to make this publication possible were received from David L. Boren; Judge Thomas R. Brett; Tom R. Cornish; Robert B. Milsten; Joe Stamper; and Dan and Dawn Webber.

BOB BURKE
DAVID RUSSELL
2002

IT WAS ONE OF THOSE LARGER-THAN-LIFE, star-studded evenings in Washington, D.C. Splattered applause from spectators lined up outside the White House gate greeted limousine after limousine as they slowed for admission to an invitation-only state affair hosted by President Gerald Ford and First Lady Betty Ford.

A sharply dressed uniformed Secret Service guard nodded his approval as the sleek black carriers of the government's elite rolled by, unloaded their passengers, and orderly parked in freshly-marked spaces.

Then, the crowd began cheering. The next vehicle awaiting approval for entrance onto the grounds of the most famous house in the world was a 1972 green and white Dodge clubcab pickup with an Oklahoma license plate. A backup Secret Service agent inside the guardhouse took a second look at the pickup that sported dog boxes in the back. He thought to himself, "Is that a saddle in the back seat? Who is this coming to the White House?"

Inside the pickup truck was a beautiful woman, dressed in a flowing white gown. That was Mary Ann West. The driver, also dressed to the nines in his black tuxedo, was Lee West, a member of the Civil Aeronautics Board. West, whose prowess as a champion bird dog trainer and bird hunter was known at the highest levels of government, showed his White House pass that lay on the sun-baked pickup dash. With a nod of approval from the guard who smiled at the sight of sweaty horse pads in the back seat, the Dodge pickup with its well-dressed occupants rolled slowly toward the portico of the White House.

Members of the White House honor guard, who had been bored by the endless stream of limousines delivering celebrated guests such as Barbara Walters and Alan Greenspan, now took note of the pickup with the dog boxes jutting above the tail gate that was slightly dented from unloading dogs on rocky hillsides. The large crowd outside the gate cheered louder as Lee drove his truck around the circle drive. Members of the honor guard, standing at attention with the shiniest rifles Lee had ever seen, had a wide grin beneath their tailored hats.

The pickup belched slightly as Lee pulled in front of the White House entrance. A full colonel opened Mary Ann's door to let her alight from the pickup. Then Lee drove his truck and parked it alongside the sea of limousines that had brought a bevy of high federal government officials to the White House dinner.

To no one's surprise, Lee's Dodge was the only pickup in the White House parking lot. As he straightened his bow tie, Lee remembered how he had decided to drive his truck to the White House. Mary Ann had desperately wanted to attend the dinner— Lee was not overly excited about it. As a compromise, they went— but Lee got to drive his Dodge.

As Lee ambled up the long set of steps that led to the White House entrance, he thought, "It's a long way from Antlers, Oklahoma, to the White House, even if only for dinner."

> *We were too poor to paint—and too proud to whitewash.*
>
> L E E   W E S T

HaRD times
in LIttLe DIXIe

THE GREAT DEPRESSION and Lee Roy West arrived in Oklahoma at about the same time in the fall of 1929. One was bad—one was good—but both left lasting, indelible marks upon the face and landscape of the Sooner State. Both are important chapters in Oklahoma's colorful and unique history.

The BAD event—the Great Depression—began in October, 1929, as the stock market crashed and launched the worst and longest period of high unemployment and low business activity in modern history. Banks failed, factories and stores closed, and millions of Americans were left jobless and homeless.

The suffering in Oklahoma almost dealt a fatal blow to the young state that was still struggling with an agriculture-based economy that was badly faltering. Farmers had little or no income—most farmland in the state was occupied by tenant farmers.

Weather contributed to Oklahoma's problems. A searing drought blanketed the state until even normally wet Pushmataha County in southeastern Oklahoma, home to Lee West's parents, was dessicated. Dust storms gave birth to the term "dust bowl" and sand blew in such quantities that travelers lost their way, chickens went to roost at noon, airports closed, and trains stopped.[1]

In 1929, Oklahoma's per capita income was nearly 70 percent of the national average. Three years later, the per capita income dropped to just $216, half the depressed national average. Oklahoma farmers quit the land and moved to town to hunt for jobs. Farm foreclosures were daily events.

Pushmataha County was originally part of the Choctaw Nation, the lands ceded to the Choctaws when the federal government drove them from their lands in Mississippi during the 1830s. One of the major districts of the Choctaw Nation that existed until Oklahoma statehood in 1907 was the Pushmataha District—named for the great Choctaw leader, Pushmataha. At statehood, the name was assigned to the odd-shaped county that encompassed the Kiamichi River and Little River valleys and the rugged, forested mountains that lay between them.

Pushmataha County was in the heart of the area of Oklahoma known as "Little Dixie." Legend has it that the counties in the southeastern corner of the Sooner State were named Little Dixie because their terrain, stifling humidity, and Democratic politics were somewhat akin to those of the Old South.[2]

The Great Depression adversely affected Pushmataha County like it did the other areas of Oklahoma. In fact, the bottom had dropped out of the rural economy in southeast Oklahoma before 1929. Farmers could not sell cotton for enough money to repay loans for seed and cheap implements which they used to till the dry soil. Cattle and hog prices were so low that ranchers could not turn a profit.

Oklahoma's legendary United States Senator, Robert S. Kerr, observed the Depression and wrote, "Like a siren of doom, wild winds screamed…blowing topsoil by the tons from the parched, dry earth. Thousands of good farm families, consisting of the best human stock of our nation, loaded their jalopies and started westward in search of a new land. The dust and the heartbreaks were a blight on our times."[3]

The West family stayed in Oklahoma and, like most people in Pushmataha County, was very poor. But the fact that the family did not leave during the Depression said something about their grit and determination. Robert E. Lee, longtime columnist for *The Daily Oklahoman*, theorized, "A lot of Okies went west...a lot of Oklahomans stayed behind and built a strong state."[4]

The Wests lived on rented land in an old farmhouse that had no running water or indoor restrooms and was heated by wood stoves. But, at least they ate well. Any family that had even a tiny patch of ground used skills of raising food taught them by their ancestors to plant and harvest corn, potatoes, okra, squash, and green beans—vegetables the women could can and place in "fruit jars" so the family could have something to eat during the long winters.

Oklahoma was hit earlier and harder by the Great Depression than almost any state. Author John Steinbeck perpetuated that fact forever in his mythical description of the Joad family being driven off their Oklahoma land and forced to find a new home in California. Steinbeck's description of the times in *The Grapes of Wrath* aptly portrayed the condition of the world that awaited the birth of Lee West in 1929. Steinbeck wrote:

> The sun flared down on the growing corn day after day until a line of brown spread along the edge of each green bayonet. The clouds appeared, and went away, and in a while they did not try any more. The weeds grew darker green to protect themselves, and they did not spread any more. The surface of the earth crusted, a thin hard crust, and as the sky became pale, so the earth became pale, pink in the red country and white in the gray country."[5]

It was Steinbeck who birthed the name "Okies" for tens of thousands of Oklahomans who left the sun-scorched land and headed west during the Great Depression, a scourge of a heritage that has taken nearly two-thirds of a century to reverse, especially in the minds of those who lived through the terrible days of the 1930s.

The West family lived in the gray country, as Steinbeck called it, so named because of its dark-colored soil that lay among the rocks that had fallen from the peaks into the valleys in some distant time.

In October, 1929, as Calvin "Cal" West and his wife, Nicie Hill West, heard bits and pieces about the stock market crash and bad times that lay ahead, they prepared for the birth of a child. They lived in Bobtown, a tiny community that has long since faded from official maps and disappeared from the northern Pushmataha County landscape. Bobtown was near Clayton, a slightly larger community, made up of farmers, ranchers, and a few merchants in northern Pushmataha County. Cal's principal occupation was that of a horse trader but he had acquired a small herd of cattle and grazed them on a piece of rented land near Clayton.

Clayton was in the Kiamichi River Valley—virtually surrounded by mountains: to the northeast, the Potato Hills, the west, the Jack Fork Mountains, and the south, the Kiamichi Mountains. The town was founded in 1887 when the Saint Louis and San Francisco Railroad, commonly called the "Frisco," was extended through the Ouachita Mountains. It was named for Clayton, Missouri, a suburb of St. Louis.[6]

The terrain around Clayton was rugged and heavily timbered. Large deer and wild turkey populations made it a paradise for sportsmen and for the Depression-laden families who depended upon wild game for their major meat supply. Many of the local residents made their sparse living at sawmills. Men labored in the forests to cut large pine trees and haul them several miles into Clayton and surrounding railroad towns such as Dunbar, Eubanks, Wadena, and Kosoma. From there, the finished lumber was transported by rail to distant markets.

Clayton had a few storefront businesses along a two-block main thoroughfare on State Highway 2 that weaved its way along the Kiamichi River from the county seat, Antlers, into the mountains above Clayton. A service station, grocery store, and old-time hardware store anchored the local economy.

Cal West had an interesting pioneer ancestry. He was born February 10, 1890, in Yell County, Arkansas, on Petit Jean Mountain in present day Petit Jean State Park, named for a young French girl who disguised herself as a cabin boy and sailed to America and the rugged Arkansas hills during the period of French exploration of the New World. She died of a fever and was buried on the mountain that bears her name.

Cal's great great grandfather, John West, was born in 1788 in Bladen County, North Carolina, but moved to Tennessee sometime after 1820. His son, Cal's great grandfather, Owen West, born in North Carolina in 1819, brought his family westward from Tennessee in 1853 and settled along the Petit Jean River near Centerville, Arkansas. At the time Owen West and his wife Jennie moved into a vacant log cabin beside a large spring that ran into Cedar Creek on top of Petit Jean Mountain, only two other white families lived in the area. The dirt-floored cabin now sets in Petit Jean State Park and is known as the "pioneer cabin." It was moved from its original location when Lake Bailey was created and flooded the area.

Owen's eldest son, James McDaniel "Mack" West, was born in 1843 in Tennessee before his father brought the family to Arkansas. At an early age, though illiterate, he believed that God had given him a special gift of being able to read the Bible. He was "called" to the ministry and served for years as an itinerant Baptist preacher, traveling the area by horseback, preaching, performing marriages, and saying words of encouragement when pioneers died.

Mack married Talitha Morris who gave birth to a son, Joseph J. West, on Round Mountain, near Ola, Arkansas, on January 26, 1863. Only a few months later Mack joined Company I of the First Arkansas Cavalry and served the Union effort in the Civil War. After the war, he moved near the rest of the West family in Yell County.

The seven sons of Owen West. Back row, left to right, Ephriam Miles West, Elijah A. West, Elisha W. West, and William Wiley West. Front row, left to right, Samuel West, John H. West, and James McDaniel "Mack" West, the great grandfather of Lee Roy West.

Joseph married Sarah Jane Hamilton in 1881 in nearby Conway County. Their sixth child was Cal West.

Cal married Annie Hampton in 1907 and had three children, William Oliver "Jack" West, Birt West, and Othel "Pete" West. Cal was an overseer for a cotton farm along the Arkansas River. After he and Annie were divorced, he met Nicie Hill James, born in Blue Ball, Arkansas, in 1894, who arrived at the farm in a wagonload of workers who came to help bring in the cotton crop. At the time, Nicie was living with her mother, Mary Margaret Morgan, and Nicie's two-year-old daughter, Allie Bernice James. Nicie's husband, Carl James, had enlisted in World War I and had never been heard of again. In 1919, Cal and Nicie were married in Fort Smith, Arkansas, and moved to Horatio, in southern Arkansas, to work on a cotton farm. Their first child, Juanita, was born March 27, 1923, at Horatio.

Soon, Cal moved his family to Clayton, Oklahoma. Deloyce West was born there on March 18, 1926, and Calvin West, Jr., was born in Clayton November 9, 1927.

It was just after Thanksgiving, on November 26, 1929, that the GOOD event of 1929 came to Oklahoma. Lee Roy West was the first of his siblings to be born in a house with a doctor in attendance. The three older West children had been born in a "top wagon" used by the family during trips to the cotton or wheat harvest or looking for horses to buy and sell. A top wagon was a regular wagon equipped with hoops, over which canvas was stretched.

Lee Roy's older siblings were responsible for much of his care and certainly his recreation in the rocky yard outside the West rent house. The children often rode a pony named Midget. Lee's first recollection is of being tied into Midget's small saddle that had been cinched tightly on the back of a huge Angora billy goat. The goat escaped his captors. Lee Roy remembered, "Since the goat had no withers, the saddle was in fact soon under the goat's belly rather than on his back. Since I was securely tied to the saddle, I was upside down under the rampaging goat."[7]

Lee Roy yelled at the top of his voice every time his head hit another rock. He was soon rescued by his mother, the first act that the youngster remembered in forming his opinion that he had the best mother who ever lived. He also recalled a "certain amount of satisfaction at witnessing rather severe corporal punishment being administered" to his siblings.[8]

Before Lee Roy was six years old, he began his formal education at the Clayton elementary school. The Great Depression was nearly six years old also and times grew harder in Pushmataha County. In the winter of 1935, Cal West gave up trying to make a living in the area and loaded the family's belongings onto a bobtailed truck and moved during frigid weather to Blanchard in south central Oklahoma. Young Lee Roy rode in the cab of the truck with his parents while his two sisters and brother lay hidden among the mattresses and bed clothes in the back, seeking escape from the cold Oklahoma winter.

Lee Roy did not handle the move to Blanchard well. He was frightened of his new school teacher and thought his classmates were unfriendly. One especially tall boy chased Lee Roy home each day, causing many tears unless Lee Roy's brother or sisters happened to be nearby to protect him. Lee Roy remembered, "I was miserable and for the only time in my life, failed academically. I was not promoted at the end of the year."[9]

Lee Roy's siblings were somewhat ashamed of their "retarded brother." When asked about him, they had a ready excuse, saying, "He was hurt while being dragged by a goat when he was smaller."[10]

Cal found horse-trading around Blanchard was as lean as back in Pushmataha County. He could not make monthly payments on his truck and lost it to the bank. Both his occupation and recreation were affected by the loss of the truck. Lee Roy and his brother enjoyed riding in the back of the truck on the open prairies around Blanchard while shooters, armed with shotguns and riding on the front fenders, shot what seemed to be thousands of jackrabbits that roamed the land looking for food. Instead, they ended up as food. Nicie West called them "Hoover Hogs," a somewhat derisive and accusatory reference to the fact that many Democrats blamed the Great Depression upon the policies of Republican President Herbert Hoover. The Wests ate rabbit until "it literally came out of their ears."[11]

Cal resumed his trading activities out of the back of a wagon pulled by a team of horses. In the fall of 1936, Lee Roy returned to the Blanchard elementary school and was not nearly as frightened of his teacher as before. However, he was still terrified of the school bully. His parents gave him conflicting advice on how to handle the situation. His father said, "Fight him instead of running and he'll soon leave you alone." His mother advised, "Make friends with him. If he thinks you want to be friends, he will quit hitting you."[12]

Lee Roy was confused—so he did both. He fought the bully and then later played marbles with him. The strategy worked—the bully stopped whipping up on Lee Roy.

Cal's business was anything but successful. He mortgaged all his trading horses for as much as the local banker would loan. Then, trying to have enough money to live on, sold the horses, one by one. However, he failed to pay off the bank and found himself in violation of the state law that prohibits the sale of mortgaged property. He was left with one team of horses and many mortgages.

To escape the trap he had laid for himself, he loaded the entire family into their one wagon and pulled out of Blanchard under the cover of night. They traveled west to Chickasha, possibly to "throw off" law enforcement officials, and then headed toward eastern Oklahoma. After several days of hard travel, they arrived in McCurtain, Oklahoma, and camped with Gene Ratteree on his ranch for a few days.

Breaking camp, the Wests began the trek to Clayton via Talihina where family friends, Jim and Zora Watley, lived. However, one night while Nicie was cooking supper on an open campfire, sheriff's deputies arrived and arrested Cal and took him to the Latimer County jail in Wilburton.

Nicie was left with her four children by the side of the creek with a wagon and team composed of a black mare and one-eyed yellow gelding. She moved her children into a vacant cabin that had no screens on the windows. The family that owned the cabin was generous and allowed Nicie to harvest vegetables from their large garden. They also put the West children to work in their sorghum mill. The only pay was enough food to keep Nicie and the children alive. Nicie fed the children a lot of cornbread, sorghum molasses, sowbelly, and vegetables—food she cooked on a Dutch oven in the backyard.

The devoted Nicie hitchhiked to the homes of friends in Pushmataha County to borrow enough money to free Cal from jail. It was not an easy task because most everyone in Little Dixie was as

Cal West was a horse trader, bootlegger, and managed roadhouses and clubs in Pushmataha County. Legendary Antlers lawyer, Joe Stamper, remembered Cal, "He was a very entertaining guy. He had a great gift of gab. If he was living today, he would be one of those fellows in a high binding real estate deal where you wrap the mortgage around twice and then bend it back over." [13]

ABOVE: Calvin "Cal" West, Lee Roy's father, right, had a difficult time making enough money to keep his family fed during the Great Depression. In this photograph with Cal is William Oliver "Jack" West, his oldest son by his first marriage.

destitute as the Wests. However, after several weeks, she accumulated enough money to meet Cal's bail.

Meanwhile, the children had enrolled in school at Talihina. But after a few days, with their father a free man again, Jim Watley loaded up the few West family possessions and moved them to Antlers, the county seat of Pushmataha County.

> *I had the best mother in the world. She was our sole moral beacon and entirely unselfish in her love and devotion to her children.*
>
> LEE WEST

settLINg DOWN *in* aNtLeRs

LIVING IN ANTLERS was a turning point in Lee Roy's young life. It was the first time he felt stability, a "settled feeling" that is derived from living in one location for more than a few months. And, more significantly, he immediately fell in love with a beautiful brunette in his second grade classroom at Brantly Grade School. Her name was Mary Ann Ellis who did not know for some time that Lee Roy West existed.[1]

From a tender age, Lee was a champion of the oppressed. While still in elementary school, his mother and sister noticed him coming home from school every day looking as if he had been in a fight. What they discovered was that Lee had been protecting a mentally impaired schoolmate, "Buzzy" Wonsch, who was being beaten up by a group of bullies on the walk home from school. Lee continued to protect the boy until the bullies finally gave up because they grew tired of having to beat Lee up also. Lee thought Buzzy actually provided protection for him on the treacherous walk home.[2]

One of Lee's classmates at Brantly Grade School was Joe Packnett, his lifelong friend. Packnett predicted Lee's greatness at an early age, "He showed signs of greatness by picking up on the colors and realizing that Dick, Spot, and Jane were somehow to be a vital part of our education even though they were not politically motivated or slanted either left or right."[3]

The Wests lived in a one-room cabin, one of several buildings known as the "Quaid Cabins," located on the east edge of Antlers. The town took its name from the antlers of a deer nailed on a tree, marking a favorite camping place beside a major spring of water. Antlers was the Record Town for Recording District No. 24 in Indian Territory. Its post office was established August 26, 1887.[4]

The West cabin had a wood-burning cook stove and two beds. The adults and the two daughters occupied the beds while Lee Roy and his brother, Calvin, Jr., slept on a pallet on the floor. There was an outdoor privy and the boys carried water from a well a half block away. Rent on the cabin was $1.00 per week.

Lee's wardrobe consisted of two pair of overalls—one striped, one blue—bought each year just before school started, usually with money Lee earned doing odd jobs for neighbors. Lee's mother always made certain he had one pair of clean overalls to wear. Each day she or Lee's older sisters washed out the dirty pair and readied it for the following day.

Lee Roy's parents were almost total contrasts. His mother had only a third grade education but was energetic and innovative in making ends meet for her family. Lee reflected, "She was entirely unselfish and totally supportive of her children and eventually her grandchildren. She was the one solid backbone of the family—no matter how dire the circumstances. With the motherly wit necessary to cope, she was the sole moral beacon we had."[5]

Nicie made most of her children's clothing, raised and butchered chickens and pigs, and cultivated a large vegetable garden. She boiled her laundry in an iron pot heated over an open fire. She not only did her family's washing but took in laundry from neighbors to earn a few extra dollars. She used lye soap that she made from hog lard rendered when butchering hogs. After Nicie washed the clothes on a scrub board and rinsed them in well water, she hung them on a drooping clothesline to dry. She starched and ironed the clothes with irons heated on the cook stove or over a fire.

When her husband was unable to work because of a broken leg, Nicie got a job with the Works Progress Administration, one of President Franklin D. Roosevelt's New Deal programs designed to help Americans escape the throes of the Great Depression. Nicie worked as a bookbinder for $21.00 per month. For more than a year, she managed to support her husband and four children on the salary, living in the one-room cabin in Antlers. Years after her death, Lee reflected, "My love and respect and admiration for my mother has increased every day of my life."[6]

Cal West was another story. He was cheerful and a joy to be around because of his "joshing, joking attitude toward everyone."[7] Even when the family was a short step from the poorhouse, there was plenty of laughter and merriment. He was a smart man, even though he could neither read nor write.

He was an especially clever horse trader who used many unethical tricks to disguise an animal's age or condition. He perfected the trick of rolling back the age on a smooth-mouthed horse. When a horse or mule reaches the age of nine, the animal becomes smooth-mouthed because the natural cups in their teeth are usually worn smooth. Cal dug out the mild cup in the smooth teeth of an animal, put a dab of caustic on the teeth to color the cup, and, as Lee recalled, "made a six-year-old horse out of one several years older." [8]

Cal also used shoe polish to cover gray hairs when mules reached advanced age. Another trick was to blow air into the sunken pocket above the eyes of a mule to make them appear younger.

Tragically for the West family, Cal was an immoral man, frequently involving himself with other women. Lee remembered his father's lack of discretion, often flaunting his relationships with other women in front of the children. Lee is convinced that Cal

Cal and Nicie West were a study in contrasts as parents. Nicie never stopped loving Cal even though he was unfaithful. She was the glue that held the family together.

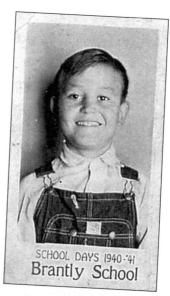

Lee's school picture at Brantly Grade School in Antlers in the 1940-1941 school year.

SCHOOL DAYS 1940-'41
Brantly School

fathered at least one or two children during one long relationship.[9]

The pain that Nicie endured because of the philandering of her husband did not show on her face. Lee remembered, "She bore it stoically, simply because she had four children and very few options. Somehow, she never quit loving my father."[10]

Cal was an indifferent parent—crude in his advice to his children. When he told Lee about the birds and the bees, he suggested that his son never bargain with a prostitute while sexually aroused (although he used much cruder language in making the statement). Cal thought such a condition put a man at a disadvantage during the bargaining process.[11]

Violence was part of Cal West's life. He frequently engaged in physical combat, especially during his stints as a bouncer in several honky-tonks or dance halls that he owned or managed during Lee's formative years. He regularly used a sap stick, black jack, or a pair of iron knuckles to maintain order in his bars and eject a reluctant customer if the need arose. His favorite mandate when fights arose in his establishments was, "Move it outside if you're gonna' fight."[12]

Lee Roy remembered the day that the United States entered World War II. He was 12 years old when the Japanese bombed Pearl Harbor on December 7, 1941. Lee Roy recalled the day because he and his brother arose before daylight that morning and walked five miles south of Antlers to hunt squirrels with a friend. The friend had two young blue tick hounds, one named Hitler and another named Mussolini. The boys killed three squirrels and a large chicken hawk. The friend's mother fried the meat for Sunday

Cal West, right, and Grover Raymond "Buck" Mantooth who married Lee's sister, Nita, in 1941. Buck died in 1966 in Yuma, Arizona.

dinner, the only time Lee Roy remembered eating chicken hawk.

At about the time World War II began, Cal turned to honky-tonks and bootlegging as his primary source of income. The term, "bootlegger," came from early moonshiners conducting much of their business at night and sticking bottles of "hooch" or "shine" into their loose-fitting boots. Moonshine whiskey was made from hops, malt, ground corn, and sugar. The ingredients fermented until a thick cap formed on the top. When the cap fell, like a cake falling, the sour mash was ready to run through a still, a contraption hidden far from the watchful eye of neighbors or law enforcement officers. Fifty gallons of mash usually made about five gallons of whiskey. It was a dangerous business because federal agents, commonly called "revenuers," could arrest a moonshiner and a federal judge might sentence him to a year busting rocks at the federal penitentiary in Leavenworth, Kansas.[13]

Southeastern Oklahoma had a different way of dealing with the sale of illegal whiskey than many other areas of the state. If Cal or

Lee's half-brother, Birt, and sister, Juanita, or "Nita" in front of the Rainbow Inn sign. The Rainbow Inn was a honky-tonk that Cal West owned outside Antlers. Both Lee and Cal, Jr., spent their teenage years dealing poker on weekends at their father's roadhouse. Lee dared not drink alcohol. His reasoning—he saw enough drunks to know that he did not want to be one.

any other local lawbreaker was to be arrested, he preferred to be arrested by local lawmen. Law enforcement officials had a reputation of great tolerance—of looking the other way if lawbreakers had timely made campaign contributions or otherwise expressed support for the local sheriff or his "relatives."[14]

Oklahoma was a dry state and state law prohibited the sale of liquor. However, federal law allowed the sale of bonded liquor. Cal bought a federal liquor stamp for a nominal fee and kept federal agents at bay, as long as they did not catch him selling illegal moonshine. But, he was in constant violation of state law which prohibited his common practice of selling commercial or bonded whiskey at the Rainbow Inn, a shady club Cal owned east of Antlers on the highway to Rattan. During the war, servicemen flocked to the Rainbow Inn from nearby Camp Maxey, just across the Texas line at Paris.

Cal had a well-earned reputation as a man who would not back down from a fight. He kept a loaded pistol behind the bar and would not hesitate to pistol whip an opponent. After a few drinks, it was not uncommon for fights to break out. Most of the brawls were moved outside and considered part of the nightly entertainment. No great harm was done except for a few skinned heads and knuckles.[15]

Lee's sister, Deloyce, or "Dee," to her family and friends.

The most violent fight Lee witnessed involved two extremely muscular brothers from Coalgate, Oklahoma, who aggressively hustled a single girl customer at the club. The girl became fright-

Left to right, Lee's sister, Juanita, or "Nita;" brother-in-law, Buck Mantooth; sister, Deloyce, or "Dee;" Nicie West; and Cal West.

ened and complained to Cal who asked the brothers to "ease off." A confrontation quickly developed. Cal pulled his handy pistol, but one of the brothers rushed him and forced him into one of the booths that circled the dance hall.

During the scuffle, Cal held the gun so tightly that both pistol grips were twisted loose from the handle. In the process, his forefinger was severely lacerated by the trigger guard. Lee Roy's

Calvin West, Jr., joined the Navy after he graduated from high school.

older sister, Juanita, rushed from behind the counter with a blackjack and laid four or five roundhouse blows to the man's head, stunning him, and preventing him from completely overpowering her father. Cal emerged from underneath his attacker and commenced to beat the man with his pistol.

At the same time, one of the West's neighbors and assistant bouncer at the Rainbow Inn, John Youngblood, was fighting the other brother. Youngblood hit the man with a heavy pistol that discharged loudly. Fortunately, the bullet penetrated the floor rather than some of the bystanders. Lee Roy, his sister, and other onlookers thought surely the second brother who lay quivering on the floor was dead. Cal said, "Damn, John, did you have to shoot him?" Youngblood said, "I didn't mean to!" Everyone was relieved when the man regained consciousness and revealed he had not been shot.[16]

Cal had his bluff in on locals in Pushmataha County. Once he bought several cartons of black market cigarettes from a man introduced by a gambler by the name of Jack Davis—cigarettes he planned to resell at the Rainbow Inn. When Cal opened the boxes, they contained nothing but sawdust. Cal was angry, and with Lee in tow, approached Davis who he considered to be his friend. Davis assured Cal he had nothing to do with the scam. Cal looked Davis in the eye and said, "Jack, you and I have been friends for a long time and I'm sure you didn't have anything to do with that, but if I don't have my money by sundown, I'll kill you." No one, including Lee or Davis, doubted Cal's threat. The money was repaid on the spot without further discussion.[17]

Cal walked a fine line with local law enforcement officials. The Rainbow Inn was once labeled a public nuisance and closed for 30 days by the sheriff because of reports that Cal pistol-whipped rabble-rouser customers.

While Cal was trying to earn sufficient money to keep his family in groceries, Lee was interested in obtaining an education. He was only slightly above average both as a student and athlete during his grade school and junior high school years. However, Lee did develop a deep love for reading. Both of his sisters began reading to him at an early age. They read *Robinson Crusoe* and *Gulliver's Travels* by the light of a kerosene lamp called a "coal oil lamp." Lee especially enjoyed Alfred Noyes' poem, *The Highwayman*, which he requested to be read over and over again.[18]

Lee also enjoyed the writings of Will James, Jack London, and Zane Grey. He slowly developed a habit as a voracious reader, a habit he still recommends to anyone who wants to succeed in life.

In junior high school, Lee harbored dreams of becoming a cowboy. He loved animals, especially horses and dogs. Because his father was in the business of trading horses, there were always animals around to ride. If there was a calf or goat roping within riding distance, Lee and his brother were probably in attendance. Many times after a roping, Lee and Cal, Jr., would strip the saddles from their mounts and challenge other riders to match races, with the winner taking home a wager of a quarter, fifty cents, or even a dollar.

Serious horse races were run out of a gate—complete with jockey saddles. Lee, weighing only 100 pounds, was a jockey on his own horse and for other horse owners in races that drew bets as high as $5 or $10.

Lack of talent ended Lee's hopes of being a calf roper. As he continued to grow and gain weight, his dream of being a jockey disappeared as well. However, he still hoped to be a horse trainer. One success at that business was the training of a buckskin named Hawk that he sold for $500 during high school, a lot of money in 1946.

While daydreaming of a life as a cowboy, Lee became acquainted with a Choctaw Indian named Pete Graham—he pronounced it "Grim." Graham frequented Lee's father's club and most often purchased only a half pint of Old American whiskey, the cheapest brand. Legend had it that Graham had been a fairly good saddle bronc rider before becoming an alcoholic derelict. When he uncapped the liquor, he ritually threw the cap over his shoulder and announced in a rodeo announcer-quality, loud voice, "Pete Grim, coming out of chute number two on Screwdriver." Then Graham proceeded to swallow the entire half pint of whiskey without removing it from his mouth.[19]

Lee once asked Graham if he had ever successfully ridden Screwdriver. Graham replied, "Never, he screwed me into the ground eight feet in front of him every time."[20]

The Old American whiskey also had about the same effect upon Graham.

Lee picked up a few Choctaw phrases from the many Choctaws who lived in Pushmataha County. Joe Packnett, John Olive, and "Dude" Coffelt became his close friends. Some of the less educated full blood Choctaws spoke English with sometimes comical results. They frequently mixed up "he" and "she" when talking about someone. When ordering cheese at the grocery store, they nearly always said, "Gimmie some of them cheese."[21]

Pete Graham once recited a traumatic incident of his life to Lee. Pete was in the woods with a woman who was not his wife. They were in a compromising position when the woman's gun carrying husband discovered them. Pete said he jumped up and ran through the woods as fast as he could with the husband firing a .22-caliber rifle at him. The wife, attempting to urge Pete to zigzag to miss the flurry of bullets, yelled, "Run winding, Pete, run winding." Happily, Pete avoided being shot but any romantic feelings he felt toward the lady dissolved during the run for his life.[22]

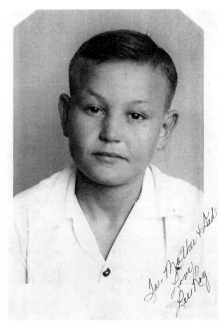

In junior high school, Lee Roy changed his name to simply "Leroy." School yearbooks and newspaper articles about his achievements in the classroom and on athletic fields reflected the change.

On one bitterly cold morning in the winter of 1946, Lee arose at dawn to run before school. When he stepped off his front porch, he saw Pete sitting on the ground with his back against the wheel of a bobtailed truck parked in the front yard. Pete wore nothing but a light shirt, blue jeans, and a pair of old cowboy boots with large holes in the soles. Lee asked Pete, "How long have you been out here?" Pete replied, "I don't know—all night, mebbe.'"

Lee helped Pete into Cal's Place, the beer joint that Cal operated near the West home. Juanita was building a fire and helped Pete to a spot near the smoldering embers. Pete asked for a drink of whiskey, a request that Juanita filled quickly. While Lee was outside running, Pete fell dead from the chair onto the floor. Lee and Juanita worried that their "thawing out" of Pete caused his early demise. Even though he qualified as a drunken derelict, they were still fond of him.[23]

LIGHTNING LEGS LEROY

AN INCIDENT AT THE ANTLERS SALE BARN during the summer before Lee entered Antlers High School resulted in a new nickname, "Lightning Legs Leroy."

Lee worked as an "alley boy" at the livestock auction on sale days helping drive livestock from holding pens into the auction ring and from the ring back to the pens when they were sold to the highest bidder. When an especially mean or wild animal was herded into the ring, someone usually yelled, "Fire in the hole!"

On one occasion, one of Lee's friends and co-workers failed to warn him that a mean and mad Brahma mother cow was headed his way. Lee remembered, "It didn't take long to scale the fence surrounding the auction ring with that ole momma in full pursuit."[1]

Thereafter, Bill Akard, the auctioneer and local wit, dubbed Lee as "Lightning Legs Leroy." The nickname stuck but was later shortened to "Lightnin' Legs" and eventually to just "Lightnin'." For several years Lee's cowboy and ranching friends referred to him by the nickname.

Lee had other close calls at the sale barn. Once, when Lee was trying to impress prospective buyers by riding a snappy little buckskin horse by them, auctioneer Akard yelled, "Well, bust him off down there and roll him over [turn him around] and let's see what kind of action he has." Lee dug his spurs into the 900-pound pony a little too deeply. Lee recalled, "My pony swallowed his head and threw me the full length of my bridle reins over his head. I did a complete somersault and landed on my back looking up at the sky." [2]

Akard walked to where Lee lay smarting from the bucking and said, "Lightnin', if you don't quit getting off that horse like that, you're gonna' ruin him." To this day, Lee cannot remember ever being more embarrassed and humiliated. The event went a long way toward convincing him that he did not have a future as a saddle bronc rider.

Another time, Lee and his friend, Lew Akard, were practicing calf roping on the Akard ranch west of Antlers. They had rigged a chute and gate to release calves into the pasture rather than into an enclosed roping arena. The pasture was cleared for about a half mile but then crossed a small creek with thick willow trees along each side and heavier timber beyond.

Lee was riding a green horse that did not have much experience with a calf roper on his back. One end of the lariat rope was tied to the saddle horn—Lee held the other end, ready to cast the loop over the escaping calf. When the calf came out of the gate, the horse broke hard, the front cinch of the saddle broke, and Lee hit the ground.

Somehow, the horse jerked all the slack out of the rope which was looped around Lee's right arm. As the horse headed across the pasture, Lee panicked. The horse was dragging him at breakneck speed toward a pasture full of almost solid trees. He knew that if the horse made the woods, he "was a goner."[3]

His friend, Lew, tried unsuccessfully to head the horse from the woods. But, in a lucky moment for Lee, the back cinch tightened around the horse's flank and the animal began to buck. That action slowed him down enough for Lee to regain his feet and get enough slack in the rope to get it off his wrist. No great damage was done except for the lasting mental image. More than half century later he still wakes up at night seeing the timber getting closer and closer.

During the same summer, Lee and several friends were riding horses toward the fairgrounds where a local calf roping contest was scheduled. They were practicing throwing loops at anything that moved. Two of Lee's other friends, Harry Ellis and Noel Page, drove by in a pickup truck. Noel waved at Lee with his hand out the passenger side of the truck. Without thinking, Lee threw his rope at Noel's upraised arm. Miraculously, the loop fell just an inch short. Lee remembered, "I was immediately nauseated upon realizing how dangerously close I came to endangering his life, or limb at least, because my rope was tied fast to the saddle horn." It was one time that Lee was grateful for his lack of talent as a calf roper. It caused him to often reflect how easy it is to cause damage to someone else.[4]

Until high school, Lee thought he would be a cowboy, a horse trainer, or an auctioneer, hoping to

High school was both an important and wonderful time of Lee's life. It was during this period that he began to believe in himself— to believe that he could accomplish things he had never even thought about before. He gained more and more confidence that he might be able to continue his education beyond high school—a thought that was foreign to his father and most of his ancestors.

earn enough money to purchase a small ranch. However, his dreams went far beyond Antlers, largely because of wonderful teachers and friends who encouraged him.

One such person was Bill Farr, assistant football coach and freshman mathematics teacher. Farr knew Lee's father and his background, yet encouraged Lee to do well in school to prepare for college. He always told Lee, "You can do as well as any of these other kids. If you want to go to college, you can, because you have a good mind."[5]

In his freshman year, Lee was elected president of his class. He made the high school football squad but did not play very much because of an excellent bunch of athletes including Orb Whaley, Sam Pace, Leonard Bryant, Bill Long, Don "Hobuck" Hendricks, and Leroy O'Quinn who were starters.

Other freshmen—Joe Packnett, Loyd Nelson, Grady Martin, Tom Olive, Charles Dale, Bill Redman—joined Lee in sorting through the dregs of leftover equipment, practiced hard, and began preparation for a future in football. Lee was encouraged to continue his football career by Farr and principal Earnest Hooser. The team won all but two of its regular season games but lost in the first round of the state playoffs.

Playing high school football was an important first step in Lee breaking out of the mold which his father's actions had cast for him in southeast Oklahoma. It was the first time that Lee had received any community attention. The bragging on his athletic skills was an encouragement to try harder—both athletically and academically.[6]

During Lee's sophomore year, his parents bought a café in the small town of Soper in Bryan County, nearly an hour's drive from Antlers. Lee's brother moved with his parents and enrolled at Soper High School. However, because Soper had no football team, Lee elected to stay in Antlers.

He lived with his sister Deloyce and her husband until they moved. He was only 15—but on his own. He worked part time repairing flats at a service station. Luckily, he was invited to live with the family of his friend, Roy Hernandez, the senior quarterback on the Antlers High School football team. Roy's father, a Mexican-Portuguese man nicknamed "Hot Tamale Jim," sold hot tamales from a cart that he wheeled around town. Even though the Hernandez family income was as low as anyone in town, they generously invited Lee to live with them. Lee donated his meager earnings to the family income. Lee remembered, "They were easily the warmest, most generous people I was ever around outside my own family. I will never be able to adequately repay their kindness and generosity."[7]

Lee was happy when his parents moved back to Antlers in the spring of 1945. Shortly after the family reunited in a small house on the west edge of Antlers, a tornado devastated the town. Lee was milking the family's lone cow when he heard the twister coming and saw the funnel pass a half mile south of him going in an easterly direction toward town.

The West house and barn suffered only slight damage but it was a different story in town. Hardly any of Antlers was standing. The twister killed 86 people. Lee, his brother, his father, and everyone they knew spent the night digging people out of the rubble and guiding search and rescue personnel from Camp Maxey.

One of the people buried in the tornado rubble was Lee's friend, David Pilley. Lee could hear David calling for help. As they got closer to him, David yelled, "You SOB's are standing on my head!"[8] Lee and several onlookers removed several feet of brick and debris and rescued David who survived with the help of a large silver plate implanted in his head. Several other people in the same building did not survive.

Mary Ann Ellis's house was demolished with her and her grandmother, Frances Medora Ellis, inside. Miraculously, Mary Ann escaped serious injury but nine people who lived on the same city block were killed.

In Lee's sophomore season, the Antlers football team was short on experience, size, speed, and talent. He was a starter both ways,

TORNADO AREA -ANTLERS, OKLA.-13 APRIL'45

Lee developed a healthy respect for the damage that can be inflicted by a tornado when he observed the twister that devastated Antlers, killing 86 people, on April 12, 1945. Lee was milking a cow when he saw the funnel heading toward downtown Antlers.

but it was a dismal campaign with only three wins. However, Lee was not disheartened. He continued to practice and train hard. He also started at shortstop on the school baseball team but admittedly had a hard time hitting curve balls.

Antlers hired a new football coach for Lee's junior year and the team performed better than the year before. George Strickland had played basketball at Oklahoma A & M, now Oklahoma State University. At Antlers, he coached football, basketball, and baseball. He was a disciplinarian who approached coaching as a teacher and a friend. "He was very effective in that almost all of us felt that he took a personal interest in us, our welfare and our future," Lee remembered, "Most athletes respect their high school coaches—but I had a genuine affection for him and felt that he did for me." [9]

During basketball practice one afternoon, Lee, called "Pud" by many of his friends, collided with fellow player Pete Holt's head. The collision broke off one of Lee's front teeth at the gums. Coach Strickland and W.A. Obuch, the school superintendent, knowing that Lee could not afford any dental work, tapped what they referred to as a "contingency athletic injury fund" and paid a dentist for the necessary repairs. Lee had to suffer a huge gap in his engaging smile for several weeks.

Definitely the best thing that happened to Lee in his junior year in high school was that he began dating Mary Ann Ellis, the daughter of a local drug store owner. Lee had been secretly in love with Mary Ann since the second grade. All of his silent efforts to pursue and impress her had proven ineffective. But in their junior year, Lee somehow convinced her to begin dating regularly, even though he had not yet persuaded her that she could not possibly go through life without him. According to Lee, "The fact that she started going out with me was the greatest morale booster I had ever received to that point in my life." [10]

The school newspaper, *The Antlers*, featured Lee as the student of the week in February, 1947. He was called, "perhaps one of the most original and striking personalities around school." The story reported that Lee had seen some interesting places like the Alamo, Fort Sam Houston, Arkansas, and Mississippi, but "says he likes Oklahoma the best and Antlers most of all." According to the report, Lee's favorite subject was typing and his favorite radio program was "The Supper Club." Hoagy Carmichael and the Mills Brothers were his favorite crooners. His favorite song was "To Each His Own." [11]

Lee's ambition, according to the aggressive high school columnist, was to be an athletic director and attend college at Oklahoma College for Women (OCW). That reference was obviously "tongue-in-cheek" because OCW only admitted women students. Lee told the reporter that he liked all types of girls but what he most

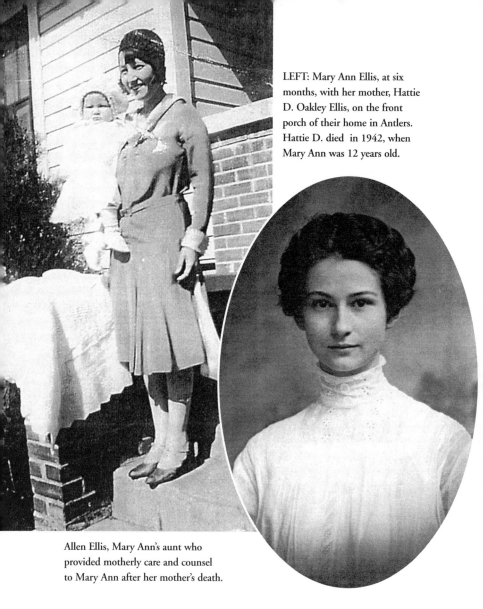

LEFT: Mary Ann Ellis, at six months, with her mother, Hattie D. Oakley Ellis, on the front porch of their home in Antlers. Hattie D. died in 1942, when Mary Ann was 12 years old.

Allen Ellis, Mary Ann's aunt who provided motherly care and counsel to Mary Ann after her mother's death.

liked was "their ability to get along with people, their personality and their friendliness." Lee also said he wanted to be a bachelor, an obvious lie.[12]

Lee and Mary Ann attended the First Christian Church in Antlers together. They were greatly influenced by Bill Pharr, a young, well-dressed minister who did not fit the stereotype of a rural Oklahoma minister in the 1940s. Pharr was dapper, almost to the point of being vain. He was well read, erudite, and an excellent speaker. He later left the ministry to head the Dallas, Texas, office of the National Conference of Christians and Jews.

Pharr's views on religious tolerance and ecumenicalism struck a chord with both Lee and Mary Ann. Pharr often spoke out against religious zealotry and frequently attacked sins that were committed "in God's name." One of Pharr's common prayers included the phrase, "Dear god, please protect us from some of your followers."[13]

Pharr had a positive impact on Lee in that he encouraged Lee's already extensive interest in reading and urged him to continue his education beyond high school.

During the summer of 1947, between Lee's junior and senior years, the West

Mary Ann as a sophomore at Antlers High School.

Bob Ellis, Mary Ann's father, owned Ellis Drug in Antlers.

RIGHT: Lee's fortunes turned positive in his junior year in high school when he began dating Mary Ann Ellis on a regular basis. He described the event as a giant morale booster.

BELOW: Lee decked out in the colors of the Antlers Bearcats. He was captain of the high school football team in his senior year. He played guard on both offense and defense. He was 5 feet 10 inches and weighed 166 pounds.

family migrated to California to work in the peach orchards. It was somewhat like a belated *Grapes of Wrath* trip made in a 1936 Ford that tended to get very hot crossing the mountains and the desert. "We resembled the Clampett family, without the oil money," Lee recalled.

When Lee, Calvin, Jr., and his parents arrived in California, they pitched a tent in the

yard of W.O. "Jack" West, Cal's son by his first marriage. Jack's generosity and patience were beyond belief as the Cal West clan lived in his yard the entire summer. Lee was able to save almost all the money he earned thinning peaches. He did not even get a haircut all summer. However, on the return trip to Oklahoma, the car broke down in Needles, California, and again in Nocona, Texas.

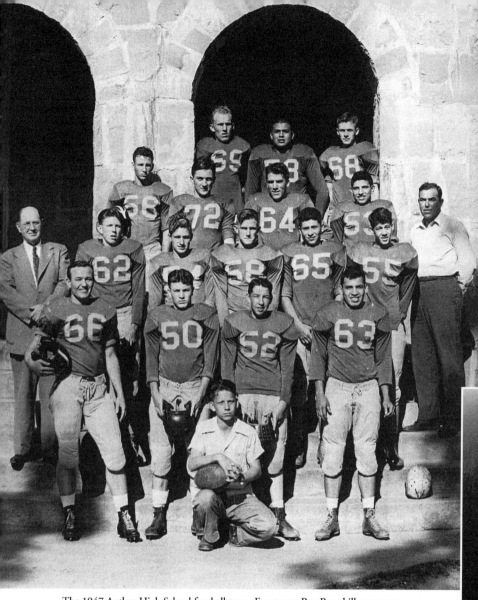

The 1947 Antlers High School football team. Front row, Ray Berryhill, manager.
Second row, left to right, Lee West, captain, Virgil O'Quinn, Pete Holt, and Joe
Packnett, co-captain. Third row, left to right, W.A. Obuch, school superintendent,
Loyd Nelson, Grady Martin, Earl "Buddy" Tucker, John Thomas Olive, Peanut
Shackleford, and George Strickland, coach. Fourth row, left to right, David Pilley,
Charles Dale, Roy Earl Jackson, and Hal Zimmerman. Fifth row, Billy Redman,
Bob Impson, and Carl Wood.

ABOVE: Lee, right, with good friend and fellow Antlers High School football player Roy Hernandez.

LEFT: Mary Ann was chosen as football queen at Antlers High School in 1947-1948. Lee considered himself to be the luckiest guy in the state to be dating such a beautiful and gracious girl.

Mary Ann's high school graduation photo.

Most of what Lee had saved went for car repairs so the family could get home to Antlers before school started.

Lee's senior year in high school was "superlative in terms of sheer enjoyment."[14]

Lee was elected president and Mary Ann was chosen as vice president of the student council. It was Lee's first entry into politics. Joe Packnett remembered, "It was a heated contest but Lee prevailed and served with dignity and honor."[15]

Packnett, who later became president of Oscar Rose Junior College in Midwest City, Oklahoma, toured Pushmataha County in a flatbed truck with Lee in their teen years, often double-dating. Packnett said he knew that Lee would somehow reach higher levels than watching the Saturday night traffic while sitting on the steps of the First National Bank of Antlers.[16]

Lee was named to both the state and national honor societies. John Olive was named outstanding senior man and Ann Amend was the outstanding senior woman. Hal Zimmerman was class valedictorian and Ann was the salutatorian.

Lee, as football team captain, called the plays on both offense and defense. Grady Martin, Loyd Nelson, Charles Dale, John Olive, Hal Zimmerman, Bud Tucker, and Bill Redman were outstanding senior players. Virgil O'Quinn, Carl Wood, Roy Earl Jackson, Bill Wyatt, Hallard Randell, and Peanut Shackleford were underclassmen who contributed to a successful 7-1-2 season.

For his efforts, Lee was named to the All-District football team. But the "crowning" moment of his senior year was when he crowned Mary Ann as football queen during halftime of the homecoming game. In other sports, Lee started on the high school baseball and basketball teams.

Lee's career in high school track was less than outstanding. Track was not a big sport in Antlers and only by trick did Lee join the team. He was earning extra money working for the United

States Soil Conservation Service—typing documents for an hour each day on a typewriter in the basement of the high school. He did not go out for track because practice was at the same time he was typing.

However, Lee's good friends, Joe Packnett and Grady Martin, two of the track team's best runners, convinced Lee that he should compete in the 440-yard dash because the star at that distance, Billy Joe Fuller, had quit the team.

As the county meet drew closer, Joe and Grady persuaded Lee to train with them, although he was skeptical that he had any chance of winning. Lee surprised himself when he was able to "stay pretty close" to Grady in the 100-yard dash and he almost beat Joe in the 220-yard dash. What Lee did not know was that his friends were setting him up.

At the last minute, Billy Joe Fuller decided to enter the 440-yard dash. There were about 10 runners in the race, including Lee who fell behind within a few steps of the starter's gun. He fell farther and farther behind. At the 330-yard mark, he overtook Fuller who was so tired that he was walking. Except for Fuller, Lee finished dead last. As he crossed the finish line, he saw Joe and Grady rolling on the ground laughing. To the amusement of everyone, when track lettermen were announced, Coach Strickland awarded Lee an "A" but it was about the size of a quarter. Strickland remarked, "Lee West has deceptive speed—he's slower than he looks!"[17]

Lee and Mary Ann graduated from Antlers High School in May, 1948. Among the 42 graduates was Wilma Coffman, now House. After receiving outstanding legal training under attorneys Joe Stamper and Loyd Benefield and United States Magistrate Ronald Howland, Wilma became Lee's administrative assistant in 1985. Lee said, "The value of her assistance has been immeasurable. Her lifelong friendship has been even more valuable to me."[18]

READING

I never remember being overly impressed with even the cleverest magician, prestidigitator, but all my life I have been enthralled by a clever wordsmith—by a writer who makes magic with words—writers such as William Faulkner, Somerset Maugham, Herman Melville, Leo Tolstoy, or Fyodor Dostoevski.

Both of my sisters started reading to me at an early age. They read Robinson Crusoe *and* Gulliver's Travels *by the light of a kerosene lamp. Alfred Noyes' poem,* The Highwayman, *was read to me over and over again. There is no doubt that what we read has an impact upon us—especially what is read in our early years. I have long held the conviction that hearing* The Highwayman *over and over undoubtedly planted a seed of empathy and concern for the "criminal." This seed grew into my lifelong concern for the basic constitutional rights of someone charged with even the most heinous crime.*

At an early age, I learned to love Will James, Zane Grey, and James Fenimore Cooper. Jack London also became an early favorite.

As I progressed through high school, my reading list expanded substantially. I had excellent English literature teachers in Flora Easton and Gladys Newcombe. Mrs. Newcombe exposed us to the classics and prompted discussion of poetry and literature in class. She encouraged my obvious interest and complimented me on my comprehension to a degree that became a little embarrassing so I had to "dumb it down" to avoid being ribbed mercilessly by my teammates.

But I was really into George Elliot's Silas Marner *and* Middlemarch. *I read John Steinbeck's* The Grapes of Wrath, *and, of course, identified with the Joads. In Steinbeck's early book,* In Dubious Battle, *I learned a great deal about the* appeal of the Communist Party and even more about the perfidy. I loved Thomas Hardy's Return of the Native *but identified most closely with Jude in* Jude the Obscure.

I read D.H. Lawrence's Lady Chatterly's Lover *but spent most of the time on the sexual material during the first reading and had no idea he was criticizing the Industrial Revolution. The same was true in Hemingway's* Farewell to Arms. *I fell in love with William Faulkner—because you could read and reread him and get something more each time. I read* As I Lay Dying, Sanctuary, Wild Palms, Intruder in the Dust, The Sound and the Fury, *and everything else I could get my hands on. He has continued to impress me more and more as being a near genius of both observation and description. His* Spotted Horses *may well be the best short story I have ever read.*

I was also an avid reader of newspapers. I frequently would walk to downtown stores to read the delivered paper before the store opened.

I did not realize then, as I did later, that reading is the easiest and best way to broaden your world.

Former Harvard College President Neil L. Rudenstine expressed the value of reading about as well as anyone when he said:

> *When we are reading* Anna Karenina *or* Dubliners… *when we are reciting Keats or Yeats or Seamus Heaney, we know that we are about as close to the vital signs of human experience as any representative is likely to take us.*
>
> *…there is nearly always…a strong pull that ultimately leads us back to an original source—a particular novel or poem or a great philosophical, historical, or religious text that can dramatize and reimagine life in ways that expand*

our vision and deepen our sense of what is possible,
delightful, terrible, or impenetrable; in short something that
can enlighten us, move us, and genuinely educate us. If we
are fortunate and alert, we may gradually learn how to see
more clearly the nature and possible meaning of situations
and events; to be better attuned to the nuances, inflections,
and characters of other human beings; to weigh values with
more precision; to judge on the basis of increasingly fine
distinctions; and perhaps to become more effective, generous,
and wise in our actions.

In college, my reading list expanded enormously. Lee Jenkins
was an avid reader and influenced me greatly. Max Schulman,
Henry Fielding, Ernest Hemingway, and F. Scott Fitzgerald
were all different and excellent. Later, Boris Pasternak,
Alexander Solzhenitsyn, Anton Chekhov, Leo Tolstoy, and
Fyodor Dostoevski provided ideas and insights previously
obscured. Other favorites were John Updike, Gore Vidal,
Tennessee Williams, and Larry McMurtry, who proved that a
writer can be both good and bad. I have enjoyed every one of
McMurtry's books, even the bad ones.

Cormac McCarthy, Richard Ford, and Norman McClean
are all good. Tom Word is the best at writing about bird dogs
and field trials. Baxter Black is an absolute favorite. For some
strange reason, I have never been able to enjoy William
Shakespeare, although he is quite quotable. This is certainly a
reflection of my shortcoming—not his.

> *Lee was always as straight as an arrow. If he told you something, you could bank on it. He never hedged his straightforward opinion about anything or anyone.*
>
> LEE JENKINS

off *to* college

LEE WAS THE FIRST MEMBER OF THE WEST FAMILY to even think about higher education. His sister, Deloyce, and brother, Calvin, Jr., had been the first of the Wests in Pushmataha County to complete high school. Their oldest sister, Nita, had to quit school early to take in washing to help the family meet its bills. Deloyce had gone to work as a telephone operator for Southwestern Bell Telephone Company after high school and Cal, Jr., joined the Navy almost immediately after graduation. College seemed only a dream for the rich or the top student-athlete—and Lee was neither.

If Lee was headed to college, he would be responsible for every dime it took to pay tuition and for a place to live. His family's finances prevented them from providing anything but moral support. Even though his parents had little formal education, both were lavish in their encouragement—for different reasons. His father, who could neither read nor write except to sign his name, repeatedly reminded Lee that if he did not get an education, he would "wind up like him."[1] Lee's mother, on the other hand, gave a different kind of encouragement. She was convinced that he was smart enough to do whatever he wanted to do, if he set his mind to it.

Lee was offered a partial football scholarship to Southeastern State College in nearby Durant, Oklahoma. However, he had dreamed of attending the University of Oklahoma (OU) in Norman—largely because of the success of their football program.

Lee had followed Oklahoma A & M's football team in his freshman year of high school. While in Oklahoma City for high school state playoffs, he had attended the 1944 Oklahoma A & M game against OU at Taft Stadium. It was the first college football game for Lee and he was impressed with the Aggies' All-American Bob Fenimore. The Aggies won the game and went on to the Cotton Bowl.

But by the time Lee was a junior in high school, the popularity of OU football was on the rise. Due to fan unrest, Coach Dewey Luster was forced out as OU football coach after the 1945 season. He gave his health as the official reason for his departure although surely his Sooners' loss to Texas and an embarrassing defeat at the hands of Oklahoma A & M, 47-0, contributed to his ills.

Thirty-nine-year-old OU president George L. Cross engineered the hiring of 32-year-old Jim Tatum, a big, brash, bearish, North Carolinian. Tatum suggested he bring with him as assistant coach, Charles B. "Bud" Wilkinson, a 30-year-old former University of Minnesota football player and assistant coach at Syracuse University in New York.

With the help of a swarthy squad of ex-servicemen returning to college on the G.I. Bill, Tatum greatly improved OU's football fortunes. Tatum took full advantage of the expanded pool of football players and successfully raided other colleges to snare discharged servicemen.

Tatum left after one year and OU President Cross and the Board of Regents hired Wilkinson. Lee liked Wilkinson and became "totally addicted" to OU football, a condition that endures into the 21st century.

Lee's best friend, Joe Packnett, was startled by Lee's hint that he might try to attend OU. Joe had always thought of OU as a school for fraternities and sororities—not for poor kids from southeastern Oklahoma. Joe recalled, "I knew that he didn't have any more Levis than I did—which was two pair—and nothing to carry them in. So I was surprised and hoped he would change his mind and either join the service with me or attend college at Wilburton or Tishomingo."[2]

Lee knew absolutely nothing about the availability of academic scholarships and consequently did not apply for any. It was in the days before student loans and he pondered just how he would pay for college. On top of that fear came Mary Ann's announcement that she and her best friend, Ann Amend, would enroll at Stephens College, an exclusive girls' school in Columbia, Missouri. Lee got a sick feeling in his stomach—fearing that she would marry some young man attending the University of Missouri, also located in Columbia. He pined, "I felt sure she wasn't likely to even remember my name after a year of being separated."[3]

After high school graduation, Lee set out to earn as much money as he could. He was given a job clearing brush from highway rights-of-way by Frank Fodge, the engineer at the Antlers office of the State Highway Department. Fodge was a great supporter of high school athletics and often hired three or four students during the summer months.

It was brutal work. For eight hours a day, Lee used a heavy headed axe in hot humid weather. He was paid 70 cents per hour, or $5.60 per day. He saved almost every penny he made. By the end of the summer, he had amassed the enviable sum of $240.

One day while clearing right-of-way between Antlers and Clayton, one of his friends from Clayton High School, Johnny Sands, stopped to talk. Johnny, whom Lee had known and played basketball against since they were in grade school, told Lee he was going to OU and invited Lee to be his roommate. Lee thought, "If ole Johnny Sands from Clayton can go to OU, so can I."[4]

Lee's boss, Frank Fodge, was encouraging and gave Lee time off to hitchhike to Norman to enroll for the fall semester. He spent the night with the daughter and son-in-law of W.A. Obuch, the Antlers school superintendent. The next day, Lee found two jobs—one waiting tables at the Lambda Chi Alpha fraternity house and the other racking balls and cleaning up at the pool hall at the OU Memorial Student Union.

Lee hitchhiked back to Atoka where he was met by Mary Ann who drove him home to Antlers. She was impressed with his plans. As Lee remembered, "That alone was pretty thrilling to me."[5]

In early September of 1948, Lee hitchhiked to Norman with his few changes of clothing in a canvas bag and a cardboard box. He showed up a few days before classes began to wait tables during rush at the Lambda Chi Alpha house. Frankly, he did not know

Left to right, Euell Griffin, Ann Amend, Lee, and Mary Ann. Griffin, a native of Baton Rouge, Louisiana, was Lee's roommate in Worcester House for part of his second semester at OU. This photograph was taken in front of Mary Ann's home in Antlers.

what "rush" was, but soon discovered it took a lot of work for him to make certain enough food and snacks were available for the social events planned at the fraternity house.

Lee was assigned to live in Worcester House, one of a series of barracks-looking dormitories just south of the OU football stadium. However, the dorm was special for Lee—it was the first place he ever lived that had indoor plumbing. He shared a room with his friend from Clayton, Johnny Sands. But before Johnny arrived, Lee met James L. Shanahan, "a mush mouth Mississippian from Vicksburg."[6] Shanahan was equally as unsure of himself as Lee but did have some valuable information. Shanahan was attending OU on a Navy Reserve Officers Training Corps (NROTC) scholarship, an option that Lee would choose his second year of college.

It was the beginning of a lifetime friendship. Shanahan went on to a 27-year career in the United States Marine Corps. He was an infantryman in Korea and a helicopter pilot in Vietnam. He retired as a full colonel. When he and Lee returned many years later to the OU campus, Worcester House had been torn down. Lee said, "No monument had been erected noting that we had once lived there. We immediately proceeded to President David Boren's house to complain, but neither he nor wife Molly were there to hear our complaints."[7]

Lee enrolled in 16 hours of courses his first semester. He studied hard and worked both of his jobs into the night. On his first day in English class, the professor gave students two days to turn in a theme explaining why they enrolled in college. Lee worked at least 15 hours on the paper and was flattened by the big red "F" that graced the paper on its return. It confirmed his worst fears. He was tempted to pack up his meager belongings and hitchhike home to Antlers that night. But he did not. It helped his feelings when he learned the next day that almost everyone in the class had the same grade. Lee assumed it was some kind of psychological ploy to scare the students. It worked! Lee completed the class with an "A," but never forgot the terror of receiving an "F" as his first college mark.

Two weeks into the semester, Lee received a call from Ed Dudley, an Antlers native who was a few years older than Lee. Dudley, the son of Pushmataha County Judge C.E. Dudley, was house manager of the Kappa Alpha fraternity house and knew of Lee's financial woes. Dudley introduced Lee to Bernard "Bernie" G. Ille, the Kappa Alpha president, who offered Lee a job of waiting tables in exchange for his meals.

Because the Kappa Alpha job would equal the pay of both of his current jobs, Lee quickly accepted and quit his jobs at the pool hall and the Lambda Chi Alpha house. In addition to improving his financial condition, Lee became lifelong friends with Bernie and "some of the wackiest people I have ever known,"[8] including Lee Jenkins and Lieutenant General Jack Merritt. Lee remembered, "Jack, after sleeping through enough classes to flunk out at OU, went into the military and became a three-star general in the Army."[9] Jenkins, later the best man at Lee's wedding, became vice president of Plough-Shering Corporation.

Ille was impressed that Lee could work so hard and still make good grades. Ille had another friend he used to argue with about who was the poorest student at OU. Ille said, "When Lee came along, he set the standard. He was really poor."[10]

When the first semester grades were released, Lee qualified for the Phi Eta Sigma Honorary Scholastic Fraternity. No one was more astonished than Lee. When the congratulatory announcement was sent to Lee's parents and was read to his father, Cal cried—the first time Nicie had ever seen him cry.

Bernie Ille and Ed Dudley arranged for Lee to "pledge" Kappa Alpha. Frankly, it took a rule change because, in the past, kitchen employees were prohibited from becoming members of the fraternity. Lee was also promoted to kitchen manager and given a $15 monthly stipend—strangely enough, the exact amount he had to

RIGHT: Lee poses in his Naval Reserve Officer Training Corps (NROTC) uniform outside Worcester House, the barracks-style dormitory where he lived in his first semester at the University of Oklahoma.

pay to the fraternity for "social fees." Lee roomed with Bernie whose assigned duty was to teach Lee how to dress. Many years after that "blown assignment," Lee said, "This is the only failure of leadership I ever observed in Bernie. He was embarrassed when I wore a polyester suit and mentioned that 'Bernie taught me how to dress.'"[11]

During the spring semester of 1949, Lee competed for and was awarded a NROTC scholarship. For him, it was huge. It paid for his books and tuition and provided a $50 monthly subsistence payment. The scholarship, combined with his employment at the Kappa Alpha house, not only guaranteed he could stay in school—he was living better than he had lived in his entire life.

In mid-April, 1949, Lee hitchhiked home to see his parents and friends. On the south edge of Norman, he was picked up by a fellow student who recognized him. William G. "Willie" Paul was on his way home to Pauls Valley to help milk cows on a dairy farm operated by his mother and his brother, Homer. It was a rare occasion for Willie to have the family's one car with him in Norman.[12]

Willie's father, Homer Paul, Sr., was a distinguished state senator who had recently died. The Pauls were descendants of Smith W. Paul, for whom the town of Pauls Valley is named. Smith W. Paul arrived in the area by wagon in 1860 with his Chickasaw Indian wife, Ela-Teecha, and opened a trading post along the Washita River. Paul became a wealthy and influential farmer.[13]

The hour-long ride south, to where Lee needed to head east to Antlers, began the friendship with Willie who became a role model for Lee. The two had a lot in common—they were both from rural Oklahoma and they wanted to be lawyers. Willie, after law school, launched a career as a prominent attorney, rising to the presidency of both the Oklahoma and American Bar Associations.

Two weeks later, on April 30, Lee was serving midnight coffee to mothers of Kappa Alpha members who were spending the Saturday night at the fraternity house. The weather had been terrible that day. An afternoon tornado had ripped apart the north base of the OU campus with several deaths and numerous injuries before moving southeastward toward Antlers. Telephone lines were down and Lee had unsuccessfully tried to call his parents all afternoon.

During the midnight coffee, Lee received a phone call. He assumed it was from his parents, announcing they had escaped the storms. Instead, it was a call from the Oklahoma Highway Patrol informing him that his father had been killed and his mother severely injured as the line of twisters demolished their frame home five miles south of Antlers on the Pushmataha-Choctaw county line.

Lee immediately started for Antlers. His fraternity brother, Fred LaRue, offered the use of his car. After college, LaRue became a millionaire Mississippi oilman and played a major role in the Watergate scandal during the administration of President Richard Nixon. LaRue pleaded guilty to Watergate prosecutors to charges of raising funds to pay for the cover up of the Watergate burglary.[14]

Because Lee did not yet have a driver's license and because he was terribly shaken, another fraternity brother, Bob Farqueharson, from Hugo, offered to drive. Another friend and fraternity brother, Bill Blakemore, just returning from a party and in a slightly inebriated condition, insisted on riding shotgun.

It was a long trip to Antlers. The roads were so flooded that Bill had to twice strip down to his shorts and wade ahead in flood waters to determine if they could get through. Lee remembered, "Needless to say, Bill was completely sober in a very short time."[15] The threesome arrived in Antlers about dawn. Bill and Bob returned to Norman.

Lee learned the terrible details of the disaster. His parents had put two grandchildren, Roy "Topper" Johnston and Sandra Mantooth, under a bed, padded by blankets and pillows. Miraculously, they were spared serious injury. The house and furnishings were blown off the foundation, along with Lee's parents. They were found near the highway some 50 yards away. Cal was killed instantly when a heavy, old fashioned icebox landed on him. Nicie received serious, painful, lifelong injuries and was rushed to the hospital at Antlers.

By the time Lee arrived, it was clear that his mother would survive. He and his sister Deloyce began making funeral arrangements for his father. They had no money but borrowed sufficient funds at a local bank. It was Lee's first experience at making a loan. He had no security but local businessman Jack Cornelius vouched for him.

Lee was upset by his father's death. As he had grown older, he had become more and more judgmental and critical of his father. Their relationship was not always a happy or warm affair. Later, Lee reflected, "I regretted my critical remarks...which served no purpose but to make him feel bad. He was never able to change very much, if any, so my criticism had not helped. I often thought that my mother had done a better job of forgiving him and loving him than I had."[16] Thankfully, Lee had a pleasant visit with his father just two weeks before his death. Although his father and he had their differences, Lee never quit craving his approval.

Lee's sister, Nita, was especially disturbed at their father's death. She was his favorite—he called her "Tuffy." She had literally "gone to war" for him in family battles and loved him without reservation. She never fully recovered from his death and was never thereafter as mentally tough as she had been before. But, Lee remembered, "She remained a loving, caring sister and mother throughout her life."[17]

Lee's other sister, Deloyce, who was divorced at the time, made arrangements to move in with Nicie in a new rent house in Antlers. After missing about 10 days of school, Lee hitchhiked back to Norman to complete his first year of college.

NavaL cruises
and
more classes

THE NROTC SCHOLARSHIP which made Lee's college life a little easier obligated him to accept a regular commission at the end of college and serve up to three years on active duty. The conditions of the scholarship also required him to take an annual summer cruise.

At the end of his freshman year, Lee had a few days off before having to report for duty. He and Mary Ann were able to see each other several times in Antlers before Lee traveled by train to Treasure Island in San Francisco, California, for his first midshipman cruise. It was the first time he had ridden in a sleeper car—"quite an experience for a kid from Antlers."[1]

Lee was assigned to the USS *Helena*, a heavy cruiser, and part of a convoy headed for the Panama Canal. Midshipmen were housed in quarters normally occupied by enlisted men on heavy cruisers. NROTC midshipmen were neither officers nor enlisted men. They were treated like enlisted men within their NROTC organization with upperclassmen serving as midshipmen officers. Regular Navy enlisted men on board the ship resented the young NROTC students who would be future officers and who crowded and inconvenienced them.

En route to the Panama Canal, the convoy visited the Galapagos Islands and crossed the equator. This required Lee and his colleagues who had never crossed the equator, known as "pollywogs," to be initiated by the "shellbacks," those who previously had been initiated.

The shellbacks, almost all enlisted men, cherished the rare opportunity to physically and mentally abuse future officers. The initiation was physically cruel and degrading. Lee remembered, "There was considerable resentment between midshipmen and enlisted personnel when we next got shore duty. I dutifully took my 'ass kicking' and went on down the road."[2]

The convoy anchored at Panama City in the Canal Zone for several days. Lee traveled across the Isthmus to Colon and Cristobal. He formed one lasting friendship on the summer cruise. Winton Winter was a "gawky clown" from the University of Kansas who won a blind man's boxing smoker. Lee decided that if he was in a fight, he wanted to be on Winton's side. Winton played center for the Jayhawk football team for three years and later entered the Marines at the same time as Lee. After college and the military, Winton became a successful banker in Ottawa, Kansas, and served in the Kansas State Senate.

Lee's sophomore year at OU was fairly routine. He roomed with Robert L. Short, a Kappa Alpha pledge from Midland, Texas. Short quickly established himself as a great comic and joined with another pledge, Bob Barry, to form a hilarious comedy team. Short later became world famous when he authored *The Gospel According to Peanuts* which sold more than 10 million copies in its first printing and continues to be a best seller. Barry became Oklahoma's best known radio and television sportscaster, serving at various times as the radio network voice of both the University of Oklahoma and Oklahoma State University football and basketball teams.

Lee dated sparingly after Mary Ann returned to Stephens College in Missouri. Early in the 1949 football season, Lee was studying in the Kappa Alpha house one Friday when a pledge, Charles Halliburton, asked him if he would like to go to the OU-Missouri game in Columbia the next day. Charles' uncle, E. P. Halliburton, the president and chief executive officer of Halliburton Oil Well Cementing Company, was flying through Norman and had extra space on his airplane and a spare ticket for the football game. It took Lee only a milli-second to say, "Yes!"

It was Lee's first experience of life on a corporate airplane. The elder Halliburton spent most of the time under an oxygen mask but was friendly and affable. Because Lee did not drink, he spent most of his time in the food line. After a quick trip, the party was met in Kansas City, Missouri, and traveled in a chauffeured van to Columbia.

Lee excused himself from dinner with the Halliburtons to eat with Mary Ann. His hosts even provided an extra ticket so Mary Ann could attend the football game. It was a perfect weekend. He was able to spend time with Mary Ann and OU won the game. Lee remembered thinking he could easily grow accustomed to that standard of living. However, he recognized that he would need to upgrade his luggage from the canvas bag that "stuck out like a sore thumb" among the Samsonite luggage carried by other members of the party.

In the spring of 1950, Mary Ann flew to Norman for the Old South Ball, an annual event at the Kappa Alpha house. She intended to enroll at OU after completing her two-year study at Stephens. The trip was Lee's first opportunity to introduce Mary Ann to the OU social scene. Lee's fellow student, Duke Logan, later a successful Vinita, Oklahoma, attorney, remembered seeing Lee with Mary Ann. With tongue in cheek, Logan said, "It was astonishing. She was easily one of the best looking women on campus

Mary Ann and Lee at the Old South Ball, held at the Kappa Alpha houses at OU each year. KAs dressed up in Confederate Officers' uniforms and escorted dates who wore long evening gowns. It was Mary Ann's introduction to the social scene at OU.

and, woefully, Lee Roy was, as Lee Roy is, just plainer than dirt. She could have done better blindfolded on a dark night."[3]

After Lee's second year at OU, he and Lee Jenkins hitchhiked from Oklahoma to New Orleans, Louisiana, on their way to Pensacola, Florida, and summer NROTC duty. They had little money and only one paperback book to occupy their time. Jenkins recalled, "Lee would read a page, tear it out, and hand it to me to read."[4]

After a few days in New Orleans, Lee and Jenkins were broke. Lee called his sister, Deloyce, who wired him $25 until he could get his first paycheck. His mother remarked, "Somebody has knocked that boy in the head and surely robbed him because he had $27 when he left here."[5]

Lee and Jenkins took a bus to Pensacola and spent most of the summer at the Pensacola Naval Air Station and on the USS *Ranger,* an aircraft carrier in the Gulf of Mexico.

In the fall of 1950, Mary Ann and Ann Amend went through sorority rush at OU and both pledged Chi Omega. The 1950-1951 year was Lee's most active socially. He and Mary Ann attended almost every dance and party on the OU campus. Bernie Ille's girl-friend, and later his wife, Mary Lou Allen, helped Mary Ann adjust to life at the Chi Omega house. Lee and Mary Ann often double dated with Bernie and Mary Lou and Fred Young and Elsie Andrew, one of Mary Ann's friends from Stephens College.

OU, under the tutelage of Coach Bud Wilkinson, won the national football championship in 1950. The Sooners were invited to play in the Sugar Bowl in New Orleans on New Year's Day against Paul "Bear" Bryant's Kentucky team. With extra money earned doing inventory at Ellis Drug in Antlers during Christmas vacation, Lee and Mary Ann headed for New Orleans in Bob Ellis' car. They attended the Sugar Bowl with Fred Young and Elsie Andrew.

Because Lee had visited New Orleans the summer before, he was quite a tour guide, introducing Mary Ann to the French Quarter, Pat O'Briens, the Absinthe House, and the Morning Coffee Call. OU lost the game but Lee and Mary Ann had a wonderful time.

One weekend, George Nigh, a visiting friend from McAlester, stayed with Lee and Lee Jenkins in their basement room at the Kappa Alpha house. It had rained during the night and clogged a drain—filling the room with more than a foot of water. At dawn, Nigh, unaware of the problem, jumped from the top bunk and landed in a heap with the waterlogged rug sinking with him. Lee West looked out of his bed and said, "George, someday you ought to make a great governor because you aren't afraid to jump into anything to get your feet wet."[6] Lee's prognostication was correct. Nigh later served four separate terms as Governor of Oklahoma, a record that probably never will be broken.

For Lee's third and final summer NROTC cruise, he was assigned to the USS *Missouri*, the largest battleship in the world and the site of General Douglas MacArthur's acceptance of the Japanese surrender at the end of World War II. The ship had recently run aground, much to the embarrassment of the Navy.

The cruise was a disaster from the beginning. Everyone was crowded and quarrelsome. Lee and Willie Paul became inseparable during the cruise.[7] Paul injured his leg and was in a cast, which shortened one leg about six inches. The cast was covered by Paul's pants and Lee and his buddies spent the summer explaining to other midshipmen how "Ole crippled Willie qualified for the NROTC Scholarship."[8]

Lee engaged in a dispute with an African American enlisted man on the ship, a verbal sparring match Lee remembered as "stupid."[9] The armed services had only recently been integrated and tensions often ran high. Lee did not use any racial terms but the enlisted man accused him of using a racial epithet. Lee vehemently denied the charge. But perhaps, because of his southeast Oklahoma nasal twang, the duty officer apparently accepted the enlisted man's version of the incident.

The following morning at general quarters, it was announced that an incident of racial bigotry had occurred and such would not be tolerated aboard the ship. Lee was not named but was terribly embarrassed, humiliated, and "mad as hell."[10] It was the only time in his life that he was accused of racial bigotry.

Later in the summer, the NROTC midshipmen took part in ship-to-shore landing exercises with the Marines in Chesapeake Bay, off the coast of Maryland. Lee was impressed with the Marines' enthusiasm and discipline. He observed the contrast between Marine and Navy personnel and liked what he saw. He, Willie Paul, and Lee Jenkins began thinking about trying to get commissioned into the United States Marine Corps rather than into the Navy. They were unable to convince the fourth man in their group, Don Symcox, later a successful Norman banker, to join the Marines. Symcox warned, "No, no, I'll tell you boys what you're going to get in that Marine Corps—a little pine box about three by six. I may get that too in the Navy—but I'm staying in the Navy." [11]

Lee learned it might be too late to switch branches of the service. The decision to "go Marine" had to be made during the third year of college. Several members of the OU NROTC unit, James Shanahan, Fred Young, and OU football stars Jim Weatherall and Jack Lockett had timely made the decision and had been assigned to an entirely different summer cruise. They had spent the summer learning to be Marines while Lee and his friends only had a taste of Marine life.

Lee gave a lot of thought to which branch he wanted to serve in. The Korean War was only a year old and he anticipated that he would be sent to active duty when he graduated from college and received his commission. He and his classmates spent much conversation time weighing the odds. It was a sure bet that if they joined the Marines, the chance of physical injury increased—but they thought it would be more exciting in the Marines.

Lee's best friend in high school, Joe Packnett, had enlisted in the Marines immediately after high school and had won great acclaim when he and his fellow Marines fought their way out of a trap sprung by the Chinese at the Chosen Reservoir in North Korea. Lee remembered, "I must confess that their bravery and determination had impressed everyone, including me."[12]

When Lee returned to the OU campus, he, Willie Paul, and Lee Jenkins approached the NROTC executive officer, a Marine lieutenant colonel named Jerry Russell, to see if they could belatedly transfer. All three had excellent academic records—Willie Paul's was the best—so Colonel Russell wanted them in the Marine Corps. He promised to help.

After being notified they could transfer to the Marines, the threesome still had some reservations. From time to time, at least one of the three backed out and expressed interest in staying with the Navy. Finally, they made a pact—they would sign as a team, or not at all.

Lee signed his transfer papers and told Paul and Jenkins what he had done. However, they doubted his veracity and Lieutenant Colonel Russell refused to tell them what Lee had decided. They reluctantly signed their transfer papers and walked out of the office. There was Lee holding a big sign that read, "JENKINS AND PAUL ARE FOOLS, WEST HASN'T SIGNED."[13] Thinking they "had been had," Paul and Jenkins physically and verbally abused Lee until Lieutenant Colonel Russell came out of his office to assure them that Lee had indeed signed the transfer papers.

Since high school days, Lee had often thought of being an attorney. One of his role models was successful Antlers lawyer Joe Stamper who, like Lee, was born in Clayton. Stamper had served as an officer during World War II and was one of the most respected young lawyers in the state when he returned to Antlers after the war. So, Lee decided to try to go to law school.

At the time, OU offered what they called a "combined degree." Students were allowed to take undergraduate courses of required subjects and electives for three years and then, in the fourth year, attend law school. At the end of the first year of law school, a student received a Bachelor's Degree.

Lee accepted the challenge, knowing that moving up to a different academic level would require greater effort as well as talent to succeed. Concerned about their inability to concentrate on studies in the atmosphere of the fraternity house, Lee, Lee Jenkins, and Lynn White moved into an apartment near the Pi Phi sorority house. Willie Paul rented a garage apartment from OU President George Cross. Paul was dating President Cross' daughter, Mary Lynn, whom he later married. Paul had drawn the president's attention when he made the highest score ever on the OU entrance examination.

The friends did most of their studying in the law library or in one of their apartments. Lee picked up a new nickname, "The Goat," according to Lee Jenkins, who remembered, "He could walk through a room and leave everything in cluttered disarray."[14]

One afternoon, the two Lees were visiting with President Cross at his home while they waited for Willie Paul. Lee West had been invited to have dinner with the Cross family. As Jenkins was leaving,

Three members of the 1951 freshman law school class at the University of Oklahoma certainly made a name for themselves. Bill Paul, left, was later president of both the Oklahoma and American Bar Associations. Fred Harris, center, served as a member of the Oklahoma State Senate and as United States Senator from Oklahoma. He was vice president of the OU freshman law school class and was later a candidate for President of the United States. Lee was president of the 1951 freshman class. Courtesy Crowe Dunlevy.

West said, "Jenkins why don't you stay for dinner too?" Cross looked at Lee West and bemusedly said, "Lee, I do believe you are a true communist." Cross was already familiar with Lee's liberal leanings toward most social issues of the day. The two often "talked out" many hot topics.[15]

Nothing about the first few weeks of law school was reassuring. As a matter of fact, it was truly a terrifying experience for Lee. For the first time, he was called upon to stand and recite the case being studied. His analysis was subject to blistering cross-examination by the professor. Almost always, Lee, and other students, were led farther and farther until their reasoning was exposed as faulty, or just plain stupid. Lee remembered, "All this, while you are learning a language and procedure with which most us were totally unfamiliar."[16]

Lee and Mary Ann were active in OU social circles after she joined him on the Norman campus for their third year of college.

Lee still served meals at the Kappa Alpha house and had great difficulty keeping up with his studies. But, he admitted, it was pretty exciting when a professor invited him to "stand up and make a noise like a lawyer."[17]

About two weeks into the first semester of law school, a first-year class meeting was called to elect officers. Fred Harris and Dan Rambo, two well-known students on campus, were quickly nominated for president. To Lee's surprise, Willie Paul nominated him. All the nominees left the room. Rambo, later a prominent Norman lawyer and political activist, and Lee were convinced that the charismatic Harris would surely be elected. But, to everyone's surprise, Lee was elected.

Lee learned that Paul had made a rousing speech on his behalf and "guaranteed" the class that he would be in the third of the class expected to graduate at the end. Paul was a great deal more confident than was Lee. Paul later reflected, "Everybody liked Lee because he had a way of making people feel he had an interest in them and what they were doing."[18]

As class president, Lee also became a member of the Board of Governors of the entire OU Law School student body. There he was promptly elected secretary—a chore more than an honor.

Left to right, Mary Ann, Lee, and Nicie West. Lee wrote on the back of the photograph, "The two greatest women of my life."

Mary Ann and Lee at a Kappa Alpha party in 1952.

Lee's mother, Nicie, right, at Lee's college graduation and Marine Corps commissioning ceremony in June, 1952.

Practice examinations at mid-semester revealed that Lee was doing pretty well, but not spectacularly. His grades at the end of the first semester verified the prediction with him barely in the top third of the class. He was disappointed—but not depressed. Fred Harris, later elected to the United States Senate from Oklahoma, was the academic star of Lee's first year class.

The second semester involved not only course study—but practice court as well. Lee joined forces with Paul and did battle with Reford Bond, III, and Henry B. "Boots" Taliaferro in two different cases. Their record was 1-1.

Jenkins and Lee teamed up to represent Mike Hughes, one of their Kappa Alpha brothers, on a real charge, possession of liquor, in Norman Municipal Court. They presented a spirited defense. The judge admitted they were "probably right" but found Hughes guilty anyway. It was Lee's first glimpse of the reality of being a defense counsel in a criminal case.

After years of pleading his case, Mary Ann finally agreed to marry Lee as soon as they could financially afford it after graduation. "It was the greatest debate I had ever won and I was deliriously happy," Lee remembered. He finally got up enough nerve to ask Mary Ann's father, Bob Ellis, for his blessing. Ellis' response was, "Well I always assumed she would marry someone, sometime."[19] Lee recognized Ellis' typical droll way of saying he had no objections. Mary Ann's Aunt Allen, Mr. Ellis' maiden sister who had served as Mary Ann's surrogate mother after her natural mother's death, also gave her blessing—and more. Because Lee could not afford an engagement ring, Aunt Allen contributed a family diamond to the cause. Lee had it mounted and it was a proud day when he placed the ring on Mary Ann's finger.

Just when everything seemed to be going smoothly, both Lee and Mary Ann got "cold feet" about their approaching marriage. Mary Ann was the most concerned because they had never dated anyone except each other. So, they got "unengaged." Lee jokingly asked Mary Ann to return the ring but she quickly pointed out that he had not given it to her in the first place. The diamond came from her aunt.[20]

The unengagement lasted only a few weeks. Both realized after a few dates with others that they were better off together than apart. Mary Ann began wearing the engagement ring again and they planned to get married the Christmas after Lee completed his Marine Corps basic training and finished paying for his father's funeral expenses.

Several of Lee and Mary Ann's friends were married as college graduation approached. Lee was in the wedding parties of both Willie Paul and Fred Young.

Lee's mother came to Norman for his graduation ceremony in June, 1952, and attended the ceremony when he was commissioned into the United States Marine Corps as a second lieutenant. Lee remembered, "I can guarantee you that there was no prouder parent in Memorial Stadium."[21]

tHe marines
and marriage

UNITED STATES MARINES TRACE THEIR LINEAGE to a tavern at the corner of King Street and Tun Alley in Philadelphia, Pennsylvania. During the Second Continental Congress in the fall of 1775, John Adams of Massachusetts and six other delegates met at Peg Mullan's Beef-Steak House to talk about the creation of a Continental Navy and Continental Marines. Marine historian Edwin H. Simmons wrote, "If there were to be a Continental Navy, then there would have to be Continental Marines. Marines were as much a part of a man-of-war's furniture as its spars or sails or guns. They preserved internal order and discipline and gave national character to a ship...Marines were also useful in amphibious expeditions, being half soldier-half sailor."[1]

Lee was proud to be a Marine. Fresh on the minds of Americans was the gallant fighting of Marines in some of the most furious battles in World War II—battles at Guadalcanal, Iwo Jima, and Okinawa.

In June, 1952, Lee and Jenkins traveled to Quantico, Virginia, to report for duty. They had opted to take regular Marine basic training at Quantico before the special basic course began in August for recently commissioned officers coming out of the NROTC program. The Marine basic was tough—a great deal of drilling, learning to break down the M-1 rifle and reassembling it while blindfolded. There was also a lot of running and physical drills. When there was free time, the two Lees explored nearby Washington, D.C. They dug deep into their salaries to pay for their own officers' uniforms.

Mary Ann and Ann Amend visited during the Fourth of July holiday. Jenkins and Lee drove to Washington, D.C. and took them out to dinner. Mary Ann could not help but notice the large number of young women everywhere they went. Because of the enormous number of government jobs available for women in the nation's capital, the ratio of women to men was uncommonly great.

The foursome, along with two other Marines, drove in Jenkins' car to New York City. It was the wildest trip Lee ever made. As the lone teetotaler, he drove all night—even though he still did not have a driver's license and had never owned a car. Jenkins mixed up a gallon of salty dogs for the passengers. Lee and Mary Ann rode in the front seat with a "gunny sergeant" who had been drilling with them. Ann had to ride in the back seat between Jenkins and Bob Anderson, a second lieutenant from South Carolina.[2]

It was the first time Lee had driven in heavy traffic and personally observed carnage on the highway. During the night, they came upon several deadly car crashes. Lee had a couple of close calls and his nerves were shot by the time they arrived in New York City.

They made an old hotel their base of operations as they saw the sights and spent a hectic weekend in Greenwich Village at bars such as Bon Soir, listening to Mae Barnes and Jack Teagarden, among others. They attended the Broadway play, "Diamonds Are a Girl's Best Friend," starring Carol Channing. They also spent a day on Fire Island with a crowd they met in one of the bars. They had a great time but "were completely strung out" by the time they returned to Quantico. At least that was Lee's opinion. Jenkins, who led that kind of lifestyle on a regular basis, saw nothing extraordinary about the weekend at all.[3]

The 15th Special Basics Class began in early August. It was an intensive training exercise with classes, drills, and numerous hikes and obstacle course challenges. It amounted to a boot camp for third lieutenants, the rank assigned the newly-commissioned officers.

Lee did not exactly enjoy the training—but he did well enough. He qualified as an expert or sharpshooter marksman on the rifle range—a feat made difficult because he had to shoot left handed to use his dominant left eye. It had never been a handicap before, but because all military weapons had bolts on the right, shooting from a prone position was somewhat awkward. Until Lee got accustomed to the left handed shooting, he drew an occasional "Maggie's drawers," a red flag signaling a miss. Lee did not score well on the pistol range but qualified as a marksman.

A few days into the special training, Mary Ann called to say that she wanted to get married before Christmas. She did not like her job at the Tulsa Shade and Drapery Company. Lee has always theorized that she may have been worried about the overabundance of single women in Washington, D.C. For both of them, the old adage, "absence makes the heart grow fonder," had real meaning.

Even though Lee was not yet totally debt free, they agreed to be married during the Labor Day weekend. Lee was assigned the responsibility of planning the wedding at Quantico with the help of Mary Lynn Paul, Elsie Young, Gerry Scheide, and other Marine wives already living on the Marine training reservation. Lee recalled, "With their help, things got out of hand almost immediately."[4]

Lee had planned a simple ceremony at the chapel with only Mary Ann's father and two aunts present. None of Lee's family could afford to travel crosscountry for the ceremony. Before Lee knew it, their friends had put together a full-scale military wedding, complete with a 10-man sword line—all in dress whites. There was a reception planned at the Officers' Club for at least 100 guests. "I had lost control completely," Lee said.[5]

Lee and Mary Ann pass through the sword line after they were married on August 29, 1952. Members of the sword line were Hugh West, Bill Paul, Fred Young, Mitch Servin, Jack Saul, Don Berg, Hillard Staton, Jack Lockett, Dick Scheide, and Frank Bell.

Lee and his new bride, Mary Ann, use a Marine sword to slice into their wedding cake.

Lee's big chore was to find dress white uniforms for himself and his best man, Lee Jenkins, and members of the sword line. That chore was easy except for the search for an oversized uniform to fit Jim Weatherall, a huge football star at the University of Oklahoma. Weatherall had just won the Outland Trophy as the nation's best lineman. When Lee could not find a uniform large enough for Weatherall, a smaller Marine, Hugh West, was substituted in the sword line.

Lee Jenkins, left, was Lee's best man for his and Mary Ann's 1952 wedding. Here Lee and Mary Ann leave the Officers' Club at Quantico, Virginia, following the ceremony.

Mary Ann, her father, and two aunts, Allen and Lenna Mae, arrived three days before the wedding. Mary Ann was delighted with the arrangements. She owned a car so Lee needed a driver's license. On their wedding day, he took a driver's test and acquired his first driver's license. He was 22 years old.

Despite being put together by committee, the wedding went off smoothly. Lee Jenkins was best man, Elsie Young served as matron of honor, and Mary Lynn Paul sang "Ave Maria," even though a heated debate ensued with the chaplain who did not think the song was appropriate in a Protestant wedding ceremony. Mary Lynn won the argument. Bob Ellis payed the bill for the reception at the Officers' Club. Lee Jenkins never forgot sitting around the reception telling duck hunting stories with Ellis.[6]

Lee thought Mary Ann was lovely and he was happier than anytime before in his life. They spent their wedding night at the aging Ambassador Hotel in Washington, D.C. Several of Lee's friends had reserved the bridal suite as a wedding gift. The next day they drove into the Virginia mountains to the skyline drive and spent the night near Luray. Two other nights were spent in a cabin on the skyline drive and in Charlottesville, Virginia.

After the honeymoon weekend, Lee and Mary Ann returned to a small, furnished two-bedroom house he had rented in Fredericksburg, Virginia. After paying the first month's rent for the house on the banks of the Rappahannock River, Lee still had $83 in his pocket to last until the next payday.[7]

During the week, Lee's military training was demanding. His weekends were usually free, allowing Mary Ann and him to attend University of Virginia football games in Charlottesville with Dick and Gerry Scheide. Dick Scheide had graduated from the university and Mary Ann and Lee attended parties at Scheide's fraternity house.

On one weekend, Lee and Mary Ann went to the Army-Navy game in Philadelphia, Pennsylvania, with Willie and Mary Lynn Paul. After the game they went to New York City for the weekend. They ate at the famous Stork Club, owned by Oklahoma native Sherman Billingsley. When Billingsley, who grew up nearly as poor as Lee near Anadarko, Oklahoma, learned the group was from Oklahoma, he showered them with gifts and mementos.[8]

The Marine training became tougher as the weather grew colder. Lee and other trainees completed 20-mile hikes with full packs. They also endured overnight bivouacs—usually scheduled when it was cold and raining hard. Near the end of the training, several days were spent in the field in a mock battle exercise. Everyone survived the rugged training although several of Lee's classmates were killed in Thanksgiving holiday traffic accidents.

During Basic School, Lee and other Marines were asked to express three preferences for a specialty, or MOS. Nearly all of Lee's classmates, including Lee Jenkins, listed "Infantry/Korea" as all three of their choices. Lee chose "Artillery/Korea" as his first choice because he knew that he would be sent to Fort Sill, Oklahoma, for training before shipping out for Korea.

In true military fashion, Jenkins was assigned to shipboard duty in the Mediterranean Sea where he often wrote of the hazards of life in ports along the French Riviera. Lee said, "Once more, the boy from Beggs, Oklahoma, had outsmarted us!"[9] Willie Paul was sent to El Toro, California, for radar training.

In December, 1952, Mary Ann and Lee loaded her small car with their meager belongings and headed toward Oklahoma.

They spent Christmas in Antlers with their families and traveled to Lawton to rent an apartment for themselves and for Dick and Gerry Scheide. Dick had also been ordered to take artillery training at Fort Sill. En route to Lawton, Mary Ann and Lee spent two days in the home of George and Cleo Cross in Norman with Willie and Mary Lynn Paul.

The basic artillery course began in January and lasted four months. Lee trained to fire 105-mm and 155-mm howitzers and learned how to call in artillery fire as a forward observer. Time was divided between the classroom and the field. The training was fairly routine except for the Oklahoma weather. Lee, as a native Oklahoman, was kidded about the sudden changes of weather. One day, they went to the range at noon in shirt sleeves because the temperature was 83 degrees. By 5:00 p.m., the temperature had dropped below freezing with a stiff breeze from the north.

The Fort Sill training punctured one myth that Lee had held his entire life. That myth was that Japanese, Koreans, and other Orientals were intellectually inferior. There were many Republic of Korea officers attending the artillery training with Lee. They spoke little or no English even though the courses were taught in English. Some of the courses involved complicated math and trigonometry calculations and everyone, including Lee, had difficulty with them.

The Koreans outscored the Americans so badly on the tests that it was embarrassing. Lee thought that the reason might be due to heightened discipline and the fact that their homeland was under siege. Nevertheless, Lee learned his lesson, remembering, "Orientals will knock the top out of a curve more often than not if given the opportunity to compete."[10]

There were a number of other foreign officers undergoing artillery training at Fort Sill. Lee became well acquainted with an Iranian officer, Hussien Hussienzadeh, or Joe Johnson in English. Hussienzadeh had graduated from the Abbas Abbad Military Academy in Tehran, an institution Lee understood to be the equivalent of the American Army's West Point. Hussienzadeh, scheduled to return to Iran as an instructor, spent a lot of time and shared many meals with Mary Ann and Lee. They had long conversations about the different cultures and religions. Lee maintained contact with his Iranian friend for many years until the United States broke off relations with Iran. Hussienzadeh had been one of the country's elite soldiers under the regime of the Shah but Lee has no idea what happened to him after the Shah was overthrown.

Mary Ann and Lee developed a close friendship with Dick and Gerry Scheide at Fort Sill—so much so that they invited them home to Antlers one weekend. Because entertainment was somewhat limited in Pushmataha County, the Wests introduced the New Englanders to a chicken fight. Cockfighting has never been illegal in Oklahoma but it was, and is, illegal to wager or gamble on rooster fights. For that reason, most cockfights occur in pits in barns in remote areas—always at night.

Lee drove Mary Ann and the Scheides to a remote rural area west of Antlers. From where they parked, they had to walk at least a quarter mile in pitch-black darkness to a barn which housed the fighting pit and arena seats for spectators. There the Scheides observed what very few New Englanders had ever experienced—combat between fighting cocks. It did not take long for the novelty to wear off and they soon left. The Scheides were somewhat amazed that the local sheriff and two county commissioners were among the most vigorous bettors and handlers.

Whether from horror or amusement, the chicken fights made an impression on the Scheides. In the years that followed, they seldom communicated with Mary Ann and Lee without mentioning that experience.

Upon completing Artillery Officers School, Lee was assigned to the 12th Regiment of the Third Marine Division at Camp Pendleton, California. Lee and Mary Ann headed for the west coast. West of Denver, Colorado, they ran into an early May snowstorm going over the Loveland Pass and had to be pushed through the snowdrifts by the highway patrol. They stopped in Reno, Nevada, and were impressed with the entertainment and the low cost of dining. They agreed with the city's nickname, "Biggest little city in the world."[11]

Fred and Elsie Young were already in California and had rented Lee and Mary Ann an apartment on Lobero Drive, overlooking the beach at San Clemente. It was near Casa Pacifica, later the residence of President Richard Nixon. There was a golf course a half mile east of the apartment, so Lee took up golf. He played at least nine holes every day. Willie Paul was stationed at nearby El Toro Marine Station so the two old friends often met on the golf course.

Life was enjoyable along the beach. Lee and Mary Ann were awakened each morning by the sounds of seals barking on the rocks below their window. There were weekly beach parties and "grunion hunting" sessions. Then, suddenly, on August 6, the entire Division was shipped out to the Far East—destination unknown, although everyone expected it to be Korea.

The Korean War had begun in June, 1950, when North Korea, the Democratic People's Republic of Korea, invaded South Korea, the Republic of Korea. The conflict quickly developed into an international war involving the United States and 19 other nations. The war was one of the by-products of the Cold War, the global diplomatic struggle between Communist and non-Communist powers following World War II.

The United States entered the war to support South Korea within days of the North Korean invasion. More than 30,000 United States troops were killed in the fighting before a truce was signed at Panmunjom in July, 1953, only a month before Lee headed to that part of the world.

Lee was assigned to the USS *Colonial*, a landing ship dock (LSD), its main function the transportation of equipment. Shortly after the vessel sailed from San Diego, California, those onboard were advised that their destination was Japan, rather than Korea. The trip to Japan took 23 days—the old flat-bottomed boat pounded the waves all the way. Lee's shipboard routine consisted of chow, cleaning equipment, reading, loafing, and more chow. As battery executive officer, Lee led the troops in Fox Battery. After a few days, the novelty of the seafaring excursion wore off—but the weather was nice.

Lee wrote to Mary Ann almost every day, usually addressing her by her nicknames of "Shorty" or "One-Shot." While crossing the Pacific, he expressed his boredom, writing, "Yesterday I did try to run down some arrangements for a smoker for the troops. Everyone thought it was a good idea but the ship only had two pairs of box-ing gloves only 8 ounces in weight and someone would have gotten killed. Also we had no equipment to construct a ring. Oh well, another brilliant idea shot to ----!"[12]

Lee's letters, tinged with his good humor, expressed his loneliness for his wife. He wrote, "I surely do love you more than any of my wives and I miss you terribly. Just hold to the rigging, Shorty, and I'll be home before you know it."[13]

Marine Lieutenant Lee Roy West sailed the Pacific, a long way from the mountains of southeast Oklahoma.

CLARENCE DARROW *of the* SECOND BATTALION

LEE AND THE MARINES LANDED AT NUMAZU, Japan, on August 29, 1953, and traveled 46 miles by land to Camp McNair, a tent camp on the slopes of Mount Fujiyama, a famous Japanese volcano and landmark. Lee was intrigued by the beauty of Japan—emerald green and every inch of land being used for farming. Camp McNair was in a mountainous region and all the mountain slopes were meticulously cultivated. For a kid from the wide-open spaces of Oklahoma, it was a revelation.

Lee's first experience with the Japanese civilians was pleasant. As the ship anchored off a small town, the curious townspeople gathered a mile in each direction along the tree line that came to within 75 yards of the water. He wrote Mary Ann, "They were very shy,

Lee was stationed at Camp McNair, a tent camp on the slopes of Japan's Mount Fujiyama. The camp consisted of about 400 tents housing the Second Battalion of the 12th Marines.

but if you smiled at them or spoke, they would grin happily and giggle childishly. There were more kids than I had ever seen…They were very clean, well-scrubbed. One lad was obviously pretty sharp. He had on a tee shirt and slacks. He could speak just enough English to tell me that he did not speak English."[1]

Lee had learned how to say "hello" in Japanese but his southeast Oklahoma drawl must have rendered the language humorous. When he tried the language, the Japanese burst out laughing. Lee's heart was tugged by the children who watched him eat his rations. One child looked so hungry that Lee gave him his entire meal.

Living and working in the shadow of the 12,000-foot Mount Fujiyama provided a challenge. There was a legend, "He who does not climb Mt. Fuji during his life is a fool—but he who climbs it a second time is a greater fool." In his first few weeks at Camp McNair, Lee and several of his buddies climbed the mountain, leaving camp on Saturday and climbing to near the top that night. Early the next morning, the Marines climbed onto the rim in time to observe the sun coming up. To Lee, it was "breathtaking."[2]

The Marines were housed in tents with concrete floors and board frames. They had the services of a Japanese houseboy who cleaned the tent and shined shoes for $2 a month. Shirts were laundered for 11 cents. Food was incredibly cheap—steaks were 85 cents and hamburgers cost a dime.

A hearty Second Lieutenant West braves the snow at Camp McNair, Japan. Shortly after his arrival in Japan, Lee was reassigned from a firing battery to Headquarters Battery. He became the Battalion Personnel Officer; Battalion Legal Officer, because of his one year of law school; Battalion Flag Football Coach; and all-around flunky for Colonel Hugh Jackson Irish, the battalion commander.

Lieutenant West is ready for action with his binoculars, an indispensable part of an artillery officer's gear. The binoculars were used to spot enemy objectives and call in fire on them.

Lee loved the Japanese countryside. Mount Fujiyama was located in a resort area, only two hours by train from Tokyo. Most of the local Japanese farmers and merchants traveled by bicycle or motorcycle. There were very few automobiles. The farmers were extremely hardworking and thrifty people—qualities Lee admired greatly.

When Lee received his first letter from Mary Ann, he learned that she had driven from California to Antlers in two days after he shipped out, contrary to her promise that she would drive only during daylight hours. At least she was safe. Shortly thereafter, she moved to Oklahoma City.

Mary Ann went to work as a secretary for the Harper Turner Oil Company. Lee had made arrangements for $250 of his $333 monthly salary to be allotted to Mary Ann. She generously gave much of the money to Lee's mother who was able to greatly improve her tiny house she had rebuilt on the county line south of Antlers. Nicie jubilantly wrote to Lee that she, with the help of neighbors and relatives, had been able to add indoor plumbing to the house. They at first had erroneously hooked up the hot water tank to the commode in the bathroom. But after that little mistake was corrected, "everything was just fine."[3]

The Camp McNair Marines discovered an orphanage about four miles from the camp. One hundred children lived in austere conditions under the supervision of four Catholic nuns in one big room. All of the children were under the age of five and each were cared for at a cost of $17 per month.

Lee and some of his friends began delivering leftover food from the mess halls to the orphanage. The children were starved for attention and swarmed over the men when they arrived. Whatever a Marine said, the children repeated. If Lee said, "Hello," a child repeated the word. If he said, "Oklahoma," the child tried his or her best but the word came out, "Otahoma." About a third of the children had one Caucasian parent and another third had one African American parent. Lee's toughest duty in Japan was tearing himself away from the children after delivering the leftover chow.

On time off, Lee explored the small villages around Camp McNair. He thought the people were surely the most polite people in the world. He quickly learned to like Japanese food that consisted primarily of rice, with small bits of meat or fish, and large amounts of vegetables and plants. He overcame his naturally occurring southeast Oklahoma squeamishness of eating sushi—raw fish, squid, and octopus.

Lee's battalion football team won the regimental championship so he became coach of the regimental team in the division championship series. Lee's squad traveled to Camp McGill and won 21-7, a victory that placed the team into a playoff with three other teams for the division championship.

As battalion legal officer, Lee prosecuted most of the courts martial and was having great success because obtaining a conviction in a military tribunal is far easier than in a state or federal court. Lee reflected, "It was not a very well kept secret that the presumption of innocence is regularly turned on its head in military courts."[4]

Lee also did some defense work. He upset his battalion commander, Colonel Hugh Jackson Irish, when he successfully defended a Marine on a charge that the colonel had personally lodged. Lee had convinced the military court that the evidence of guilt was inadequate.

Shortly after the acquittal, Colonel Irish called a meeting of the battalion officers in his tent. Looking directly at Lee, he made it clear that did not want any "Perry Masons" in the outfit. Another officer, Bob Middlekauf, remembered the moment, "There followed an awkward pause and then an almost diatribe about how Colonel Irish had to have discipline in the battalion and he could not do it if some smart ass officer took on a case like that and beat the rap."[5] When men charged with crimes in other battalions requested Lee to defend them, Irish turned down the requests. He

In September, 1953, Lee experienced his first typhoon. His tent was spared, but many tents at Camp McNair were blown down. Water was ankle-deep in the floor and for six hours he and his tent mates waited for the worst. He remembered, "Compared to an Oklahoma tornado, it was a piece of cake." In this photograph, Lee wades water left by the passing typhoon.

kept asking Lee if his "fees" were cheaper than other available defense counsel. Irish called Lee the "Clarence Darrow of the Second Battalion."

Despite Lee's success as a defense counsel, Irish was fond of him and repeatedly tried to get him to become a career Marine.

During the fall of 1953, Lee visited Tokyo and Yokosuka, Japan. The Army-Navy Club in Tokyo provided cheap accommodations. Lee was intrigued by the fact that an English woolen suit could be fitted, tailored, and delivered for less than $100. He took his football team to Yokosuka to play in the division championship. The team lost the first game but won the second contest to place third in the division. Lee presented the Regimental Championship Trophy to Colonel Irish at a dinner and party at a posh resort hotel near Camp McNair.

On December 6, 1953, Lee was promoted to first lieutenant. The weather turned cold and snow came early in the Japanese mountains. Spending more and more time inside, Lee grew restless. In a letter to Mary Ann, he reported an incident involving one of his tent mates, "Captain Wiley Tipton just stumbled in drunk as a skunk. He reports that he has had three fights with Captain Demmons and that he was ahead, 2 to 1. He has numerous lumps all over his head and his knuckles are skinned up badly. Captain Demmons also just stumbled in, blood streaming from his face. They laughed awhile and have gone back out to fight awhile again. Such is our exciting life in Japan."[6]

On December 7, 1943, Lee startled Mary Ann with a letter that revealed he had spent all afternoon in a whorehouse. Quickly, Lee explained, "Actually it's not quite what you just thought." It turned out that he was there on official business. The weekend before, two Marines had done severe damage to the house of ill repute and local civilian authorities were trying to prefer charges because Marines were subject to civilian jurisdiction.[7]

Lee was sent to the house to try to arrange a settlement. The very friendly girls wanted 10,000 yen, about $40, but Lee persuaded

Lee, right, and his gunnery sergeant, on the way to a re-invasion of Iwo Jima in March, 1954.

them that their case was weak. Eventually, the girls accepted 2,000 yen, about $8, as full settlement of their damages. Lee reported to Mary Ann, "It was fun and we left the best of friends—remind me to sometime introduce you to some of my friends who are whores."[8]

Lee missed American music. He asked Mary Ann to air mail him some 45-rpm records of the latest hits to play on a record player some Marine had acquired. Lee requested records by George Shearing, Nat King Cole, and Billy May.[9]

For the first time ever, Lee was away from his family for Christmas. He missed them terribly—especially Mary Ann.

Cold weather artillery training was excruciating in Japan. Lee's battalion spent a lot of time in the field preparing for a practice invasion of Iwo Jima scheduled for March, 1954. The famous island had been invaded by American troops during World War II but would be recaptured in a division-sized amphibious landing exercise.

Lee thought the landing might get a lot of publicity and reminded Mary Ann to watch the Pathe newsreels. He wrote, "If you see a guy charging across the beach with gritted teeth, you will know it wasn't me. I'll come ashore in a jeep."[10]

On March 11, 1954, just before the battalion shipped out for Iwo Jima, Lee sat for the first time as a member of a court martial panel. He wrote Mary Ann, "It was really easy. I just sat there and made all sorts of rulings and watched counsel sweat. Remind me to be a judge someday—you can really be a bad ass then."[11]

Later in March, the Marines again stormed the shores of Iwo Jima. Lee landed on the west beach with Mount Suribachi on his right and, as predicted, rode ashore in a jeep "rather than with gritted teeth like John Wayne." The exercise went smoothly and Lee was convinced that the Third Divison could conduct itself fairly well in combat.[12]

Lee had been requesting a transfer to Korea for some time, a request finally approved by Colonel Irish in April, 1954. On April 9, he and Bob Middlekauff flew to Seoul, Korea. Middlekauff, one of Lee's tent mates at Camp McNair, later became a distinguished historian and author, teaching at Yale and Oxford universities and the University of California at Berkeley. Middlekauff introduced Lee to J.D. Salinger and other writers of interest.

Lee and Middlekauff were sent to the Third Battalion of the 11th Marines, all in the First Marine Division. It was the most forward battalion and overlooked the Imijin River and the Korean demilitarized zone. They were stationed only 10,000 yards from Panmunjom, where peace talks were being conducted, and two miles from Freedom Gate Bridge. Lee was assigned to G Battery and Middlekauff reported for duty in H Battery.

Korea was dusty during the dry season and very muddy during the rainy time of the year. The living conditions were about the same as Lee had experienced in Japan—except the tents had wooden floors, rather than concrete. There was always a shortage of water and the Marines slept under mosquito nets. Almost immediately after arriving in Korea, Lee's unit began planning another amphibious landing exercise down the coast near Inchon. He was reunited with several of his old buddies, James Shanahan, Wint Winters, and Willie Paul.

Most members of G Battery were trucked out of their camp on the Imijin River on April 27, headed for Inchon. Lee was left behind to travel with a small contingent of 50 Marines scheduled to leave for the exercise the following day. The only other officer in his tent was First Lieutenant Ned Mingle from Syracuse, New York, who was scheduled to leave for liberty in Japan the next day.

Lee and Mingle were fast asleep when Lee was awakened by someone moving around inside the tent. He drowsily asked, "Who's there?" Immediately, a light was shined in his eyes by a Korean who somehow had gotten by Marine sentries and gained entry into the officer's tent. Lee's question had frightened the man from the tent. But on his way out, he calmly picked up a small handbag Lee had filled with an extra pair of dungarees and several pair of "skivvy drawers."

As soon as Lee could extricate himself from the mosquito netting, he grabbed his pistol, ran to the door, and fired one shot at the fleeing Korean who was disappearing into the trees inside the compound. Lee remembered, "I would have been more likely to hit the man if I had thrown the pistol at him."13

Lee's gunfire started quite a "ruckus" around the compound but the burglar escaped with Lee's skivvies, and Mingle's $170 in cash and pistol. Korean civilians were allowed to come into the area during the day but were required to move out at night. Obviously, the man who stole from Lee did not. However, Lee later mused, "I am glad I was such a poor marksman. I would have hated going through life feeling guilty about shooting a man over a few sets of skivvy drawers."14

Because of the "battle" experience, Lee momentarily thought about applying for a Medal of Honor—but never did.

The following day, Lee and the remaining Marines were trucked to Inchon and boarded an APA-212. The landing went without incident and Lee and his unit were soon returned to their quarters on the Imijin River.

The peace talks at Panmunjom continued at a slow pace. Ever so often, the ceasefire would be violated by accident, but from all appearances, the heavy fighting would not resume.

Lee heard rumors that Marines like him, who had received a regular commission and were obligated to serve three years, might be released early. Because he was anxious to get home to Mary Ann and to return to law school, he quickly made application for the early out. Within a month, he was advised that in August, 1954, he would be returned to Treasure Island at San Francisco for the purpose of resigning his regular commission and then be discharged from active duty. He developed a "short timer's attitude" and thought of little else except going home.

Prior to his departure from Korea, several of his friends treated him to a farewell champagne party. He fulfilled his obligation of trying to drink all the champagne within sight. For the first time in his life, he became nauseated by reason of drinking too much. He became so sick that he has not been able to tolerate champagne since that time—but he likes most wines.

On his way back to America, Lee, Middlekauff, and Bill Wood spent two days in Hawaii. While on Waikiki Beach, they encountered Van Heflin, the Oklahoma City native and popular movie star, who had just completed filming "Battle Cry." Lee had his photograph taken with Heflin who, according to Lee, "acted very much like a nice old boy from Oklahoma."[15]

When Lee checked in at Treasure Island, his paperwork had not arrived. His only duty was to call in each weekday morning to see if his reserve commission had arrived. If the answer was no, he was free until the next morning, as well as on weekends. Mary Ann drove from Oklahoma to San Francisco to meet Lee. They spent nearly 30 days on a second honeymoon, first at the famous Mark Hopkins Hotel, then to the Olympia Hotel downtown, and later to a motel in Berkely. During the month, Lee and Mary Ann explored San Francisco, went to Lake Tahoe, Nevada, twice, and visited Lee's half brother, W.O. "Jack" West and his family in Hughson, California.

Lee was promoted to captain when his reserve commission arrived. In September, 1954, he was discharged from active duty. He was committed to serving an additional six years in the inactive reserves but his service as a Marine was over. But, as the saying goes, "Once a Marine, always a Marine."

Lee and Mary Ann drove frantically across country to Norman where Lee was already a few days late to enroll in law school.

> *I had no one but myself to blame if I didn't do well in school.*
>
> LEE WEST

HITTING
the BOOKS

WITH HIS MARINE ACTIVE DUTY BEHIND HIM, Lee returned to law school determined to be a top law student at OU. He quickly discovered that his second year of law school was tougher than the first year, especially after a two-year absence from the classroom.

Lee was well aware of the rich heritage of the OU School of Law. The school had admitted its first students in 1909. Regents selected Julien C. Monnet, a Harvard University graduate, as dean, a position he held until his retirement in 1941. Monnet assembled a faculty from the country's leading law schools and built an exceptional library. By the 1920s, most attorneys in Oklahoma were graduates of the OU College of Law.[1]

For the first time as a student, Lee was not required to hold down a job. Mary Ann worked and Lee received full benefits of the G.I. Bill. There was no one to blame if he failed to do well as a student.

Several of the second year law students were former classmates. Among them were Willie Paul, Lee Jenkins, Reford Bond, III, Jack Gardner, and Boots Taliaferro. But many members of the class were new, having begun their studies while Lee was in the military. The new faces included Leo Winters; Bob Milsten; Temple Bixler; Bill Goffe; Donald Winn; Lewis Mosburg, Jr.; Mark Holcomb; and Richard "Dick" Fowler.

Willie Paul had rented Lee and Mary Ann an apartment across the hall from his and Mary Lynn's at the Parkview Apartments. The arrangement allowed Willie and Lee to carpool to classes and study together. Lee was in awe of Willie's excellent study habits and was determined to try to match his friend's efforts.

On October 5, 1954, Lee and Willie were invited to join in the work of the *Oklahoma Law Review* by Editor-in-Chief David L. Fist.[2] The *Law Review* provided training in legal research and writing, and more importantly, was a prerequisite for membership in Order of the Coif, an elite legal scholastic fraternity that admitted only students who finish academically in the top 10 percent of their graduating class.

Lee and Willie accepted Fist's invitation to be a part of the *Law Review*. Lee was certain Willie could pass muster in writing notes or articles to be published in the quarterly *Law Review*, but was far less certain about his own abilities. Lee realized that he had to raise his academic standing to get into the top 10 percent of his class if he had a reasonable chance of making Order of the Coif. Again, he looked for leadership from Willie. They both joined the Phi Delta Phi legal fraternity along with Lee Jenkins; Boots Taliaferro; Reford Bond, III; and Lewis Mosburg, Jr.

J. Duke Logan, a year behind Lee in law school, observed Lee's gravitation to a new group of friends. Logan said, "He had clearly defined academic goals on a much higher plane than those of his former associates. This was an uncommonly intelligent move that apparently resulted in some sort of osmotic association creating faculty confusion when handing out grades. Lee did well."[3]

Lee's hard work paid off. He performed splendidly on first semester exams, improved his class standing substantially, and was named to the Dean's Honor Roll.

On April Fool's Day in 1955, Leo Winters and Robert "Bob" Grove staged a Frontier Day Rodeo for OU students. They entered Lee and Willie Paul in the wild cow milking contest. Lee was the roper and Willie was to be the milker because of their respectable backgrounds of "wanna' be" ropers and dairy farmers.

Unfortunately, Lee's roping skills had not improved since high school. He was able to catch only one horn of the cow. Willie frankly was relieved because the cow was wild. Lee's miss meant Willie did not have to milk the cow. The team tied for first place because none of the other four entries qualified. After the roping, Winters, later Oklahoma's lieutenant governor and state treasurer, gave Lee and Willie some advice. Winters said, "You two guys had better stick to the law—you ain't gonna' make it as rodeo cowboys."[4] Lee had made that solemn conclusion years before.

During the second semester, Lee and Willie competed for positions on the moot court team that was slated to argue before Justices of the Oklahoma Supreme Court on April 21, 1955, as part of the annual Law Day celebration. Faculty members selected Lee and Willie as one team and Lewis Mosburg, Jr., and Dick Fowler to oppose them in arguing an imaginary case concerning a television news commentator who questioned a person's loyalty and was being sued for defamation. Marcus Holcomb was selected as alternate in the event any of the team members fainted or became ill when faced by members of the highest court in the state.

Lee and Willie worked hard on their presentation for the plaintiff in *Charles R. Orr vs. William H. Gilbert*, the moot court case. They were understandably nervous about arguing the case before the Supreme Court justices. Their only redemption was that the argument was to take place in Meacham Auditorium on the OU campus, rather than in the intimidating chambers of the Supreme Court in the State Capitol—intimidating at least for second-year law students.

After the argument before a large crowd of fellow students, parents, and nearly 500 lawyers and judges attending Law Day

Rivals in the 1955 moot court competition at OU, held in celebration of Law Day. Left to right, Dick Fowler and Lewis Mosburg, Jr., Tulsa; Marcus Holcomb, Buffalo; Willie Paul, Pauls Valley; and Lee West, Antlers.

activities, the decision was announced that Willie and Lee won the $60 first prize, "by a very narrow margin."[5] Mosburg and Fowler took home $40 as the second prize.

Lee surmised that maybe one of the reasons he and Willie won the moot court competition was that two of the justices were from their hometowns. Justice Ben T. Williams was from Paul's hometown of Pauls Valley and Justice Earl Welch was from Antlers. Years later when Welch was convicted of income tax evasion and taking bribes while a member of the Supreme Court, Lee quipped, "I'll swear to my dying day that he [Justice Welch] did not get a nickel of our $60 prize money."[6]

Lee was a hero in his hometown when *The Antlers American* ran his photograph and front-page story about his winning participation in the moot court case. Shortly thereafter, he and Mary Ann traveled to Antlers for a weekend visit. In the Ellis Drugstore, Lee encountered local poultry producer Ross Orr, a man he had known for his entire life. Orr made the mistake of mentioning that he had read about Lee winning "something or another."

It was the only excuse Lee needed to unload on Orr. Lee described the competition in detail and gave most of his court argument verbatim. Orr listened quietly through the entire tirade and then remarked, "I always knew if it didn't take anything but talkin', you would do OK!"[7]

Lee's second semester grades were the best of his law school career. He made an A of some kind in every course except for a C+ in federal practice. Much to his surprise, he was awarded the American Jurisprudence Award for receiving the top grade in his taxation course. The excellent grades raised his class standing to a level that would allow him membership in Order of the Coif if he maintained his position.

The way in which Lee learned about his grades that semester is interesting. Legendary OU School of Law Professor George Fraser, with whom Lee had developed a friendship, called Lee into his office. Fraser began the conversation with, "I guess you know you made some sort of an A in every course except one." When Lee was informed that he had made a C+ in Fraser's federal practice course, he was shocked. Lee said, "I hope our friendship didn't cause you to be tougher on me when you handed out the grades." Fraser replied, "Hey, just the opposite. If we hadn't been friends, you wouldn't have made even a C+!"[8]

Lee was honored by the OU faculty in his selection for a cherished summer internship for upcoming seniors in the legal department at the Gulf Oil Corporation offices in Tulsa, Oklahoma. The job, which paid handsomely, was designed to educate law students about the job of corporate counsel in a huge oil company.

Lee shared an apartment in Tulsa for the summer with fellow law student Bill Goffe, later a judge on the United States Tax

Court. Mary Ann, who had a good job in Oklahoma City, continued to live in the apartment in Norman where she and Lee spent the weekends.

Gulf Oil furnished Lee a nice office, with his name on the door. He was so proud that he used all sorts of excuses to lure his friends and classmates to Tulsa so they could see his name on the door—certainly an ego builder.[9]

Members of the OU Phi Delta Phi chapter had elected Lee their president the previous spring. That made him eligible to represent the fraternity at the national convention at the Stanley Hotel in Colorado to be held just before the fall semester convened. Lee and Mary Ann drove to Colorado for the convention, spending a night en route in Hooker, Oklahoma, with fellow student, Leo Winters.

Staff members of the *Oklahoma Law Review* in 1955. Left to right, Willie Paul, Pauls Valley, article and book review editor; Henry "Boots" Taliaferro, Jr., Oklahoma City, managing editor; Lee West, Antlers, case editor; and Reford Bond, III, Chickasha, note editor. Seated are Jean Johnson, Norman, editorial assistant, and Donald Winn, Amarillo, Texas, editor-in-chief.

Lee, right, and Mary Ann, center, admire a $500 check given to Lee by the Liberty National Bank and Trust Company of Oklahoma City. Presenting the scholarship check is Liberty President Harvey P. Everest.

Lee and Leo had become good friends when Leo had offered to share milk from a goat which he had staked out at the Parkview Apartments in Norman. Lee recalled, "Leo easily qualified as one of the wackiest yet delightful people I ever knew."[10]

Lee's senior year in law school was a replica of his senior year in high school—everything was perfect. He was elected president of the Student Bar Association Board of Governors, the governing board of the OU School of Law student body. He was also named to the Student Honor Code Council and as Case Editor of the *Oklahoma Law Review*.

In February, 1956, Lee was awarded a $500 scholarship presented by Oklahoma City's Liberty National Bank and Trust Company for outstanding ability to perform legal research and scholarly legal writing. Lee joined the elite group of former winners—Robert Looper of Oklahoma City; Fred Harris of Lawton; and Gordon F. Brown of Oklahoma City.

The $500 check was presented to Lee by bank President Harvey P. Everest at a lavish banquet attended by bank officials, city dignitaries, and senior law school students and their wives. The affair was held in the President's Room of the Oklahoma Club in Oklahoma City. It was the first time Mary Ann and Lee had been featured at an event that was to be given special television coverage. Mary Ann was excited but "calmed her nerves," according to Lee, by spending most of his scholarship money on her dress from Balliet's, an exclusive Oklahoma City dress shop. Lee remembered, "It was worth it because she looked stunning on the video tapes of the banquet presentation."[11]

In the spring of 1956, Lee was selected as the outstanding law graduate from the OU chapter of Phi Delta Phi. The award was made on the basis of grades, activities, and personal character. In March, Lee was notified by Dr. Eldridge Phelps, Secretary of the Oklahoma Chapter of Order of the Coif, that he was selected for induction into the ancient and honorable group. For Lee, it was the realization of a specific goal during his final two years of law school. He was inducted into the Order of the Coif with Willie Paul; Lewis Mosburg, Jr., considered by Lee to be the best of his class academically; Reford Bond, III; and Don Winn.

Senior honors continued to mount for Lee. He was given the Harry Allen-Leroy Allen Prize, awarded to the author of the top *Law Review* article in the 1956 edition. Lee had written a *Law Review* article entitled "Municipal Corporations—Liability for Medical Service to Prisoners," prompting Assistant Tulsa City Attorney John W. Hager to write, "Your grasp of the legal issue involved is good and your treatment thereof is quite excellent. In a very close sense, what you have said in your article parallels the arguments which I made in a brief to the Supreme Court and in oral arguments before that body. However, you have treated the subject much better than I did."[12]

Lee's greatest prize of his senior year was the S. T. Bledsoe Award, given to Lee as the outstanding graduate of the class of 1956. The award was made by Adelaide Bledsoe Kingman and Virgil T. Bledsoe of Phoenix, Arizona, as a memorial to their father who had offered the same prize for many years. The Bledsoe Award was based on all elements of merit in a student's record for the entire three-year law school curriculum.

Both Mary Ann and Lee's mother were present when he received the Bledsoe Award. Lee was proud—and could not have been happier.

pRACTICINg
Law

LEE GRADUATED FROM THE OU SCHOOL OF LAW
in May, 1956. Antlers Postmaster Robert Nash was among the
townspeople who sent their congratulations. Nash wrote, "The
warmth of friendship that goes out to you from our little church
and the entire community should sustain you under the severest
circumstances...I want you to know that we are proud of you and
the record you have made."[1]

Within a few weeks of graduation, Lee was invited to join one
of Ada, Oklahoma's largest law firms—Busby, Stanfield, Busby and
Deaton. For a salary of $350 per month, Lee joined former
Oklahoma Supreme Court Justice Orel Busby; W.V. Stanfield;
Austin R. Deaton, Jr.; and David Busby, a member of the firm on
a leave of absence while serving on the Washington, D.C., staff of
a United States Senate subcommittee, a post Busby was appointed
to by Oklahoma United States Senator Mike Monroney.

In addition to the "lofty" salary for the fresh-from-law-school Lee, he and Mary Ann were allowed to live in David Busby's house, rent-free. The house was rather elaborate with the cost of utilities and lawn upkeep rising to more than rental on a small apartment. However, it was an impressive place that would be Lee and Mary Ann's home until they built a new house after living in Ada for two years.

Ada, called the "Queen City of the Chickasaw Nation," was founded in 1890 when William Jeff Reed built a combination of log stores and dwellings in an area that had been occupied by Chickasaw Indians since their removal from native homelands in Mississippi in 1837.

In 1891, a post office was established and Reed named the town after his daughter, Ada. At statehood, Ada became the seat of Pontotoc County, named after a county of the Chickasaw Nation and a Chickasaw settlement in northern Mississippi. In Chickasaw, "Pontotoc" means "cattails along the prairie."[2]

Cotton was king in early-day Ada—the streets were as white as a snowy day during cotton-picking season. After cotton played out, oil was discovered in the Fitts Field, bringing renewed vitality to the area. As the new economy dawned following World War II, leaders joined together to seek new industry for the city.

After six months in Ada, Lee was made a partner in the firm that changed its official name to Busby, Stanfield, Deaton and West, and handled a wide range of legal problems including personal injury, probate, divorce, and other cases that small-town law firms must take to stay in business and serve their clients.

As the youngest lawyer in Pontotoc County, Lee was elected secretary treasurer of the county bar association. Within his first three months as a lawyer, Lee, and the next oldest lawyer in the firm, Austin Deaton, Jr., argued a case before the United States Court of Appeals for the Tenth Circuit in Denver, "a terrifying experience" for Lee. However, with Deaton doing the "heavy lifting," the tandem successfully obtained a reversal of a lower court decision against their client.[3]

Mary Ann and Lee tried to start a family during their first years in Ada—without initial success. In April,1957, Mary Ann gave premature birth to twin boys. One lived only one hour and the other lived less than 24 hours. The shock and sadness was enormous.

The next few years was filled with happiness and sadness— beginnings of life and endings of life. Mary Ann's father, Bob Ellis, whom Lee called "a good man and my good friend," died of a heart attack on March 20, 1958. A month later, on April 22, Mary Ann gave birth to their first daughter, Kimberly Ellis West. Within months of Bob Ellis' death, Lee's older brother, Cal, Jr., was killed May 18, 1958, in an automobile accident, leaving his widow, Hilda, a three-year-old daughter Katie, and a son, Charles Calvin West, from a previous marriage. Charles Calvin, later adopted by his mother Daphene's second husband, John Snuggs, was the last of the male descendants of Cal West.

A second daughter for Lee and Mary Ann, Jennifer Lee West, was born May 23, 1961.

When Bob Ellis died in 1958, his sister Martha Allen Ellis, vice president of the First National Bank of Antlers and owner of an insurance agency, was left alone on the 160-acre Ellis home place. Lee's mother, Nicie, was also living alone on her property five miles south of Antlers.

Aunt Allen decided to sell the farm property and build a duplex in Antlers. She invited Nicie to move into the other side of the duplex. It was a great plan that made it easier for the entire family to gather at holidays at one location. The duplex provided both Allen and Nicie with a kitchen, living room, and two bedrooms. The huge backyard provided plenty of room for children to play and hunt Easter eggs.[4]

Both Allen and Nicie benefited from the arrangement. Neither had to live alone and Allen, for the first time, had an extended family. As Kim and Jennifer grew up, they spent some of their summer vacations in Antlers. They were able to be independent and walk downtown, ride bicycles on the sidewalks, and be home in time for blackberry cobbler. It was a childhood most would only dream about.

Lee and Mary Ann formed wonderful friendships in Ada. Austin and Liz Deaton, Jim and Evie Gassaway, John and Bobbe McDonald, and Oliver and Z.D. Parker formed the nucleus of young married couples with whom they socialized.

Lee always carried on humorous correspondence with friends from law school. Sam Crossland, a year behind Lee at OU, sent Lee a letter that he alleged had been sent to Fred Mock, the chairman of the Board of Bar Examiners, the entity that administers the bar examination to aspiring lawyers in Oklahoma. Crossland, with tongue-in-cheek, was asking for Lee to be disbarred.

The Tulsa native, who later served as legal counsel to Oklahoma Governor J. Howard Edmondson and as general counsel of the Morrison-Knutson Corporation, wrote, "Lee's feet stink and he doesn't love Jesus. But…we must help him if we can and I believe that disbarment would be no solution." Crossland also said, "My feelings toward Lee Roy are those of a harried father whose only son and heir has left the security of the family hearth only to fall into a life of sin and dissipation."[5]

Kimberly Ellis West at age six months.

Life was busy for the young West family. As Lee was learning the reality of the practice of law, he and Mary Ann began acquiring land that made up the Barshoe Ranch and began purchasing horses to stock the ranch. Lee was also active in OU alumni affairs, serving on the Board of Directors of the OU Alumni Association. He and

Lee, in his cowboy hat, and Kimberly
Ellis West at their Ada ranch.

Mary Ann and Jennifer Lee West.

Mary Ann seldom missed an
OU home football game.

When Lee arrived in Ada, he
encountered one of the truly
remarkable characters who ever
crossed his path in his lifetime.
His name was Ralph Evans--but
everyone called him "Fireball." He
had a number of occupations—
candy salesman, high school
Spanish teacher, assistant football
coach, real estate agent, insurance
salesman, and loan shark. He helped start the weight training program that has been largely responsible for Ada High School's football team winning 19 state championships in the 20th century. That
fact has been confirmed by former Ada coaches Elvan George and
Craig McBroom and McBroom's sons, Larry and Gary.[6]

Fireball was the most incredible practical joker Lee ever met.
They became close friends through their mutual interest in Ada
High School and OU football. Later they became co-owners of

several race horses, "none of which could outrun a fat man wearing rubber boots," Lee said.[7]

Lee and Fireball constantly exchanged insults. Lee called Fireball a "right wing racial bigot." Fireball spread the word far and wide that Lee was a "dirty Conumist," his way of pronouncing "Communist."[8]

In 1961, Lee and Fireball had a filly named "Flapper Chick" at LaMesa Downs, a small racetrack in Raton, New Mexico. She quickly proved she was the slowest horse at the track so Fireball and Lee decided to travel to New Mexico and bring the horse home to Ada. They were driving Lee's Chevrolet coupe and pulling a one-horse trailer.

Early in the evening, they drove by the home of Bill Broadrick who had recently had been named as United States Marshall for the Eastern District of Oklahoma. Broadrick and his wife, Emma Joyce, were having a drink on their patio when Lee and Fireball pulled up. Fireball said, "Come go with us…we're just going out west of town." Broadrick got in the back seat and the three friends headed west.[9]

Broadrick became suspicious by the time they went through Shawnee—but Fireball would not stop until they arrived at Sayre in far western Oklahoma. There, Broadrick called his wife and tried to explain how he had been "kidnapped." In Amarillo, Texas, Broadrick purchased a fifth of whiskey and drank most of it before they stopped in Clayton, New Mexico, for what little was left of the night. Broadrick, somewhat "drowsy" in the back seat, was given a motel room key as Lee and Fireball left for their room. When they arose several hours later, they found Marshall Broadrick still asleep in the back seat.

The Oklahomans arrived in Raton in time for the afternoon races. Broadrick, normally a dapper dresser, was much less than that—unshaven, hung over, and wearing the same clothes he had on when he left Ada the day before.

As soon as the races were over, they checked into a cheap motel where Lee and Fireball cleaned up to eat at an adjoining restaurant.

Bill was taking a nap but promised to join his friends as soon as he showered, shaved with Lee's razor, and put back on the same clothes.

As Lee and Fireball left the motel, they informed the lady at the front desk that their "friend" was having a mild seizure and should be detained if he tried to join them in the restaurant. When the lady expressed concern, Fireball said, "He won't hurt anyone, but he might fall and hurt himself." A short time later, Broadrick appeared at the restaurant, somewhat agitated, and insisting that they check out of the motel because the woman at the main desk was "as crazy as a hoot owl."[10]

The next day, Lee and Fireball delivered Broadrick to his home in Ada. Broadrick was never able to totally convince his wife that Lee and Fireball had kidnapped him against his will.

During Lee's first years of private practice in Ada, he agreed to represent a defendant in a criminal case. The firm usually did not handle criminal cases, but Lee was anxious to get involved in a case arising out of the robbery of an Ada grocery store building which had burned after the safe had been blown.

Jim Gassaway, later Lee's law partner and president of the Oklahoma Bar Association, was the assistant county attorney at the time. He worked for County Attorney W.B. "Barney" Ward who was very effective despite being blind.

Gassaway and Lee just happened to be traveling to Oklahoma City together the morning after the robbery and drove by the robbed building which was still smoldering, even though a light snow had fallen during the night. As they left Ada on State Highway 19, they crossed Sandy Creek and saw Sheriff Bill Broadrick, later the United States Marshall, engaged in a spirited snowball fight with several state highway department employees alongside the road.

During the day, police officers in Tulsa had stopped a car for a traffic violation and found inside three men and money suspected of being stolen in the Ada robbery. All three were returned to Ada and charged with robbery. One of the men was Lonnie Pointer, whom Lee agreed to defend. It was Lee's first felony case and he was "really uncertain" about what he was doing.[11]

During the preliminary hearing, Ward and Gassaway presented evidence that mud taken from Pointer's shoe "matched" the mud around the store that had been robbed. They also had "some very unlikely" testimony that Pointer had been seen in the vicinity of the store the night of the robbery. It was also revealed that Pointer had been picked up in Tulsa by Sheriff Broadrick the day after the robbery and returned to Ada in the sheriff's car.

The sheriff testified that he had brought the prisoner directly from the jail in Tulsa to the jail in Ada—establishing a reasonable assumption that the mud from Pointer's shoe that had been "forensically" examined, matched the mud in and around the robbed store.

Even though Lee was inexperienced as a criminal defense lawyer, he knew he had to find some explanation for a Tulsa resident having Pontotoc County mud on his shoes. In cross-examining Broadrick, he asked the sheriff if he allowed Pointer to get out of the car anywhere in Pontotoc County where he could have picked up the incriminating mud. The sheriff repeatedly assured Lee that he had not.

Lee then questioned Broadrick about whether there was any mud in his car which might been transferred to the suspect's shoes while being transported to Ada. Over and over, the sheriff denied ever getting out of his car to get any mud on his shoes that somehow was tracked to his car. For the first time in his legal career, Lee learned that police officers, even good men like his friend Sheriff Broadrick, sometimes forget certain things in their zeal to convict a criminal.[12]

With Gassaway, who had observed the snowball fight the day after the robbery, squirming in his chair at the prosecutor's table, Lee allowed the sheriff to repeat several times the disclaimer that he had ever left his car. Then, Lee dropped the bombshell. He asked the sheriff if he remembered the snowball fight on the side of the road. Lee said, "If you can't remember it, then I will ask Assistant County Attorney, Mr. Gassaway, to take the stand and refresh your memory."[13]

A short time later, a plea agreement was reached. Lee's client escaped doing jail time in exchange for his agreement to testify against the other defendants. Pointer was quite willing to make the deal. He told Lee, "You have got to keep me out of prison at McAlester if I testify. For $100, they can arrange to have me killed and left sitting in the theater some night after the movie has ended down there."[14]

In Pointer's testimony at trial, he incriminated himself and both of the other defendants who were convicted. But the identification testimony previously presented was thoroughly impeached, just as the sheriff had been. In his first felony case, Lee had developed a certain amount of skepticism toward eyewitness identification and forensic evidence.

After five years in his first law firm, Lee, Austin Deaton, and Jim Gassaway decided to establish a younger firm of lawyers. In trying to make the decision, Lee counseled with Earl Sneed, dean of the OU School of Law. Shortly after the discussion, Sneed called and offered Lee a job as a special lecturer in the OU law school.

The post was to be a one-year appointment, primarily to replace Professor R. Dale Vliet, off on sabbatical in Helsinki, Finland. The offer included allowing Lee and his family to live in the completely furnished Vliet home.

After consulting with Mary Ann, Deaton, and Gassaway, Lee accepted the OU job. They went ahead with the formation of the Deaton, Gassaway, and West law firm, with Lee teaching full time but practicing part time. Lee, Mary Ann, and their two girls moved to Norman in August, 1961. Lee returned to Ada at least one night each week and almost every weekend to work in his law office and on the ranch. His secretary, Kay Brown, made his job much easier by communicating with clients and keeping his files in order while he was at OU during the week.

> *Needless to say, I was extremely unsure of myself as a law professor.*
>
> L E E   W E S T

acaдemia

THE ONLY GOOD THING ABOUT TEACHING in law school only five years after graduation is that the new teacher still remembered the routine. Lee worked very hard to stay ahead of his students, many of whom he considered to be much brighter than himself. After a few weeks behind the lectern, he was having a wonderful time. "You learn more law in attempting to teach a subject than in any other way," Lee remembered.

Lee's three semesters at OU as a professor were gratifying for many reasons, including the good fortune that some of his students have gone on to outstanding careers. At the head of the class is Andrew "Andy" Coats, former mayor of Oklahoma City, and now the dean of the OU School of Law.

A major stress for Lee was in grading lengthy exams. He said he taught classes for free—but was paid for grading papers each semester.

One somewhat unusual event occurred during one of Lee's lectures. He was discussing the legal concept of *res ipsa loquitur*, "the thing speaks for itself," when an adult walked into the classroom carrying a strange looking device and sat down. Lee was not alarmed but believed, in the back of his mind, that surely it was a practical joke played by Fireball Evans or some other of his Ada friends.

Lee ignored the man and continued with his lecture and discussion. After a while, the man joined in the discussion and "held forth," displaying an obvious deep knowledge of the somewhat esoteric doctrine of law. Lee invited the man to leave, saying, "You are obviously better versed in the subject than the teacher or the students."[1] The man left without incident and, strangely, Lee never did know why the stranger picked his classroom, that day, to show off his prowess on *res ipsa loquitor*.

In November after Lee began teaching at OU, one of the full professors, William Bandy, died of a heart attack. Dean Earl Sneed offered Lee the job of replacing Bandy. Lee thanked Sneed but felt inadequate to be a full professor in the law school without an advanced degree. Also, Lee was not certain that he wanted to spend the rest of his life in the classroom.

Jennifer West, left, age six months, and Kimberly West, right, at three years old.

Mary Ann, Lee, and Kim, at a Christmas party hosted by OU Law School Dean
Earl Sneed in December, 1961.

Sneed understood Lee's concerns and suggested that he look
toward obtaining a graduate degree in law. Lee's first thought was
about supporting his family. How could he return to school and
expect his family to have anywhere near the standard of living they
enjoyed because of his early success in the Ada law practice and as
a lecturer at the OU School of Law? Again, Sneed had the
answer—apply for an academic grant.

Without any high degree of expectation, Lee applied to the Ford
Foundation for a fellowship in law teaching. To his amazement, he
was notified in June, 1962, that he had been approved as a "Fellow
in Law Teaching" for one year at Harvard Law School. Again, after
consulting with Mary Ann, Austin Deaton, Jr., and Jim Gassaway,
Lee enthusiastically accepted the offer from Harvard, a fellowship
in law teaching assignment that would allow him to earn a master's
degree in law.

After completing his teaching duties during the OU summer session and practicing law part time in Ada, Lee packed up his family and headed for Massachusetts.

The Harvard Law School is a prestigious and imposing place. Harvard, the nation's oldest institution of higher learning, was founded in 1636, at Cambridge, Massachusetts, just 16 years after the arrival of the Pilgrims at nearby Plymouth. Harvard College was established by vote of the Great and General Court of the Massachusetts Bay Colony and was named for its first benefactor, John Harvard, a young minister who, upon his death in 1638, left half his estate and his library to the new school.

Six American presidents, John Adams, John Quincy Adams, Theodore and Franklin Roosevelt, Rutherford B. Hayes, and John F. Kennedy, were graduates of Harvard, which had grown from 9 students with a single master to more than 15,000 degree candidates in nearly a dozen professional and graduate schools.

Many of Harvard's early graduates became ministers of Puritan congregations throughout New England because of the school's heavy teaching of the prevailing Puritan philosophy. An early brochure justified the college's existence, "To advance Learning and perpetuate it to Posterity; dreading to leave an illiterate Ministry to the Churches."[2]

Lee was not at Harvard to become a minister or be tutored on Puritan principles. He was there to increase his knowledge of the law—to give himself options for the future. If he had an advanced legal degree, he would have sufficient academic credentials to hold down a full law school professorship—if he chose that direction.

Lee and Mary Ann took up residence in a summer beach home opposite the Nahant Island in Revere, Massachusetts, named after the famous Paul Revere who made the midnight ride that all school children learn about. The house, about 15 minutes from the Harvard campus, was the summer home of a Mr. Monahan who lived in the nearby town of Arlington. It was a huge, aging home right at the edge of the water with numerous upstairs bedrooms to accommodate Monahan's large family, most of whom lived in the area.

Lee's Ford Foundation grant provided his family with a decent but not lavish standard of living. They ate quite well because fresh lobster could be purchased at reasonable prices just a short distance up the beach. It was the only time in his life Lee was able to eat all the lobster he wanted, "for hamburger prices," so they "overindulged" on the rich food.[3] Nearby Durgin Park and a number of good restaurants provided excellent food at good prices. Locke Ober was a superb restaurant also, but Lee and Mary Ann only occasionally sampled its fare because "the prices were not all that reasonable."[4]

Shortly after arriving in Massachusetts, Mary Ann asked Lee to keep open the first weekend of October so they could go on a foliage tour in New Hampshire and Vermont. Lee objected, pointing out that the only hills he wanted to see were the hills around Antlers in southeast Oklahoma. Lee did not relish the idea of spending an entire weekend just looking at leaves on trees. He remembered, "As you might guess, we went on the foliage tour."[5]

Lee was afforded faculty status at the Harvard Law School. He was also given office space in the library portion of Langdell Hall. His privilege of eating in the faculty dining room meant that he was allowed limited association with members of the law school faculty, one of the most distinguished faculties in the world.

Lee chose personal injury litigation as the topic of his graduate program study and wrote his graduate thesis on the collateral source rule, a rule of law that involves the payment of damages from two or more sources. For example, in Oklahoma, the collateral source rule prevents a jury from knowing about workers' compensation payments received by an injured person in a lawsuit against a negligent third party. The legal theory is that the negligent party may owe damages to the injured person despite the latter receiving payment from a "collateral source."

The title of Lee's thesis was "The Collateral Source Rule Sans Subrogation, a Plaintiff's Windfall." The paper was written under the supervision of Professor Louis Jaffe, an outstanding and widely recognized scholar and teacher.

Lee's teaching consisted of appearances before his seminar students to explain the developing law of the collateral source rule throughout the different jurisdictions of the United States. Lee worked hard in researching his paper and completed it well before the end of the year. The paper was thoroughly discussed and critiqued, both by the seminar students and by Dr. Jaffe. The final paper was approved by Dr. Jaffee and was later published in the *Oklahoma Law Review*.

Lee's grant allowed him to enroll in several law courses at Harvard. He studied estate planning under A. James Casner, a vain but very brilliant scholar and teacher. Professor Clark Blyse, an extremely likeable and wonderful teacher, taught Lee administrative law. He took a Russian law course from Harold Berman and a course on creditors' rights from Detlev Vagts.

Lee sat in on lectures by Dr. Henry Kissinger, whom he had never heard of before arriving at Harvard, and Charles Fried, later Solicitor General of the United States under President Ronald Reagan. Kissinger became a household name in America as a presidential counselor and secretary of state for three presidents. The dean of the law school was Erwin Griswold, also later solicitor general, who, in Lee's mind, spent much of his time flipping the lights off in the library stacks which were already very dark at best.[6]

Lee made friends with Professor Bob Keeton who later became a federal trial judge in Boston and Roger Fisher, an authority on negotiation and mediation.

Lee's Harvard graduate class was made up of 82 students working toward a Master at Law (LLM) or Doctor of Jurisprudence (SJD) degree. Only 13 members of the class were from the United

States with the remaining 69 students representing 46 different countries.

Lee gave his best effort to get to know as many of his classmates as possible. He and Mary Ann became friends with Dan Goyder and his wife from Ipswich, England. The Goyders later visited the Wests in Ada. Lee became acquainted with Brian Tomerlin of Sydney, Australia; Father Dan Degnan, a Jesuit who later was dean of the Seton Hall Law School; Bernard Wall, a Chicago bank trust officer; Jeremy Shea and Mike McCann, outstanding lawyers from Wisconsin; and Willis O'Leary of Calgary, Canada.

RefLections *of* Lee west

HARVARD

When I was at Harvard, my small office was situated near a larger office occupied by the former dean of the Harvard Law School, Roscoe Pound, a legendary legal scholar. He was 92 years old at the time and his secretary was also quite ancient. They were both rather deaf, the result of which was that they had to shout at each other in order to communicate. Those of us in the graduate program who occupied the nearby offices could not help but hear their conversations.

Pound and his secretary had apparently worked together for many years because their discussions often became heated. On one occasion, I heard her shout at him, "Roscoe, you old fool, you are doing all the work on this project and you know you are not going to get any of the credit for it."

There was a lengthy period of silence before Pound replied, "If we waited for things to get done by the people who get credit for it, not much would ever get done." That may have been the most profound statement I heard during my entire stay at Harvard.

A few of the friends met Lee every day at Harkness Commons, a popular campus spot, for coffee and tea. Lee often brought his latest copy of *The Antlers American*, his hometown weekly newspaper. The paper was carrying a weekly account of a cowboy from Antlers who was trying to ride horseback from Antlers to Los Angeles, California.

Several of Lee's learned classmates waited expectantly for the weekly update on the cowboy's progress as he moved across Texas and New Mexico. Unfortunately, the trip came to a bloody end somewhere near the Arizona border because the cowboy developed a bad case of hemorrhoids. The story had a happy ending, however, because the cowboy later married his nurse.[7]

Even in Massachusetts, Lee and Mary Ann avidly followed OU Sooner football. Lee had become good friends with Assistant Coach Eddie Crowder during Lee's years as an OU student and law school professor. Lee was honored that Crowder would call him long distance from the OU locker room after each home game to brief him on the outcome and the highlights of the game. After the first game against Syracuse University, Crowder called to tell Lee that OU was trailing with only minutes to go in the game when a somewhat strange young man named Joe Don Looney told OU Coach Bud Wilkinson, "Coach, give me the ball and I'll score." They gave the ball and Looney promptly ran about 75 yards for a touchdown, winning the game, just as he promised.[8]

In the spring of 1963, Lee received a call from District Judge John Boyce McKeel in Ada. McKeel had been diagnosed with cancer and the long-term prognosis was not good. McKeel knew that Lee someday wanted to be a judge and said, "If you want to succeed me, you better get back down here pretty soon."[9]

Since his second year in law school, Lee had secretly wanted to become a federal trial judge. He believed that a logical step in that direction would be to gain experience as a state district judge. Even if a federal appointment never came in life, he thought, a career on the state bench would be fulfilling.

He did have options. He interviewed with several law schools who were anxious to hire Harvard graduates. But Lee never gave serious consideration to any of several interesting offers.

After final exams and before graduation exercise, Lee, Mary Ann, and the girls headed home to Ada. Shortly after their return, Lee received an impressive degree, altogether in Latin, wherein the *Universitas Harvardiana Cantabrigiae* granted a Master of Laws degree to *Lee Regem West*. Since that time, Lee's favorite niece, Sandra Mantooth, has referred to him as "Uncle Rectum."

Lee was very proud of his degree from Harvard. He mused, "Harvard is such a great institution that any graduate's resume is enhanced. Certainly mine has been. It almost immediately bestows a degree of intellectualism, whether deserved or not."[10]

Lee believes that his Harvard degree has served him well through the years, offsetting what United States Court of Appeals for the Tenth Circuit Judge Robert Henry refers to as Lee's "Little Dixie diphthong." Lee had to look that word up in the dictionary. He found it meant that he talks through his nose with a Little Dixie accent.[11]

Not all of Lee's Oklahoma friends have been that respectful of the Harvard degree. Former United States Marshal Bill Broadrick once remarked, "Ol' Lee must have a flat learning curve. He had to go to law school well past 30 to learn enough law to make a living practicing law in Ada. All the other lawyers did it in a shorter time."[12]

OU Law School Dean Andy Coats, Lee's former student, said, "It has been said that a Harvard degree gives rise to the presumption that one is, at least, not a damned fool. Down in Antlers, Oklahoma where Lee West grew up, it doesn't even shift the burden of proof."[13]

> *Just in case anyone wonders how the star of this book got started in the judge business, you can give me the blame for that.*
>
> FORMER OKLAHOMA GOVERNOR
> HENRY BELLMON

appointment
to the BENCH

LEE, MARY ANN, KIM, AND JENNIFER returned to Ada—glad to be back in Oklahoma. Lee's law partnership with Austin Deaton, Jr. and Jim Gassaway flourished, especially in the area of personal injury litigation. The firm obtained several large verdicts for plaintiffs and word got out to anyone hurt in that area of the state that Deaton, Gassaway, and West would do them a good job.

Gassaway remembered a case in which they represented an old cowboy named Don Wilkins in a case against an insurance company. Gassaway thought Lee had made a huge mistake when he asked the jury to award Wilkins $75,000 for his broken ankle. Lee had turned down a $17,500 offer and Gassaway was worried that the jury would not come in that high. Lee's convincing closing argument obviously made a difference—the jury awarded $35,000, the largest personal injury verdict in Pontotoc County to that time. On the way out of the courthouse, one juror told Lee, "Mr. West, I done all I could to get you that $75,000."[1]

Leverett Edwards, a member of the National Mediation Board, arranged for Lee to do considerable work as an arbitrator and mediator for the National Labor Relations Board. Lee spent a great deal of time in Chicago, Illinois, in 1964 and early 1965. Lee flew to Chicago for a week each month, staying in a hotel in the city's Loop area near his office in the Consumer Building. He frequented Berghoff's, Chicago's well-known German restaurant.

Lee served as the "neutral" to resolve labor disputes between the railroads and their employees. Basically, a claim was filed by the employee through the union. If the claim could not be settled, it was presented to Lee at a hearing by a representative of the union and defended by a representative of the railroad, all in accordance with a detailed regulatory scheme. After hearing the presentations, Lee wrote an opinion, ruling for either the employee or the railroad.

While in Chicago, Lee presided over two hearings each day. He took his notes and evidence received in the hearings back to Ada where he wrote his opinions. The pay was excellent. Mary Ann occasionally accompanied Lee on the trips, giving them an opportunity to thoroughly explore the Windy City. They saw both Louie Armstrong and Maurice Chevalier perform at the Palmer House Hotel.

On one trip to Chicago, Lee went out to dinner with another Oklahoma lawyer, William "Bill" Christian, a former Oklahoma Secretary of State who was also mediating disputes. Christian had grown up in Broken Bow, even farther into the heart of Little Dixie than Antlers. Both were in their "normal southeast Oklahoma wardrobe" wandering around the near north side of Chicago when they were spotted by a taxi driver.

The driver said, "Are you boys looking for something?" Christian said, "We sure are." When the driver asked, "Well, just what exactly do you have in mind?" Christian answered, "A big bowl of peach ice cream." Christian remembered, "Lee and I were then subjected to language that even we had not previously been exposed to."[2]

Ada District Judge John Boyse McKeel, an able and popular judge, died in 1965, creating a vacancy in the district judgeship, in Judicial District 22, headquartered in Ada. Lee immediately applied for the appointment along with Bob Macy and Calvert Cannon of Ada. Macy, who later became the District Attorney in Oklahoma County, had recently switched his registration from Democrat to Republican. No doubt Macy thought that move would help him land the judgeship in Ada because the decision was left up to Oklahoma's first Republican governor, Henry Bellmon. Both Lee and Cannon were Democrats.

Bellmon's election in 1962 was a new day, the beginning of a new era in Oklahoma politics. He was a true grassroots politician, born near Tonkawa, Oklahoma, in 1921. He bought the suit he wore for high school graduation with money he raised selling skunk and opossum hides. After graduating from Oklahoma A & M, he served in the Marines in World War II, earning the Silver Star and Legion of Merit for service on Iwo Jima.

From his Billings farm, Bellmon campaigned in every town and village in Oklahoma in 1962 and overcame incredible odds to be elected governor. By 1965, Bellmon had won the hearts of many Oklahomans with his humble attitude, complete honesty, excitement about economic development, and promises of no new taxes.[3]

Lee had never met Bellmon and none of his close supporters for the judgeship were well acquainted with the governor. However, Lee contacted friends from law school and other acquaintances that had been involved in Bellmon's campaign. He asked them to put in a good word for him with the governor's office.

In early August, 1965, Lee was summoned to the governor's office at the State Capitol in Oklahoma City to meet with Governor Bellmon. Even before the interview, Lee knew he was facing an uphill battle. Bellmon's administrative assistant, Drew Mason, was brutally frank. He told Lee, "You have a large number of friends and supporters, but I am not one of them." When asked why, Mason informed Lee that he was encouraging the governor to

BELOW: Kim, right, age six, uses her newly-discovered reading skills to entertain her sister, three-year-old Jennifer, at their Ada home in November, 1964.

LEFT: Jennifer began the first grade while Lee was district judge in Ada.

appoint only Republicans to vacant posts in state government.[4]

The interview with Bellmon went well but Lee left the Capitol believing that Republican Macy had the inside track, if for no other reason than he was a Republican. Bellmon looked for a Republican, later revealing, perhaps with tongue in cheek, "In Little Dixie, it was pretty hard to find a Republican. I looked, I looked, and I looked. I didn't look for qualifications or anything. I just looked for a Republican. Failing to find one, it fell to me to seek the least offensive Democrat I could find. And, also, a man who is without peer as a quail hunter."[5]

A few days after his meeting with Governor Bellmon, Lee was notified that he was the choice of the governor to be the new district judge in the 22nd Judicial District. Lee was sworn in by Oklahoma Supreme Court Justice Denver Davison of Ada on August 25, 1965.

OU Law School Dean Maurice Merrill could not attend the swearing in ceremony for his former student, but wrote, "The newspaper says you are the new judge of the Pontotoc County Court. Quite as accurate as journalists usually are."[6]

For the next eight years, Lee spent possibly the best years of his life, in terms of fun and excitement, on the state bench in Ada. For the first year, he learned the trade of being a state district court judge without any serious blunders, but certainly not pleasing everyone.

Bob E. Bennett, an Ada lawyer who tried many cases in front of Lee, was impressed with Lee's ability to see through ulterior motives of witnesses who testified in his courtroom. Bennett said, "He could read witnesses and evaluate testimony better than anyone I've ever known. He just knew if they were telling the truth or not."[7]

Bennett and Lee showed up most every morning before court at a local restaurant for coffee—an informal "coffee club." Bennett remembered, "Lee has an uncanny ability to communicate with people from all walks of life. He likes to be around people of different views and different backgrounds."[8]

There was never a shortage of unusual happenings in Pontotoc County. Shortly after Lee became a judge, he made some rulings that were not appreciated by a character named Elmer West, who was no relation. After one hearing, West ran into Francis Mayhue, an Ada lawyer, later a judge, and Lee's friend. Elmer West, who did not have a great understanding of the language of the judicial system, said, "Somebody ought to give that damned Lee West a sanitary hearing and appoint him a gardeen."[9]

Mayhue related the story to Lee who asked, "Did you defend me?" Mayhue reported that he had "sort of" defended the new judge by saying that Lee "might pass a 'sanity' hearing but would surely fail a 'sanitary' hearing."[10]

"Uncle Elmer" West continued to disapprove of rulings made by Lee from the bench. In the one grand jury investigation Lee presided over in Ada, he later discovered that the first witness who volunteered to testify to the panel was none other than Elmer West. District Attorney Gordon Melson laughingly told Lee that "Uncle Elmer" said Lee was by far the dumbest, most corrupt judge who had ever served on the bench." The grand jury did not return any indictments but Melson often joked that "Uncle Elmer's" testimony came close to getting Lee thrown out of office.[11]

"Uncle Elmer" was later engaged in an altercation with Escal Myer at the Ada sale barn. In the scuffle, Escal's pistol fired. No one was hit by the bullet but Elmer fainted from fright. He later attempted to get prosecutor Melson to file charges against Escal for assault and battery. Melson declined, suggesting instead that he file charges against Escal for missing Elmer.

"Uncle Elmer" had a tough time getting along with anyone. Once, he was aggravated with Melvin Chilcoat, a local real estate agent. Elmer walked up behind the smallish Chilcoat and hit him in the ear with his fist. What Elmer did not know was that Chilcoat was holding a tire tool which he promptly used to "crack Elmer right between the horns." Several stitches were required but no charges were filed by anyone.[12]

In 1966, Lee attended the National College of State Trial Judges held at the University of Nevada-Reno. State trial judges from across the land were assembled to be subjected to a month of intensive study and discussion of problems confronting them. It was easily the best month of education Lee received anywhere. It was also a wonderful time for the family because Mary Ann and the girls were able to accompany Lee to Reno. During the conference, Lee made friends with Bob Jones of Oregon and Jack Shanstrom of Montana, both of whom were later appointed federal judges.

OU FOOTBALL

Since I was a junior in high school, I have been addicted to OU football. By the time I enrolled at OU in 1948, the Sooners were a national power. After I enrolled, they had a 31-game winning streak and shortly thereafter a 47-game winning streak that still stands a half-century later as a record in major college football.

While I was in school, Jack Lockett and Jim Weatherall, two of the outstanding players on the team were in my NROTC program so I got to know them well. Later, Lockett was in my wedding party and Jim was scheduled to be but we were unable to find dress whites large enough to fit him.

Through Jack and Jim, I got to know several of the players. Eddie Crowder and Merrill Green became very close friends and later on I helped them recruit players in Ada.

When I returned to teach at the OU Law School, Eddie Crowder and Bob Ward, another assistant football coach, became close friends. While at Harvard, Eddie would call me from the dressing room with the final score. Coach Wilkinson and Hugh "Duffy" Daugherty of Michigan State University appeared at a coaching clinic in Boston and Bud invited me to have breakfast with them, a real treat. Daugherty was one funny Irishman. I heard Bud telling him about Joe Don Looney as best he could. Bud surmised then that Looney would not stay hitched despite having unlimited ability and his prediction proved correct.

Merrill Green was an assistant coach at Texas Tech University while Mary Ann and I were at Harvard. The Red Raiders played Boston College in Boston and we went to the game. That night Merrill joined Mary Ann and me for dinner at Durgin Park, a rowdy restaurant in the Market Area of Boston. Merril captivated and regaled a huge crowd of Bostonians with anecdotes about how, despite his outstanding coaching, the Eagles had beaten his Texas Tech team 46-0 that afternoon.

In 1960, I was made an honorary member of the "O" Club by Coach Wilkinson, mainly through efforts of Eddie Crowder.

After returning to Ada in 1963, I continued to help recruit for OU. When Coach Wilkinson left, Gomer Jones became head coach and Jay O'Neal, a good Ada lad, was named assistant coach. But they lasted only until 1965 when Jim McKenzie was named head coach.

My first contact with the new group came almost immediately. Ada High School coach Craig McBroom called to invite me to the signing of an OU commitment by Ada defensive star Gary Jamar. It was the first OU signee for a very brash young assistant coach, Barry Switzer. I thought Barry was the cockiest guy I had ever met. Yet, he was charismatic.

McKenzie died after one season as head coach and Chuck Fairbanks succeeded him. Chuck and Barry both recruited Ada and on occasion I attended a game with one or both of them. Bobby Warmack, a fine athlete and even a greater kid, was the starting quarterback for Ada High, and Fireball Evans and I took almost full credit for getting him to OU. Whether true or not, he led OU to an Orange Bowl championship.

When Chuck left to coach the New England Patriots, Barry succeeded him "with a bang." Barry was accused of offering an illegal inducement to a recruit. He called me in Ada and wanted to know how he could go about taking a lie detector test to prove his innocence. I expressed my concern about the reliability of such tests and told him the skill of the operators varied considerably. He wanted to know where he could get a good and honest operator.

I did not know an operator but recommended he contact Larry Derryberry, my former student, who was Attorney General of Oklahoma. I then called Larry on Barry's behalf and Larry agreed to help. Barry passed the test with flying colors and he and Larry became good friends. Barry tracked me down by telephone while I was bird hunting in Valentine,

Nebraska, to jubilantly report that he had passed the lie detector test.

When I moved to Washington, D.C., in 1973, my close association with OU football ended. Even after I returned to Tulsa and Oklahoma City, I was not nearly so involved as before.

I still follow the Sooners religiously. As the saying goes, I have stuck with them through thick and thin—but I confess that I am a typical fan in one regard. I tend to stick with them a lot stronger through the thick of winning than I do through the thin of losing.

I really enjoyed the 2000 national championship year— even more than any of the previous national championship campaigns.

> *McCarthy had about as much of a chance of escaping as an elephant in a snowstorm with a real bad nosebleed.*
>
> VERNON ROBERTS

emmit Ray mccarthy

IN 1967, LEE PRESIDED OVER a highly publicized criminal case, *State of Oklahoma vs. Emmit Ray McCarthy.*

McCarthy was a rare combination of comic and con man. He was six feet eight inches tall with a personality somewhat like Elwood P. Dowd and Andy Griffith, all in one. McCarthy had spent most of his life incarcerated because of failed attempts at conning people, burglary, or other nonviolent crimes. He had a great ability to endear himself to everyone, including jailers and prison guards.

In early 1967, McCarthy was being transported from jail to a hospital in Oklahoma City by a law enforcement officer for the purpose of getting medical treatment. McCarthy somehow managed to get the officer's pistol from him, confiscated the police car, and headed south, leaving the unharmed police officer stranded. Sometime during the night, he worked his way to Stratford, in Pontotoc County, evading a rather massive effort by state troopers and local law officers.

Knowing that he had to change automobiles to escape capture, McCarthy stopped at a house on the east side of Stratford to steal another car. However, as his bad luck would have it, the house McCarthy chose was the home of Stratford's only police officer. McCarthy attempted to hide the stolen police car and entered the house with gun drawn when the police officer answered the door.

McCarthy took the police officer, his wife, and two daughters hostage and drove them in the officer's car south to Ardmore. By that time, the Oklahoma Highway Patrol had discovered the missing police car in Stratford and put out an all points bulletin for the Stratford policeman's car.

Again needing to change cars, McCarthy and his hostages stopped at the home of an elderly lady in Ardmore. The lady was hard of hearing and at first refused to hand the keys to her new car in the driveway over to McCarthy. In fact, she held out until McCarthy agreed to transfer several flower pots and vases from the car to her home. The entire Stratford police officer's family, hoping to avoid violence, helped McCarthy move the flower pots.

McCarthy headed south again. Miraculously, he was captured near Marietta, in southern Oklahoma, without injury to anyone. He was returned to Ada and charged with kidnapping the family in Stratford.

Gordon Melson was the district attorney and Lee appointed local lawyers, Vernon Roberts and Ken Johnson, to represent McCarthy because he could not afford to retain private counsel. Both Roberts and Johnson were excellent civil attorneys but lacked experience in criminal law. However, being true professionals, both worked hard representing McCarthy, even though they suffered financially, giving up a lot of civil work for the meager fee allowed for representing the indigent defendant.

The late Vernon Roberts, one of Lee's all-time favorite lawyers, and McCarthy were a perfect match. Roberts had a strong desire to love and help anyone who needed love and help. Lee reflected,

"And, Emmitt needed more of both than almost anyone I have ever met."[1]

Roberts and Johnson provided McCarthy legal help and Roberts provided books, cigarettes, and companionship for the incarcerated suspect. Roberts and McCarthy early recognized that they were kindred spirits and spent long hours discussing life, literature, and philosophy.

On the morning the trial was scheduled to begin, Lee received a call from the sheriff's office reporting that McCarthy had escaped during the night. Lee immediately suspected that Roberts may have had something to do with the escape. Roberts denied the accusation and expressed concern for his client's welfare. The concern was well founded because McCarthy had left the jail wearing only a thin shirt and trousers. It was winter and the temperature was well below freezing.

McCarthy escaped into a wooded area west of Ada and somehow endured the cold while an embarrassed sheriff, Burl Griffin, and other lawmen mounted a manhunt. The entire population was on alert because a known kidnapper was on the loose.

Overcome by hunger on the second day of freedom, McCarthy approached a rural home west of Ada. Fortunately, the home's residents saw him coming, vacated the premises, and called the sheriff from a neighbor's house. McCarthy calmly entered the house and ate his fill. While he was engaged in filling his empty stomach, the local highway patrolman, John Wayne Smith, who lived nearby, was alerted.

The trooper was joined by rancher Marvin Barnes who was armed with a .410 shotgun. When he saw the officer coming, McCarthy hid behind the living room couch. In attempting to load his gun, an excited Barnes accidentally fired his shotgun into the ground. No one was hurt, but the gunfire convinced McCarthy to give up without a fight. McCarthy walked from the house with his hands held high, saying that he had elected to surrender before "someone out there hurts themselves."[2]

As a result, McCarthy became even more of a local celebrity. With Vernon Roberts serving as the conduit, McCarthy became the beneficiary of the community's largesse. A steady deluge of food, cigarettes, and reading material was provided. McCarthy, of course, generously shared his bounty with his fellow inmates in the Pontotoc County jail.

Lee rescheduled McCarthy's trial. But shortly before the date with justice, McCarthy escaped again. This time, he convinced jailer, Don Kaiser, that he had a lethal weapon. In the middle of the night, Kaiser released McCarthy who ended up in the home of an Ada resident with whom he drank coffee most of the night and negotiated a deal. The deal was that the Ada man would drive McCarthy to the Texas state line and let him out. Shortly thereafter, all six feet eight inches of McCarthy climbed into the man's trunk and thought he was headed for Texas. However, the man drove to one of several roadblocks sheriff's deputies had set up and delivered McCarthy.

When McCarthy was turned over to Sheriff Griffin, the sheriff was openly hostile. He said, "Emmit, I guarantee you will not escape again even if I have to handcuff myself to you until you go to trial." McCarthy calmly replied, "You shouldn't do that, Burl. You might wake up some morning and find both of us gone."[3]

A jury finally convicted McCarthy and sent him to prison for the minimum sentence of 10 years. During closing arguments, Roberts, trying to explain the curious escape attempts to jurors, said, "Emmit, I hate to say this in your presence, because you are my friend, but you are kind of a nut. You had about as much chance of escaping as an elephant in a snowstorm with a real bad nosebleed."[4]

Lee often misquotes his friend George Short, "There once was a lawyer, Vernon Roberts, but only once."[5]

Lee presided over another slightly unusual murder trial in Pontotoc County. In *State of Oklahoma vs. Dub Jones*, Jones was charged with shooting a younger man to death at the entrance of his beer joint west of Ada. Melson, later a respected district judge, was still district attorney and prosecuted the case. The defense counsel hired by Jones was Bob Macy who was practicing law in Ada at the time.

The trial took several days. Closing arguments came at the end of the day and Lee decided to let the jury spend the evening deliberating the case. While jurors met to decide Jones' fate, Lee invited Melson, Macy, and the defendant to dinner at a local restaurant. Everyone enjoyed the meal although Lee remembered that Jones was somewhat distracted because a jury was at that moment deliberating his guilt or innocence of a first degree murder charge.

The case was never mentioned during the meal. Everyone involved in the case was present and none thought the dinner was improper, including Lee. Looking back on the event, Lee said, "I can only imagine the outcry if that were to happen today."[6]

When the dinner companions returned to the courthouse, the jury found Jones not guilty of the murder. Macy, in Lee's opinion, had done an excellent job of providing an effective defense. Of Macy, Lee says, "As a defense counsel, he was good enough to occasionally acquit defendants who were guilty. Unfortunately, as a prosecutor, he proved to be even more effective at convicting defendants who were innocent."[7]

Lee once presided at the parole revocation hearing of a young defendant who was accused of burglarizing the automobile of Lieutenant Governor Leo Winters who had stopped for coffee on the edge of Ada on his way back to Oklahoma City from a speech in Atoka. Winters saw the parolee entering his car and rushed from the restaurant to tackle and apprehend him. The Lieutenant Governor held the suspect on the ground until police arrived.[8]

At the hearing, Lee advised the young man that he had no discretion—his parole had to be revoked. However, Lee said if he could have discretion in the matter, he would free the parolee because it was punishment enough to be subjected to Winters' jokes while being held captive. Winters incorporated the story into many of his speeches in Oklahoma during the next decade.[9]

Lee believes it is more difficult to serve on the state bench than on the federal bench, especially if a district judge or associate district judge serves in a rural area of Oklahoma. Even though a judge is initially appointed by the governor, he or she must run for re-election on a non-partisan basis every four years. "The longer you serve," Lee said, "the more vulnerable you become for the simple reason that almost every dispute you rule on will make someone mad. Frequently, a ruling makes everyone mad, especially if it is a particularly good and fair ruling."[10]

In a rural area, a judge knows a high percentage of the litigants. It is a well-known fact that parties to lawsuits who know the judge tend to get madder at him or her if a ruling is not altogether favorable. Total strangers are much more understanding of adverse rulings than acquaintances.

famiLiarity
Breeds
contempt

THERE ARE DISADVANTAGES TO BEING A JUDGE in a
court where the practicing attorneys are all old acquaintances. Lee
found that to be true in his eight years on the state bench in Ada.
Many of the local lawyers were Lee's best friends. Some were former partners and combatants since law school graduation. Lee had
socialized with them, played poker with them, hunted with them,
and occasionally "did some social drinking" with them.[1]

However, when Lee became a judge, the roles with some of his
best and warmest friends changed. Lee was required to rule on matters according to the law and also had to maintain dignity and
decorum in the courtroom. The latter often required him to
"remind" his friends of their professional responsibility as officers of
the court. The attorneys were normally receptive on rulings on the
law and the facts of a case, but were less understanding when they
were reminded of their professional shortcomings. In fact, Lee said,

"They sometimes 'come unglued.' They can hardly handle an old drinking buddy sitting up there on high pointing out that they have behaved unprofessionally."[2]

An example is an incident involving Austin Deaton, Jr., one of Lee's best friends and with whom he practiced law from 1956 to 1965. Lee knew that Deaton was an excellent, able, and ethical lawyer in every respect.

After taking the bench, Lee appointed Deaton to represent an indigent criminal defendant. However, at a scheduled hearing for the accused, Deaton sent over an associate from his firm to represent the man. Lee sent word to Deaton through the associate that he had appointed Deaton as the defense lawyer and he was expected to represent the man in person.

Deaton apparently perceived Lee's message as an attempt to tell him how to run his law firm. He was "mad as hell" and it took some time after Lee left the state court bench before the two old friends renewed the warm relationship they had shared before.

Another somewhat comical example involved Lee's good friend, W.B. "Barney" Ward. Ward, although blind, had successfully served several terms as district attorney in Ada before changing sides to become the leading criminal defense lawyer in the area.

Ward had a persistent habit of being late for scheduled hearings or proceedings. Lee had mentioned the lateness problem to Ward on several occasions—without any effect. During one lengthy trial, Lee scheduled an evening session of court. He recessed at 5:00 p.m. and directed jurors and attorneys to return promptly at 6:30. He repeated the time, for Ward's benefit.

Everyone, the jurors, the defendant, witnesses, and the district attorney were all in place at 6:30. But Ward was nowhere to be found. Lee's blood pressured mounted as the minutes passed. Finally, an hour late, Ward arrived. Lee recessed court to hold a session in chambers with only District Attorney Melson, Ward, and the court reporter invited to attend.

Lee recited in great detail what he perceived to be Ward's short-comings. He pointed out that Ward was acting unprofessionally as an officer of the court and was abusing their friendship and tolerance as well as the jurors and the district attorney. Lee administered a heated tongue lashing, the best he was capable of, but concluded that even though Ward's conduct probably amounted to contempt of court, he would "let it go" this time with a warning.[3]

Ward sat through Lee's tirade without saying a word. When Lee completed his heated admonition, he asked Ward if he wanted to respond on the record. Ward said, "No." Lee then excused the court reporter, leaving only Ward, Melson, and himself in his chambers.

Ward asked, "Are we off the record?" Lee assured him they were. Ward then asked if anyone else was in the office except Melson and Lee. He was told no. Because there was no court reporter present, the exact text of Ward's comments have not been preserved for history. However, Lee and Melson, clearly remembering Ward's opening salvo, have pieced together their version. Ward said:

> Well, let me tell you something, you fat son-of-a-bitch. I've wasted more time sitting outside your office while you talk on the phone about your damned bird dogs than you have ever wasted waiting on me.[4]

Then, Ward pointed out Lee's shortcomings in much greater detail and for a much longer time than Lee had used to outline the blind lawyer's problems. Melson, who had witnessed and heard both outbursts, was both apprehensive and amused by the incident. Melson was even more surprised when Lee said, "Well, now that we have that all cleared up, let's get on with the trial." And they did.

Shortly before he left the bench in Ada, Lee finally was compelled to find Ward in contempt of court for being late. Ward simply did not show up for a scheduled jury trial because he had announced the week before that his client would waive the empaneling of a jury and try the case just to the judge. Ward said, "It was pouring rain that morning and I did not want to get wet walking a block to the courthouse, so I just didn't go." Lee called Ward and said, "Get over here right now!"[5]

At first, Ward thought Lee was kidding and failed to show. A day later, he received a visit from a deputy sheriff carrying a contempt citation signed by Lee. Ward was very angry with Lee. However, when agents of the Federal Bureau of Investigation interviewed Ward when Lee was being considered for a federal job in Washington, D.C., Ward gave Lee a glowing recommendation. Ward later confided to Melson that he had done so because, "I was afraid Lee wouldn't get that job and move to Washington."[6]

Later, Ward's contempt citation was reversed by the Oklahoma Court of Criminal Appeals. The decision was written by Judge Hez Bussey, himself almost totally blind. Ward had apparently not intended to appeal the contempt citation. However, he saw Bussey, who was a friend to both Lee and Ward, and the appeals judge said, "You can't have that on your record. You need to appeal." For reasons that Lee still does not fully understand, he was pleased that his decision was reversed.[7]

A year after Lee left Ada, Ward called Lee's home in Virginia. When informed that Lee was in Argentina, Ward asked Mary Ann to tell Lee to please visit him the next time he was in Ada. Mary Ann said, "Barney, does that mean you have forgiven him?" Ward said, "Hell no, but I do miss him!"[8] Lee and Ward remain close friends. In an interview for this biography, Ward said, "Lee's the best trial judge I ever appeared before. He kept control, but let you try your own case. There was never any doubt who was in charge of the courtroom."[9]

After such experiences, Lee was more appreciative than ever for the wisdom of the nation's founding fathers in providing for an independent judiciary by requiring that federal judges be given a lifetime appointment.

In 1968, Lee's nephew, Roy "Topper" Johnston came to Lee's office at the courthouse in Ada with news that he was deserting the

Lee's nephew, Roy "Topper" Johnston, left, and his mother, Lee's sister, Deloyce, in 1998. On occasion, Topper remembers to thank Lee for turning him away from the wilds of Canada during the Vietnam War.

United States Army and was enroute to Canada. Topper felt strongly that the war in Vietnam was illegal and immoral and he did not want to risk his life fighting it.

Lee advised Topper against deserting and running off to Canada. He agreed with Topper that the war was tragic—he even disagreed with the policy that allowed America to be mired in the conflict. However, he told Topper that if he deserted, he would regret it for the rest of his life. Lee explained that when a family or tribe was engaged in battle, the warriors of that family or tribe were obligated to fight until the battle was resolved. He said the United States was just an extension of the family. Lee said, "You should never engage in inhuman behavior, but if combat is required, you just have to take your chances."[10]

After considering the matter, Topper authorized Lee to call his commanding officer to explain that, while he was absent without leave for a few days, he would report for duty the following

Monday. Topper kept his word and received only a light punishment for his unexcused absence from the military.

Lee did some deep soul searching over the advice he had given Topper. He truly feared that if Topper was killed in the war, it would deprive Lee's sister, Deloyce, of her only child. Fortunately, Topper went on to Officer Candidate School, was commissioned, and served the remainder of his time in service stationed in Hawaii. He went on to a successful business career in California.

The Oklahoma

Lee's mother, Nicie West, never remarried after her husband's death in 1949. She suffered a heart attack in the late 1960s and moved in with her daughter Nita and her husband Alex. When Nicie died in 1971, the tiny First Christian Church in Antlers was filled with many friends and family members. In this photograph, Nicie is escorted by Kim, left, and Jennifer, at her home in Antlers. Kim and Jennifer have wonderful memories of their grandmother who had a positive influence on their young lives.

Supreme Court assigned Lee to preside over a much-publicized murder trial in 1971. A young African American, Jerry Fowler, had been charged with the first degree murder of a white Oklahoma City police officer, Richard "Dick" Radican. Racial tension was high in Oklahoma City and the trial was moved to Pauls Valley. It was the first in state history that a change of venue was granted to a county outside or adjacent to the judicial district where the crime occurred. The move was necessary because of intense pre-trial publicity of the officer's murder.[11]

Marian Opala, then the Administrative Director of the Courts, and later a Justice and Chief Justice of the Oklahoma Supreme Court, explained why Lee was chosen to hear the Fowler case, "We knew Lee was extremely well-versed in the [U.S. Chief Justice Earl] Warren Era changes in criminal constitutional law. In those days, state judges were normally not current in the day-to-day changes in criminal law. But Lee was always curious and would polish up his tools."[12]

Opala continued, "Because of the tensions that surrounded the case involving the murder of a police officer, I asked the Chief Justice to assign the case to Lee. We needed a judge like Lee to make certain the trial was fair."[13]

Kim, left, and Jennifer adorn the West family Christmas card in 1966.

The high profile case was prosecuted and defended with zeal and diligence. Curtis Harris, the veteran district attorney in Oklahoma City, was the prosecutor—assisted by James McKinney. The defense attorney was Stephen Jones, who later was called upon to represent, by court appointment, Timothy McVeigh, charged and convicted of the bombing of the Alfred P. Murrah Federal Building in Oklahoma City on April 19, 1995.

Lee remembered, "Jones was a very young attorney, without a lot of experience, but with enormous skill and determination."[14] Lee took notice of Jones' first motion in the case, a motion to force the prosecution to turn over reports and other materials generated by the police in its investigation. Lee sustained Jones' motion, a rare occasion for trial judges in the 1970s.[15]

It was not disputed that Fowler had shot Officer Radican to death. Frankly, the only question in the minds of most observers was whether the defendant would be executed or not. The odds seemed to favor Fowler's death rather than life imprisonment.

At the close of the evidence, Lee instructed the jury and it came time for the lawyers to make their closing arguments. Jones notified Lee that the defendant wanted to say something to the jury. Lee questioned Fowler outside the presence of the jury to make sure that he wanted to participate in the closing argument. Lee made it clear to the defendant that he ran great risks with the chance of aggravating the jury with some unintentional remark. Lee also told Fowler that he had never personally experienced a defendant making part of his closing argument in a capital case and cautioned him about doing so in this case.

In the end, because Lee believed that the law allowed Fowler to speak to the jury, he gave the defendant permission to do so. However, Lee had grave misgivings.

Fowler first thanked jurors for their service. He reminded them that they had promised to be fair and impartial and said he trusted them to live up to that promise. He then told them:

> To me you are a combination. You are the judges of the facts and to me you are God himself. Not only do you have the power in your hands to determine the guilt or innocence of me, you have the power in your hands to determine whether I should live or die.
>
> Now as my judge, will you consider each and every evidence that you have heard from this witness stand, and consider it carefully? You are the 12 disciples of justice and

righteousness. Now not only does Mr. Jones sit here in my defense. God himself is present in this courtroom, mentally, in my defense. Now I pray that God will guide you in the right way to a proper decision in this matter, and right now I stand before you and I enter a plea of not guilty to the charge of murder. My plea is not guilty and I would like to bring to each of your attention that I am not the cause of this tragic accident—I am its victim.

Defense attorney Jones also made an eloquent plea on behalf of Fowler—asking the jury to let him live. After the jury retired to deliberate, Judge Haskell Paul, who had observed the proceedings, went to Lee's chambers and said, "I believe he may well have saved his own life." Paul was right. The jury returned the expected verdict of guilty but recommended a sentence of life in prison. More than 30 years later, Fowler remains incarcerated in the Oklahoma prison system. Later, when Lee was appointed federal judge, he received a letter from Fowler, congratulating him and wishing him well.

Jones later reflected upon his first experience as a trial lawyer in Lee's courtroom, "I found him to be unfailingly courteous and considerate of all persons before him, including defendants, members of their families, witnesses, and everyone else. If Judge West has ever embarrassed or humiliated any person appearing before him…I never heard about it. He is a great and noble man and a judge in the finest tradition."[16]

"Judge West genuinely likes lawyers and a good lawsuit," Jones said, "he has never been imperial and he has never lost his sense of humor."[17]

pRactical jokes
and fate

MAINLY BECAUSE OF HIS ASSOCIATION with Fireball
Evans, Lee developed a serious reputation as a practical joker.

While serving as district judge in Ada, Lee became acquainted
with Deputy Sheriff Frank Vincent who owned a ranch at
Fittstown, south of Ada. A number of limestone outcrop ridges on
Vincent's ranch were home to dens of rattlesnakes. In the spring,
Vincent would catch the snakes while they were still somewhat
lethargic. He would take the largest snakes to rattlesnake hunts in
towns such as Waurika and Okeene. He entered the snakes in contests and auctioned them off or donated them to the rattlesnake
hunt cook-off.

For some strange reason, Lee agreed to hunt snakes with Vincent.
They caught many rattlers using a herp stick and gunny sack.
Vincent even taught Lee how to handle the snakes without being
bitten and how to defang them with a pair of fingernail clippers. Lee
learned that the uneasy process had to be repeated every three weeks
because the snakes grew a new set of fangs in that short time.[1]

Vincent allowed Lee to keep some of the smaller snakes to train his bird dogs to avoid being bitten by them. Lee used an electric shock collar to teach the dogs. When they approached a planted snake, he shocked the dog lightly. After a few shocks, a dog quickly learned to avoid the snakes. Lee kept the live reptiles in a wire cage. They could live and prosper on water and an ample supply of dry dog food.

The snakes played a pivotal role in one of Lee's practical jokes when football star Norman McNabb came to Ada. McNabb was an All-American and captain of OU's 1950 national championship team. He later was an assistant to OU football coach Bud Wilkinson.

Lee and McNabb had become good friends in college and were hunting buddies when McNabb worked for the Oklahoma Wildlife Department. McNabb was invited to speak to the Ada Kiwanis Club and Lee was asked to introduce him.

Lee concealed one of his larger defanged rattlesnakes in a paper sack, secured by a clothes pin, and took it with him to the luncheon. Because of publicity about McNabb's appearance, a large crowd or 200 to 300 people gathered. Lee introduced McNabb in a highly laudatory fashion and McNabb pleased the crowd with an excellent speech on Oklahoma wildlife.

After the speech, Lee told McNabb that it was customary for the Kiwanis Club to present its guest speakers with a gift. Both were sitting at the head table, pressed closely against the wall because of the large crowd. Lee told the audience that he selected a special gift for McNabb— in keeping with the wildlife theme. Lee then dumped the rattlesnake onto the table in front of McNabb.

The snake was agitated and its 10 or 11 rattles began to buzz. It attempted to strike at glasses, cups, and plates. The snake was moving so fast, no one could see that it could not open its jaws, much less bite anyone.

Pandemonium broke out as McNabb tried to fall back in his chair to escape. Fireball Evans, the only person "in on" the joke with Lee, made matters worse by rushing to the front of the room with a starter pistol loaded with blanks. He began firing at the snake. He lined up the snake directly in front of McNabb so every time he fired a round, McNabb thought he, too, was being shot.

After the panic subsided, Lee caught the snake and put it back in the sack and gave it to McNabb to take to a reptile exhibit at a zoo. But, McNabb never fully recovered from the incident and decades later repeats a series of expletives whenever Lee's name is mentioned or when they meet.

Kiwanis President Bill Lee was not enthralled with Lee's performance. He said, "You crazy SOB, what would you have done if that fellow had had a heart attack and died?" Lee replied, "Why we would have buried him—that's the only decent thing to do."[2]

The Kiwanis leader was not the least bit mollified and required Lee to pay for $65 worth of dishes that had been broken during the panic. Needless to say, Lee was never again asked to introduce a guest at Kiwanis Club.

Troy Melton was another well-known character in Ada. He and his wife, Jerry, ran an insurance agency from an office on the first floor of the American Building, across the street from the county courthouse. One day Lee walked into the office carrying a defanged rattlesnake in a sack and asked for Troy. When Lee was informed that Troy was in the bathroom, he opened the door of the bathroom and poured the snake onto the floor. There was a loud shout and Troy immediately emerged with his trousers unzipped, screaming, "Jerry! Where's my pistol?" She said, "Troy, don't shoot the snake. It can't bite you." He said, "Snake, hell, I'm gonna shoot Lee West."[3]

On two other occasions, Lee "inadvertently" let a snake crawl out of a sack in his courthouse chambers. One time was when young Ada attorneys Frank Jacques and Charles Heard were visiting with Lee. While each of them was temporarily distressed at the sight of a rattlesnake, neither reported Lee to the Council on Judicial Complaints. Fortunately, Lee's snake antics were never brought up at either of his later confirmation hearings before the United States Senate.

Good advice from Mary Ann and Lee's better judgment prevailed. He abandoned his live rattlesnake demonstrations thereafter except to train his dogs to be snake shy.

There is a law of nature—practical jokes have a way of being reciprocated. Once, Lee was presiding over a car bombing case in Tulsa. Judge Fred Nelson's car had been wired to an explosive and, when ignited by him turning on the switch, almost took his life. After Lee was assigned to the case, he was the object of rumors and jokes in Ada.

Troy Melton started the rumor that Lee required Mary Ann to start his car each morning—in case it was wired. One day when Lee turned on the ignition in his pickup parked at the courthouse, a huge cherry bomb exploded. Fireball Evans, Melton, and half the firemen in Ada were peeping around the corner of the fire station, observing Lee's reaction. Lee later presented Fireball with his laundry and cleaning bill—but Fireball refused to pay.

During his years in Ada, Lee became acquainted with an elderly character who lived in the Aldridge Hotel. The man was very much like W.C. Fields and had an unusual sense of humor. He imagined himself to be quite a storyteller, stories that Lee enjoyed. The courthouse was across the street from the hotel so Lee frequently had coffee or lunch with the raconteur.

As the years progressed, the old man became more and more feeble. So far as Lee knew, the man had no relatives. One day the man called to ask Lee a favor. He said he was moving from the hotel to a nearby nursing home and asked Lee to bring his pickup to "move my things."

Lee agreed and carried the man and a pitiful box or two of his worldly possessions across the railroad track to a terribly rundown nursing home. Lee was getting depressed as he led the man into a large waiting room lined with chairs in which several very elderly ladies sat or slept, some with their mouths open. The odor was a combination of antiseptic and other smells that almost nauseated Lee. As the man shuffled across the room beside Lee, he said cheerfully, "Damn, Judge, there are a lot of good looking women here. I intend to have a very active social life." At that moment, Lee realized that life really and truly does depend upon outlook.

Lee discovered another great truth in Ada. Occasionally, events occur which seem routine, perhaps even trivial, but later prove to be monumental events in one's life.

Two events, totally disconnected at the time, became significant events in Lee's life. In the one grand jury investigation that Lee presided over while on the state bench in Ada, a well-known local citizen, Bert Payne, was foreman. After the grand jury was excused, Payne approached Lee with a request. He had a young friend, Molly Shi, was who was a schoolteacher in the area but was contemplating attending law school.

Molly, according to Payne, was uncertain about her chances of succeeding in law school and in the legal profession which was still very much a man's world. Payne asked Lee to counsel with Molly because of his position as judge and as a former law school professor.

Lee readily agreed and Molly came to his chambers. He found her to be extremely intelligent and outstanding in every respect and assured her that she would excel in the study of law and would likely find success as a practitioner or judge someday.

Because of her great ability and determination, aided by his enthusiastic encouragement, Molly was a great success. She excelled at the OU School of Law, enjoyed notable success as a young lawyer, winning against such experienced lawyers as State Senator Gene Stipe, and was named Special District Judge in Pontotoc County shortly after Lee left the bench in Ada in 1973. In 1977, Molly left the bench when she married Governor David L. Boren and became First Lady of Oklahoma.

While in Ada, two of Molly's best friends were Fireball Evans and Vernon Roberts, later the chairman of United States Senator

David Boren's nominating committee for federal judges. Lee's mentorship of Molly was just part of the story.

The other seemingly disconnected story involved David Boren who grew up in Seminole, the son of veteran Congressman Lyle H. Boren. Young Boren attended Yale University, was a Rhodes scholar at Oxford University in England, and graduated from the OU Law School. He was later Governor of Oklahoma, United States Senator, and president of the University of Oklahoma.

But in 1966, Boren opted to run for his first public office. He filed for a state House of Representatives seat in Seminole County. Bill Wantland, a well-known young lawyer, was his opponent and both conducted a spirited campaign. When the votes were counted, Boren held a small lead but Wantland demanded a recount. Lee was required to preside over the recount in Seminole.

The recount was uneventful, Boren picked up a few more votes, and was declared the winner. The outcome was accepted without rancor on Wantland's part but he did later leave the legal profession to become an Episcopal priest, which he considered "a higher calling."

Lee has often pondered what course his career would have taken if Molly Shi had not become his friend. He also has thought what would have happened if young Boren had not won that recount. Lee believes that each of them might well have gone on to outstanding careers because of their immense capabilities. However, he is certain he would never have had the rare opportunity of serving on the federal bench in the absence of those two events.

Boren later publicly acknowledged that while he was making his very first federal judge appointment after becoming a United States Senator, the last words he heard every night from his wife Molly were, "Lee West, Lee West, Lee West."[4]

Lee truly enjoyed his years as district judge in Ada. He was fortunate to serve with many outstanding trial judges—Alan McPheron, Jess Miracle, Ralph Hodges, Don Barnes, Rudolph Hargrave, Robert Simms, Hardy Summers, Robert Howell, Lavern Fishel, Dean Linder, and others.

The annual judicial conferences were enjoyable because of the antics of the judges. For three years in a row, Lee observed McPheron and Merle Lansden persuade a somewhat inebriated judge from eastern Oklahoma that he was to be elected president of the judges' association. McPheron and Lansden assisted the judge in writing his acceptance speech and critiqued him in several rehearsal runs before their poker playing colleagues. On all three occasions, the "heir apparent" got "deeply enough into his cups" that he failed to appear at the meeting the next morning and someone else was elected president.[5]

The conference of judges had a serious side and a seminar was always part of the meeting for continuing education of the judges. In 1967, Lee was asked to share the program with United States District Judge Fred Daugherty who had been a distinguished state trial judge before being appointed to the federal bench.

Lee and Daugherty were scheduled to discuss the impact of United States Supreme Court decisions on state trial proceedings. Daugherty had to cancel at the last minute and Lee had the entire seminar to himself.

Lee presented his paper, titled, "A Survey of the Impact of Federal Decisions on State Trial Proceedings." He outlined the federal courts' use of habeas corpus to correct apparent wrongs committed by state judges in criminal cases. He said, "There is a clear indication that the federal courts are and will continue to supervise our procedures to be sure that we are complying with the standards of the Federal Constitution."[6]

He gave a textbook presentation to the state judges about mistakes that often brought about reversals of criminal convictions. Among the problem areas Lee spoke of were involuntary confessions, denial of counsel at trial, the state's failure to disclose exculpatory evidence, trial influence by mob rule, illegal search and seizure, and prejudicial publicity. Lee told the judges, "If we, willingly and enthusiastically, look to the improvement of our procedures, then we can avoid [federal court] intervention."[7]

Lee believed that friction between state and federal courts might be ameliorated if the states would look upon recent federal court decisions as an opportunity to provide state procedures, direct or collateral, for a full airing of federal constitutional claims.

Lee was also concerned about tainting a prospective jury pool in rural areas where everyone read the local newspaper, especially accounts of what evidence had been uncovered, either legally or illegally. He told the state judges, "Personally, I have talked this matter over with the law enforcement officials and the news media in our area. I believe I am getting pretty good cooperation. The news people aren't happy with this, but it is far better than some of the more drastic restraints that are indicated." Lee warned that federal courts might, in the future, use contempt citations to thwart press interference with jury trials.[8]

After Lee gave the trial judges 25 pages of material, a discussion ensued, often with a great deal of heat.

It was the first time Lee recognized how resentful some of his colleagues on the state bench were of what they considered the federal courts "meddling" in how state judges conducted trials. Lee encouraged them to learn from the intervention, to avoid constitutional pitfalls.

After the discussion of Lee's paper, someone suggested that it be published to assist state judges to avoid problems some of them had previously been unaware of. One irate judge vehemently objected, saying, "If you publish that damned paper, half the prisoners in the state penitentiary will go free on writs of "habus scapus." The judge meant, of course, habeas corpus. The paper was published and distributed with none of the predicted dire consequences. It may well have prevented a few constitutional deprivations along the way. [9]

Governor Henry Bellmon appointed Lee to serve as a special justice on the Oklahoma Supreme Court to hear a case involving a Cleveland County millionaire, Dexter G. Johnson. A decade earlier, Johnson had died and his will was the subject of a probate action in Cleveland County court. After much legal wrangling, the case rulings were in question because charges of bribery and corruption had been leveled at three of the Supreme Court Justices who originally decided the case. Justice N.B. Johnson was impeached and removed from office by the State Senate. Justice N.S. Corn was convicted on a federal charge of income tax evasion and resigned from the Court and Justice Earl Welch also resigned.

Lee served with a distinguished panel of regular Supreme Court justices—Pat Irwin, Don Barnes, and Ralph Hodges--and Special Justice, Maurice Merrill, who had been Lee's constitutional law professor at the OU Law School. Lee had found Merrill, during law school, to be a brilliant scholar but had difficulty understanding what he said. The same was true in hearings and in deciding the Supreme Court case in question. Lee authored the opinion and all justices, including Dr. Merrill, concurred with him.

During his last years of service as district judge, in 1972 and 1973, the Oklahoma Supreme Court assigned Lee to try several high profile criminal cases, both in Tulsa and Oklahoma City. While he was flattered by the confidence the high court apparently had in him, it kept him very busy. He was actually spending more time on the special cases than on his own docket in Pontotoc County.

Several cases involved Thomas Lester Pugh and Albert McDonald, in Lee's opinion, "Not Boy Scouts, to say the least." [10] They were convicted arsonists, bootleggers, and robbers who were charged with murdering Cleo Epps, a notorious bootlegging queen, and Arless Delbert Self. The lawyer who was defending Pugh and McDonald was running for district judge against the incumbent, Judge Fred Nelson, who was presiding over their pending trials.

On the morning of the election, Nelson turned on his car's ignition and exploded a bomb. The blast destroyed the car and Nelson suffered near fatal injuries. However, he was easily re-elected by Tulsa County voters.

Pugh and McDonald were both charged with attempting to murder Judge Nelson. All of the district judges in Tulsa County disqualified and Lee was assigned to try the cases.

Both Pugh and McDonald were convicted on multiple counts and were sentenced to long terms in the state penitentiary. Pugh is still incarcerated. McDonald went to the state prison in McAlester where he died when his throat was cut in a love triangle dispute.[11]

Lee presided over another murder trial in Tulsa in which the defendant was found guilty of first degree murder. The jury hung up on the prosecution's plea for the death penalty so Lee sentenced the killer to life in prison. It was the closest Lee ever came to personally sentencing a man to be executed.

tHe CIVIL aeRONauTICS BoaRD

LIFE IN ADA FOR LEE, MARY ANN, AND THE GIRLS
was wonderful. For Lee, his job as district judge was both fulfilling and challenging. Then, in 1972, a phone call came—it was from Oklahoma United States Senator Henry Bellmon. Bellmon, the former Governor of Oklahoma, who had appointed Lee as district judge seven years earlier, had been elected to the Senate in 1968 after a stint as campaign manager for Republican presidential candidate Richard Nixon, who was also elected in 1968.

Bellmon informed Lee of a possible vacancy on the Civil Aeronautics Board (CAB). Bellmon, always on the lookout for an opportunity to place Oklahomans on regulatory boards in the federal government, asked if Lee and Mary Ann would consider coming to Washington, D.C.

Lee was stunned by the suggestion. He was a Little Dixie Democrat—President Nixon was a Republican—so was Bellmon. Lee told Bellmon, "I thought I had broken you of the habit of appointing me to anything."[1] The two old friends, despite being at the opposite ends of the spectrum on some political issues, joked about the possibility. "I have no choice," Bellmon said, "The vacancy on the CAB is for a Democratic member, and one Democrat is about as bad as another."[2]

On the serious side of the conversation, Bellmon said he did not want to advance Lee's name for the job unless he was interested. Lee asked for a couple of days to talk over the idea with Mary Ann. After considering the suggestion, Lee called Bellmon back and said he was interested. Thinking such an appointment was a long shot, Lee forgot about the CAB. Then, another phone call came.

This time, it was from Oklahoma's Third District congressman, Carl Albert, who had risen through the ranks to become one of the nation's most powerful leaders, as Speaker of the United States House of Representatives. Albert said he had just learned that Lee's name would be submitted to the White House for consideration of appointment to the CAB and that he, Albert, was in enthusiastic support of the move.

Lee apologized for not informing his good friend, Albert, about Bellmon's earlier offer. He said he really did not think there was much chance of him being in line for the position. Albert, who had established a legendary record of boosting citizens of the Third District, said, "Don't worry about that. There is nothing I enjoy doing more than trying to help someone who needs help."[3]

The CAB was created by Congress in 1938 to regulate and promote the airline industry in the United States. The Federal Aviation Act of 1958 had given the CAB jurisdiction over active air carriers in the country, including the right to set rates for domestic transportation. Seen as a powerful federal agency, the CAB also had authority to represent the nation's interests in agreements with foreign countries. One of the architects of the 1958 revamping of the nation's airline laws was Oklahoma United States Senator Mike Monroney for whom the Federal Aviation Administration's center in Oklahoma City is named.

The CAB was composed of five members appointed by the president and confirmed by the United States Senate. Its headquarters was in Washington, D.C. Among its bureaus were government specialists who settled complaints against the airlines and analyzed the economic impact and stability of the airline industry. In signing the law that created the CAB in 1958, President Dwight Eisenhower asked the agency to encourage, promote, and develop adequate, economical, and efficient air service for Americans. Eisenhower also believed the CAB could play a major role in promoting air safety.[4]

Before Lee's possible appointment to the CAB was announced publicly, he received a call from White House Special Counsel John Dean. Dean asked Lee about any conflicts of interest that would prevent him from holding the CAB job if he was nominated by President Nixon. Lee said he knew of none—he owned no airline stock and was willing to unload his meager stock portfolio if nominated, just to avoid the appearance of any conflict of interest.

Dean also asked about any foreseeable problems in being confirmed by the United States Senate. Lee, knowing that he had the backing of Republican Henry Bellmon, and the fact that he had no skeletons in his closet except for the practical jokes with Fireball Evans, told Dean he knew of no problems. During their long conversations, Dean never mentioned that there was a cancer—Watergate—growing on the Presidency.

In the following weeks, in early 1973, Lee received calls from the Office of Counsel to the President, asking him the same questions that Dean had asked. Lee became somewhat exasperated by the in-depth probing and said, "I have already gone over all of this with Mr. Dean, where is he?"[5] A White House spokesman, Peter M. Flanigan, informed Lee that Dean was involved in other matters. A few days later, Dean resigned his position at the White House, announced he would not be a scapegoat for anyone, and launched a dark day in American politics—the Watergate scandal.

Dean, a man whom Lee had never heard of when they first conversed, quickly became a household name, appearing for days of testimony before the Senate Select Committee on Presidential Campaign Activities, informally called the Ervin Committee, after its chairman, United States Senator Sam J. Ervin, Jr., a North Carolina Democrat. For what seemed like weeks, Dean's testimony was broadcast live by the nation's television networks as he gave details of the events leading to the Watergate scandal.[6]

Despite dealing with the rigorous demands of Watergate as its tentacles moved toward him, President Nixon formally nominated Lee to the $38,000-a-year post on the CAB on March 12, 1973. The news, that had been rumored in Washington circles for days, came in a routine press release from the White House. The release said Lee had broad bipartisan support—from Republican Bellmon and the country's top Democratic elected official, House Speaker Carl Albert.

Normally, CAB appointments generate little comment or excitement. However, Lee's nomination set off a flurry of high-level political and corporate activity, much of which was far from the public view. *The Wall Street Journal* announced the nomination and predicted that Lee would meet "tough going" in the Senate confirmation process. The newspaper outlined the reasons for its opinion that Lee might not be confirmed.[7]

Much of Lee's problem, not of his own making, was centered around whom he was replacing on the CAB. Robert T. Murphy of Rhode Island had angered the Nixon administration because he had taken the lead in a July 28, 1972, CAB decision rejecting a proposed merger of American Airlines and Western Airlines. Officials of American Airlines, strong supporters of President Nixon, had let the White House know that they wanted Murphy off the CAB.

Murphy, a Democrat, and 12-year veteran on the board, frequently dissented with the CAB's Republican majority and opposed moves of the airlines to cut back on flights to improve earnings. American Airlines was not the only airline upset with Murphy because of his advocacy of increased recognition of labor interests, anti-monopolistic practices, and industry competition.[8]

Back in Ada, Lee was an instant celebrity as his phone rang constantly with calls from well-wishers and reporters. Oklahoma Attorney General Larry Derryberry, Lee's former student, wrote a tongue-in-cheek endorsement of Lee for the aeronautical position. Derryberry said, "As a direct result of the appointment, my wife, Gale and I have terminated our memberships to the American Airlines Club, TWA Travelers Club, and Altus Airlines Flying Circus, and we have invested heavily in Greyhound and Amtrak."[9]

As soon as Lee's nomination was announced, supporters of Murphy went on the attack. United States Senator Norris Cotton, Republican of New Hampshire, warned that Lee would have a long wait, in fact would have "a long, white beard" before he would get a hearing on his nomination before the Senate Commerce Committee that held hearings and recommended or rejected nominations to the CAB.

Lee was the subject of many national news stories. The country's best-known political columnist, Jack Anderson, covered the story in his Merry Go Round column titled, "Lawmaker Fights White House Pick."[10] Anderson related the story of White House Special Counsel Peter Flanigan phoning Senator Cotton with news that New Englander Murphy would not be reappointed. Angrily, Cotton told Flanigan that he would fight Lee's selection and would do everything in his power to hold up the nomination.[11]

Cotton's opposition to Lee was a formidable barrier because he was a Republican and a strong supporter of most programs of the Nixon administration. In addition, three other members of the Senate Commerce Committee also publicly expressed their support of Murphy's reappointment. The three other Senators were Democrats—Warren Magnuson of Washington, the chairman of the committee; John Pastore of Rhode Island; and Howard

Cannon of Nevada. Part of the opposition from New England Senators came from the realization that Murphy was the last New Englander on the CAB and had blocked a proposed merger between Delta Airlines and Northeast Airlines, a merger that some thought would weaken airline service in the region.

Newspapers quoted reliable sources that charged that the White House badly mishandled the nomination, adding to the views of some congressmen that Nixon had absolute disdain for the Congress.[12] The headline of *Aviation Week & Space Technology*, a leading airline industry publication, read, "West Nomination to CAB Spurs Hostility."[13] Harold D. Watkins, who wrote the article for the publication, put forth the theory that Murphy was being replaced because he was the former counsel to the Senate Commerce Aviation Subcommittee, chaired by Senator Mike Monroney, whom Bellmon had defeated in 1968.

Bellmon denied the charge. An aide to the senator said there was no effort to get rid of Murphy but rather that Bellmon stayed alert to government vacancies and wanted to fill them with qualified Oklahomans. As in most press reports of the controversy, Lee was painted as an innocent bystander, "an obscure district judge who lives 90 miles from an airport in Oklahoma."[14]

Because his future in Washington, D.C., was cloudy at best, Lee held on to his district judgeship in Ada. He tried to ignore weekly newspaper stories and go about handling his court docket in a normal manner.

Lee received support from all over. Oklahoma Supreme Court Chief Justice Denver Davison, in a letter to Senator Bellmon, said, "In the 36 years I have spent on the Supreme Court bench, I have known few trial judges who equal Judge West in intellect and ethical fitness."[15]

Florence K. Murray, a justice of the Superior Court of Rhode Island, who knew Lee from judicial conferences, wrote to her own Senator Pastore, "It is not my purpose to be impertinent but merely to suggest to you that if…you have reason to consider Judge West's nomination…you will bear in mind my good representations as to his character, integrity, and ability and give them that weight which might incline and scale in his favor. To know him would be to like him."[16]

Justice Murray, who had worked for Senator Pastore early in her career, knew she was going out on a limb to oppose Murphy, also a resident of Rhode Island. She wrote Lee, "I may have lost my innocence but I have not lost my zest to fly in the face of a bull."[17]

Lee heard from many of his friends about his possible move to the nation's capital. R.H. Coleman, the president of the Remington Arms Company, wrote, "I cannot understand how you were ever talked into this because undoubtedly it will take quite a bit of your time away from bird shooting."[18]

One of the state's veteran district judges, Lavern Fishel, of Coalgate, wrote Lee, "Tis' Sunday night and I am in the office working on jury instructions. I want you to know that I have full and complete confidence in your honesty and integrity. But, Judge, they play rough in Washington and seemingly have no respect for another, his character or his reputation. Politics there is different than that which we learned in southeastern Oklahoma."[19]

Judge Fishel was right. Charges and countercharges flew over the next few weeks as Murphy's supporters accused American Airlines of manipulating Lee's appointment, especially because American had a large maintenance depot in Lee's home state, in Tulsa. Then, a bombshell allegation hit the press.

It was revealed that American Airlines had made a $55,000 illegal campaign contribution to Nixon's election effort, a contribution later refunded. Because of the Watergate investigation, it was easy for Lee's opponents, or rather Murphy's supporters, to get airtime with allegations of impropriety. Senator Pastore implied that the contribution resulted in Nixon appointing Lee who might be favorable to American's position in future CAB actions. Pastore said he had no proof but he suspected "corruption of the appointing power."[20] Pastore called for an investigation by Archibald Cox, the famed lawyer who had been appointed as a special prosecutor to investigate corruption charges flowing from Watergate.

Lee, and his primary supporter, Senator Bellmon, vehemently denied any connection between Lee's appointment and American Airlines. Lee said he had no contact with American before his appointment and had only casually met the president of the airline once.

Bellmon was angry. He accused his fellow Senator, Pastore, of "impugning the integrity of an outstanding Oklahoma jurist, the House Speaker, the President, and himself."[21] Bellmon requested that Cox's investigation into the matter be commenced immediately, writing, "This unwarranted cloud of suspicion must be quickly removed from the affected parties."[22] Lee wholeheartedly agreed.

Senator Bartlett was also angered by Pastore's call for the special prosecutor's investigation. He called Pastore's suspicions "disgusting" and labeled Cox's acceptance of the probe "likewise disgusting." Bartlett said, "It makes you wonder if Cox is going to be the political hatchet-man for a lot of his friends."[23]

Lee's hometown newspaper, *The Ada Evening News*, took the opportunity to blast Pastore and give a reason why that the senator's allegation was being investigated. An editorial said, "Well, things are pretty touchy these days in Washington and they'll investigate anything at the drop of a hat."[24]

The newspaper's editor, George E. Gurley, defended Lee in the editorial, especially Lee's friendship and good relations with Bellmon, Senator Dewey Bartlett, and Speaker Albert. "Truth of the matter is," the editorial stated, "that the Judge is an extremely friendly man, gregarious even, and he knows all kinds of people in all sorts of places and conditions."[25]

Gurley saw some good coming out of the publicity, writing, "We knew it. We knew it. We knew it. Fame would come to Ada. In a remote sort of way, it even came along via Watergate. Very remote. At least, the Watergate special prosecutor, Archibald Cox, is involved."

"Pastore's Cheap Trick" was the title of an editorial in the *Tulsa World*. The newspaper called Pastore's "vicious smear attack" on Lee "straight out of the Dark Ages of American politics." The editorial continued, "Pastore is notorious for his hot temper and quick tongue. But up to now, he has enjoyed a reputation for honesty and fair play. Maybe he's just caught up in the general Watergate hysteria."[26]

The *Tulsa World* tried to reason why Pastore had leveled the charges and accused the Senator of McCarthyism, writing, "We are led to believe that since West lives in Ada and American has a maintenance center in Tulsa, and American officials have talked to Bellmon, then West must have been transformed into a leper. Baloney."[27]

Behind the scenes, top-level White House aides tried to resolve the sticky impasse. Senator Cotton visited with Presidential Counselors Melvin Laird and Bryce Harlow. Harlow was a native of Oklahoma City who Secretary of State Henry Kissinger called the most effective power broker in the 20th century.[28]

Harlow and Laird proposed that Murphy leave his post and be appointed for one year to another vacancy on the CAB to replace Secor D. Browne who had resigned with a year left on his term. The deal would serve the dual purpose of silencing critics of Nixon for not reappointing Murphy and open the door for Lee's immediate confirmation. Murphy declined the offer.

Bellmon suggested that Lee make courtesy calls on the leading senators who would, hopefully, soon be asked to confirm him to the CAB position. Bellmon escorted Lee to the office of Senator Cotton, who was gruff but courteous. Cotton assured Lee his opposition was nothing personal but was tied to his support for Murphy who had fought vigorously to maintain decent air service into the smaller cities of New England.[29] Lee also met with Senator Cannon, Senator Magnuson, and Senator Russell Long of Louisiana who said, "Judge, you tell Carl Albert and Henry Bellmon that I will help any way I can to get you a confirmation hearing."[30]

Meanwhile, Special Prosecutor Cox announced his office could find no evidence that Lee's nomination had been used as a bartering item. Assistant Attorney General Henry E. Peterson wrote, "The officials of American denied, with no evidence to the contrary, that they either proposed or supported the selection of Judge Lee R. West."[31]

With that news, Pastore knew his fight to keep Murphy on the CAB was over. A Pastore aide said, "Once we got that information, there was not much else we could do."[32] On October 15, 1973, Murphy resigned from the CAB and became director of the Association of Local Transport Airlines. Once Murphy bowed out, Senators Pastore and Cotton withdrew their opposition to Lee's appointment.

Lee began to prepare for the Senate confirmation hearing. One of his hunting friends, Jack Weiss, when informed that the appointment had something to do with airplanes, quipped, "Hell, he don't even know how to hook up a horse trailer."[33]

Weiss's statement was partly true. Lee knew almost nothing about the airline industry and the government's regulation thereof. Fortunately, he had a good friend, Keith Kahle, who had founded a commuter airline, Central Airlines, in Oklahoma City. Central had merged with Frontier Airlines and Kahle was a knowledgeable player in the industry.

Back in March, Kahle, who stammered badly, called Lee and said, "Lee, the President has non-nominated a Lee West to ser-serve on the CAB—that's not you is it?" When Lee said it was him, Kahle replied, "What the hell do you know about airline regulation?" Lee honesty said, "Absolutely zero." Then Kahle gasped, "Oh my God!"[34]

In a great act of friendship, Kahle took it upon himself to prepare Lee for the confirmation hearing. During the summer, he had sent Lee volumes of reading material. After reading the information, Lee asked questions which Kahle promptly answered. To Lee, it was like starting law school all over again. The aviation jargon was new and unknown to him.

As the confirmation hearing approached, Kahle held a two-day dress rehearsal for Lee. Kahle was so knowledgeable of the views of the senators on the Commerce Committee that he assumed the role of each and posed questions to Lee. To Lee's astonishment, and to Kahle's great credit, Lee was not asked one question at the actual confirmation hearing that he had not faced from Kahle in practice.

Lee's date with the Subcommittee on Air Transportation of the Commerce Committee came on October 30, 1973. The Subcommittee convened to consider Lee's nomination and the nomination of Richard J. O'Melia, a Maryland Republican, who had been nominated by the president for the other CAB vacancy.

Senator Bellmon introduced Lee and quoted from letters of support from Chief Justice Davison, Oklahoma Administrator of the Courts Marian Opala, and Senator Dewey Bartlett. Bartlett said he regretted seeing Lee leave Oklahoma, but "he will be a real asset to the CAB and the federal government."[35]

Bellmon said he had known Lee for a long time as a personal friend and knew him to be a fine lawyer and a jurist of great ability and the highest possible integrity. Bellmon related how he had appointed Lee to the state bench in 1965. He told his fellow Senators, "Since that time, Judge West has proven himself to be one of the most highly regarded and able jurists in the southwestern United States. He is one of the very few district judges called upon regularly to serve on special assignment as a member of the Supreme Court of Oklahoma and the Court of Criminal Appeals….any time there is an especially difficult or complex case which calls for the assignment of a special judge, it is Lee West that the Oklahoma State Court system calls upon.[36]

When it came time for Lee to talk, he was naturally very nervous. He remembered, "I didn't embarrass any of the Senators and, more importantly, I didn't embarrass myself."

Lee began with a prepared statement in which he confessed that he was not an expert on air transportation. However, he told the Senators that he believed his experience as a practicing attorney, a

Lee, left, is congratulated on his confirmation as a member of the Civil Aeronautics Board by Oklahoma Congressman Tom Steed.

law school professor, and as a judge, would qualify him to interpret and apply the Federal Aviation Act. He promised that he would do so "fairly and impartially."[37]

When questions from senators began, Lee was ready. Senator Cotton asked about airline service to small towns. Lee, noting that he grew up in a town of 2,000 and lived in a town of 15,000, said he would be sensitive to the plight of people in small cities in America who needed airline service. Lee also reminded Cotton that he had to either drive 90 miles to the nearest airport or ride a Greyhound bus to get to his own confirmation hearing.[38]

Apparently satisfied that Lee's integrity and intelligence outweighed any inexperience in government regulation of the nation's airlines, members of the Subcommittee unanimously confirmed Lee to a six-year term on the CAB.

Speaker Albert held a reception for Lee and Mary Ann in the Speaker's chambers. It was attended by Senators Bellmon and Bartlett and a host of others, including Congressman Charles Halleck of Indiana, and Congressmen Tom Steed, James Jones, and John "Happy" Camp of Oklahoma.

Lee's longtime friend and Washington kingpin J.D. Williams, a native Oklahoman, hosted a victory banquet at a posh club. It was indeed a day of victories. The huge reception resulted in Mary Ann's picture appearing on the front page of the society section of

Lee, right, and Mary Ann, center, visit with Oklahoma United States Senator Henry Bellmon in preparation for Lee's Senate confirmation hearing in October, 1973.

Senator Henry Bellmon, right, administers the oath of office to Lee, left, while Mary Ann looks on.

the *Washington Post*. And, Lee received a call informing him that his hunting dog, Barshoe Suddenly, had won the American Field Quail Futurity.

Lee was sworn in during a ceremony at the CAB Building on North Connecticut Street, just across the street from where President Ronald Reagan was later wounded by John W. Hinckley, Jr. Immediately after he was sworn in, Lee officially resigned as district judge in a letter to Oklahoma Governor David Hall.

Lee and Mary Ann returned to Ada, began packing, and listed their home with a realtor, Fireball Evans. They looked forward to the change in their lives with both anticipation and apprehension.

aiRLiNe ReguLatOR

WHILE MARY ANN AND THE GIRLS STAYED IN ADA to see through the sale of the house, Lee assumed his federal post in Washington, D.C., and lived in an apartment with Tom and Jeannie Prather until he could buy a house.

Lee had hired Jeannie as his secretary while he was a state judge. At first, he was apprehensive about hiring her when she applied. Jeannie was the daughter of one of his best friends, District Judge Lavern Fishel of Coalgate. Fishel was an excellent judge known for his bit of temper and propensity to not suffer fools lightly. Lee had practiced in front of Fishel and quail hunted with him after Lee took the state bench. When Jeannie answered his advertisement for a secretary, he thought, "If this doesn't work out, I might lose a good friend as well as a secretary."[1]

Lee called Jeannie's former employer, Elvan George, a friend who coached the football team at East Central State University in Ada. George said, "If you can get her, you better hire her. She's the best secretary I ever had."[2] Lee followed George's recommendation and hired Jeannie, a decision he never regretted. Upon going to Washington, D.C., Lee hired Jeannie and put Tom to work at the CAB also.

As Jeannie helped Lee set up his office at the CAB, she quickly intimidated the "bean counters" of the bureaucracy. Lee frequently arrived at work to see bureaucrats coming out of her office in full flight with terror-stricken faces. Lee said, "They had just learned that she was indeed Lavern Fishel's daughter."[3]

Lee found a house for his family in Fairfax, Virginia, in an area called Mantua. It was a large colonial house on a cul-de-sac in a nice neighborhood. It cost twice as much as the better home that he sold in Ada, but fortunately appreciated in value by 50 percent while the Wests lived there.

Mary Ann, Kim, and Jennifer joined Lee and the girls were enrolled in local schools. Mary Ann kept busy as a mother and wife and joined the CAB wives' organization which was quite active. She worked part time for Bloomingdale's Department Store in the interior design department and later co-managed an art gallery in Georgetown.

Lee hired Charles "Chuck" Palmer as his administrative assistant and Elizabeth "Libby" Meade, who had served on the staff of Lee's predecessor, as his second secretary. Palmer most recently had been on the staff of Senator Henry Bellmon. Lee also hired Charles "Chuck" Raines, a native of McAlester, Oklahoma, as his law clerk. Raines had graduated from the OU School of Law and the London School of Economics. While working for Lee, he received his LLM from the George Washington University Law School. Raines was later replaced by Juliana Winters, an Emory University Law School graduate and daughter of Leo Winters, Lee's good friend and Oklahoma's state treasurer and former lieutenant governor. Juliana, who was the first woman law clerk at the CAB, had inherited a lot of her father's sense of humor and was a delightful addition to the staff. Lee enjoyed breaking new ground with the appointment of Juliana. Later, as a federal judge, Lee hired H.G. Prince as the first African American law clerk in the Western District of Oklahoma.

After Juliana worked at the CAB for only a few months, Lee called her into his office one day. He casually said, "I want you to go home and spend the afternoon thinking about how we can get rid of cigarette smoke on airplanes in this country."[4] Lee had a notion that secondhand smoke was somehow harmful to other passengers, especially children, and let it be known to other members of the CAB that he was in favor of stiff anti-smoking regulations. Lee's standing offer was that he would support any restriction on smoking on domestic airline flights, including a total ban, if any two of the other members would agree to the action and constitute a majority.[5]

Eventually, smoking was eliminated on domestic airline flights in the United States. However, it was technically a con-

Dignitaries who honored Lee at a reception after he was confirmed as the newest member of the Civil Aeronautics Board included, left to right, Congressman James Jones of Oklahoma, Congressman Charles Halleck of Indiana, Congressman John "Happy" Camp of Oklahoma, House Speaker Carl Albert, Oklahoma United States Senator Dewey Bartlett, and Keith Kahle, the former airline owner who prepared Lee for questions from senators in his confirmation hearing.

cern of the fire hazard on board aircraft that resulted in the ban on smoking.

With staff in place, Lee began performing his duties as a member of the CAB. The routine day-to-day matters such as considering fare increases, charter permits, and increasing or decreasing airline flight schedules were so new to him that he had to do background research on everything.

Lee learned quickly to like the other members of the CAB. Robert Timm, who was from the state of Washington, was the new chairman of the board. He later resigned under fire because

RIGHT: Chuck Palmer, left, served as Lee's administrative assistant for the first two years Lee served on the Civil Aeronautics Board.

ABOVE: Left to right, Keith Kahle,
Lee, and Lee's administrative assistant
Chuck Palmer. Kahle was a valuable
advisor to Lee before he was appointed
to the Civil Aeronautics Board.

Jennifer, left, and Kim, center, settled in to a normal school and family life in Washington, D.C. Here they pose with their cousin, Katie West, right.

he accepted gratuities from an airline in the form of a golfing vacation.

Whitney Gilliland, a former state judge from Iowa, was a gentleman of the old school who Lee got along with well—even though they often cast their votes differently on issues coming before the board.

Timm and Gilliland were both Republicans. The third Republican was Richard O'Melia, from Wisconsin, who had served in several staff positions with the CAB before becoming a member of the board. Lee and O'Melia had appeared at the same confirmation hearing and shared an interest in both the outdoors and in athletics.

The fifth member of the board was Lee's fellow Democrat, G. Joseph Minetti of New York. He and Lee became close friends, almost "kindred spirits."[6] Minetti's wife, Jean, had been married to the infamous Wisconsin Senator Joseph McCarthy. Jean and Mary Ann became close friends and Kim and Jennifer adored Jean.

Lee, left, and G. Joseph Minetti, who served on the Civil Aeronautics Board for more than 20 years, a record for service on the important board that governed the nation's airlines. Lee and Minetti became very close friends, humorously citing their similarity in backgrounds—Lee from Antlers and Minetti from Brooklyn.

Lee and Mary Ann pose for Keith Kahle's camera outside the United States Capitol in Washington, D.C.

Minetti was Lee's mentor at the CAB. He was a Fordham University Law School graduate—not only intelligent but extremely wise of the ways in Washington. It was from Minetti that Lee first learned how to avoid the sort of problems that CAB member Timm had encountered. Minetta said, "Lee, the airlines will seek ways to ingratiate themselves to you and you must be on constant guard or they will do something for you or your staff that will embarrass you, at least, and perhaps even disqualify you from serving as a member."[7]

Minetti summed up his warning to Lee, "If it would look suspect if printed on the front page of the *Washington Post*, don't let them do it for you."[8]

Lee took Minetti's advice and developed a well known reputation for his rigidity about not accepting gratuities from the airlines that he regulated. Bob Six, the president of Continental Airlines, and husband of actress Jane Meadows, was a strong University of Colorado football fan. The head coach at Colorado was former OU assistant, Eddie Crowder, Lee's longtime friend. Six and Crowder invited Lee and Mary Ann to attend an OU-Colorado game at Boulder. Knowing about Lee's policy, Six wrote at the bottom of the letter, "You can get your own damned ticket."[9]

Lee's policy once had a humorous ending. He and Mary Ann were traveling coach from Oklahoma City back to Washington, D.C. While waiting for their flight at the Braniff Airlines ticket counter at Oklahoma City's Will Rogers World Airport, they encountered and visited with Lee's old friend and bird dog buddy, Ray Thompson, who worked as a telephone repairman at the airport.

Shortly thereafter, the Braniff desk agent asked to see Lee and Mary Ann's tickets. The agent began writing on the tickets and said, "I'm upgrading you both to first class." Lee advised him that he could not permit that because he was a member of the CAB and could not accept a gratuity of any kind." The agent said, "Hell, fellow, I was just doing it because you are a friend of Ray Thompson, the telephone repairman."[10]

A great perk of Lee's position on the CAB was the opportunity to travel. Each of the four members of the CAB headed a team of negotiators who joined officials from the Department of State to negotiate treaties with foreign governments regarding aviation rights. For example, the United States had formal agreements with many countries such as Canada, Mexico, Great Britain, the Soviet Union, and West Germany, outlining the rights of both countries to land airliners at certain cities at specified intervals. Such treaties were called bilateral agreements.

The CAB divided the globe into four quadrants with four members assigned a specific quadrant to monitor the bilateral agreements for that part of the world. Normally, the chairman of the CAB did not participate in bilateral negotiations.

Lee was first assigned to bilateral negotiations in the Western Hemisphere which included Canada, all of South and Central America, and the islands of the Caribbean Sea. Shortly after he took office, Lee was sent to Barbados, Curacao, and Venezuela.[11]

Soon, Lee headed the CAB negotiation team on trips to Rio de Janeiro, Brazil; Buenos Aires, Argentina; Montevideo, Uruguay; and Asuncion, Paraguay. Later, he traveled to Santiago, Chile; Lima, Peru; and Quito, Ecuador. He spent a lot of time in Mexico City and Ottawa, Canada, because the United States was trying to improve both the number of cities served and the frequency of flights to those countries.

The high level negotiations did not frighten Lee. He frankly found negotiating airline agreements with foreign governments no more difficult than trading horses, as he had done with his father growing up in southeast Oklahoma. The language barrier made the new style of trading more difficult, but with good interpreters, he learned to adjust well.

As vacancies occurred on the CAB, and news got out of Lee's friendliness and ability to negotiate agreements, he was assigned responsibilities outside his quadrant of the world. He traveled to Australia, New Zealand, the Philippines, Japan, Iran, Italy, Russia,

In 1974, Kim accompanied Lee on Aeroflot's inaugural trip to the Soviet Union. When they boarded an Aeroflot jet at Dulles Airport outside Washington, D.C., on their way to Moscow, Lee quipped that at least half the airline's flights actually made it safely to their destination. Kim, only interested in seeing the sights of Russia, said, "Well, I hope if we crash, it's on the way back."

Great Britain, France, the Netherlands, West Germany, Afghanistan, Pakistan, and China. In just a few years on the CAB, Lee traveled extensively throughout every continent except Africa.

Mary Ann often accompanied Lee on some of the shorter trips, especially to the resort cities of Manzanillo and Cancun, Mexico. They visited the now world-class vacation destination of Cancun when it consisted only of an air strip and a hotel under construction.

Aeroflot, the Soviet national airline, introduced a regular flight from Moscow to Dulles Airport in 1974. The airline invited Lee and other dignitaries to fly on the inaugural flight in April, 1974, from Dulles to Moscow, and stay for a week as guests of Aeroflot. Lee and Mary Ann agreed to go. They were to visit Moscow, Kiev, and Leningrad, now St. Petersburg.

Shortly before the scheduled departure, Mary Ann became ill. Aeroflot allowed Kim, only 15 at the time, to accompany Lee. To say it was the time of her young life was an understatement. As the only teenager on board, Kim immediately became everyone's favorite. Kim and Marshall B. Coyne, owner of Washington's famous Madison Hotel, became good friends and were inseparable. Kim also became a favorite of Ivan Shtefan, the American representative for Aeroflot.

Lee wrote Kim a personal note on the official trip itinerary. Quoting Carl Sandburg, Lee said, "I love you for what you are—I love you yet more for what you will be."[12]

Lee and Kim visited Moscow, Kiev, and Leningrad. Other dignitaries on the trip were Washington, D.C. Mayor Walter Washington; Oklahoma Congressman John Jarman; Astronaut Charles "Pete" Conrad, Jr.; and Floyd Hall, president of Eastern Airlines.

On still another CAB trip, Lee went to India and stayed in the famous Uberoi Hotel in New Delhi. Lee made a side trip to the Taj Mahal. American Ambassador to India William Saxbe, whom Lee

Lee, resting on the famous Ipanema Beach in Rio de Janeiro, Brazil—with a Brazilian maid taking care of his food and drink. When friends saw this photograph, they asked, "The girl from Ipanema?"

Lee's years on the Civil Aeronautics Board were filled with receptions of airline officials. Left to right, CAB members Joseph Minetti and Elizabeth Bailey; Sir Freddy Laker, president of Laker Airlines; and Lee. "Sir Freddy" was a popular Englishman who ran a discount-fare airline that served Europe and the United States from London.

had met at the Grand National Quail Hunt in Oklahoma, offered to take him on a tiger hunt, but Lee's schedule would not permit.

Lee returned to Japan for the first time since he was there as a Marine. This time, he was lodged in the Okura Hotel across the street from the American Embassy. He paid $12.50 for a cup of coffee and orange juice, just 25 years after he could buy a complete Japanese meal for 85 cents.[13]

Lee made news in the *National Enquirer* in October, 1975. The newspaper published a "super secret" list of 200 top Americans who supposedly had been chosen to be whisked to safety in the event of a nuclear attack on America. The newspaper said that only the

President and a few top bureaucrats knew the identity of the planned survivors. However, "the chosen few, selected by virtue of their position and not as individuals," would be airlifted to one of the several underground bunkers buried deep under the Appalachian Mountains in Maryland and Pennsylvania.[14]

Lee was listed along with the President, members of the cabinet, and directors of major government agencies. The report said, "These people virtually amount to the entire federal government in micro-mini form."[15] At the time, Lee was more amused than impressed.

Lee was reminded of the *National Enquirer* story after the September 11, 2001 terrorist attack on New York City and Washington, D.C. and the hiding out of key government officials at unknown locations. Had such clandestine "hiding" been done during his time in the nation's capital, Lee said he would have wanted to be "hidden out" near the quail fields of South Georgia and South Texas.[16]

Despite Lee's early success in international aviation negotiations, he was clearly in the minority at the CAB on domestic policy—particularly in regard to airfares and more competition. Lee and Minetti favored increased competition and lower fares to benefit the traveling public. However, the Republican majority on the board favored higher fares for trunk carriers.

That attitude changed when Gerald Ford became President after the resignation of President Nixon. In President Ford, Lee and Minetti had an ally. Very soon, Ford was reversing fare increases approved by the majority. One newspaper report questioned who was the minority, Minetti and Lee, or the three Republicans.[17]

Ford replaced Timm as chairman with John Robson of Chicago, Illinois. Robson's close friend and former high school classmate was Donald Rumsfeld, then and now, the Secretary of Defense. Robson was president and chairman of the Export-Import Bank at his death in 2002.

Lee, left, and R. Tenney Johnson, a fellow member of the Civil Aeronautics Board, on a trip to McGrath, Alaska, in 1976 to monitor subsidized bush routes.

For the first time ever, Lee had an almost total failure in a personal relationship. He was initially impressed with Robson but soon learned that the new CAB chairman was neither candid nor forthright. In his first years on the CAB, Lee had a warm relationship with every board member, even when they disagreed on issues. But, Robson was different.

When a CAB decision drew criticism from airlines or other interested parties, Robson would disavow his part in the decision and leak erroneous information to the press.[18] Lee grew so frus-

Lee, on a snowmobile in the middle of summer, near Kotsobue, Alaska, north of Nome on the Bering Sea.

Lee, second from right, and Chuck Palmer, left, discuss airline matters with officials of the Mexican government.

trated that he once admonished Robson in a board meeting that he "needed to decide which side of his face he was talking out of."[19]

Matters reached a boiling point when Robson began hiring outside consultants to perform tasks that the CAB staff should be doing. The other members of the board also began to grow weary of Robson's tactics but expressed their discontent only privately. Lee was more vocal. During one board meeting, he described Robson's pet consultant, Constantine Menges, as being "Constant Menace" and "useless as tits on a boar hog," an old southeast Oklahoma expression that points out the uselessness of mammary glands on a male hog. The other members of the CAB had not heard the expression but readily agreed once they understood it.[20]

Fortunately, Robson did not last long and resigned after two years. The struggle for power at the CAB made the headlines in both general newspapers and trade publications. Jim Hartz, a native of Tulsa, Oklahoma, and former host of NBC's "Today Show," was a television anchorman at WRC TV in Washington. He and reporter Stan Bernard ran a series of reports on the power struggle.

President Jimmy Carter, who replaced President Ford in January, 1977, appointed Lee as Acting Chairman of the CAB in May of that year. Lee immediately went on the offensive, criticizing the policies of his predecessor, Robson. In a May 20 speech before the spring regional meeting of the Association of Local Transport Airlines in Minneapolis, Minnesota, Lee blasted Robson, without mentioning his name.

Lee said Robson's actions in thwarting expansion of charter flights and farming staff responsibilities to outside consultants was a low point in the history of the CAB. He described the previous year as an era in which "we have been saddled with a leadership that preferred one-man rule to a five-man consensus."[21]

Lee reiterated that the CAB did not favor total deregulation of the airlines and stressed the need for a controlled and carefully monitored transition toward greater reliance on the forces of competition. Lee believed that the CAB could oversee the airline

In April, 1977, Robert Hill, the American ambassador to Argentina, hosted a cocktail party in the ambassador's residence in Buenos Aires. Lee, fourth from right, headed the United States delegation for bilateral aviation talks with Argentina.

The Civil Aeronautics Board in 1977. Lee, center, was acting chairman. Other members were R. Tenney Johnson, left, and longtime member, G. Joseph Minetti.

industry and avert the perils of disruption and any possible monopoly of air carriers.[22]

In retrospect, Lee's opposition to total deregulation of the airlines was well founded. Many observers believe government actions in the 1970s and 1980s moving toward deregulation of major services and industries have fallen woefully short of expectations.

The debate over decontrol of the airlines caught the attention of House of Representatives Speaker Jim Wright of Texas. Wright, who frankly did not know whether deregulation was good or bad for the country, included the entire text of Lee's speech in Minneapolis in the *Congressional Record*.

Lee worked closely on the deregulation issue with Steven Breyer, a member of United States Senator Edward Kennedy's staff who was on leave from Harvard University. Breyer was later appointed to the United States Supreme Court by President Bill Clinton.

In June, 1977, Lee was invited by Secretary of State Cyrus Vance to represent the CAB at the Civil Aviation Attache Conference in

Paris, France. After presenting the CAB's position on international airline issues, Lee and Mary Ann served as American representatives at the Paris Air Show, an enormous international aviation event. There, Lee renewed his acquaintance with Oklahoma astronaut Thomas P. Stafford and met the Soviet members of the Soyuz joint flight with Stafford and other American astronauts.

After several days at the air show, Lee and Mary Ann were allowed the use of an American embassy car and driver for a trip into the Loire River Valley and the Chateau region of France. The weather was great. While being driven on the "wrong" side of the road through France, Lee thought, "Mary Ann is finally living the life she had expected when we were growing up in Antlers."[23]

In his new role as Acting Chairman of the CAB, Lee moved swiftly. Within hours, he gave former Chairman Robson's special counsel, Howard Cohen, 30 minutes to vacate his office and relieved Constantine Menges, the former Robson consultant who had been given a permanent agency position as director of the bureau of international affairs.

Lee named a new executive assistant, John T. Golden, who he believed was one of the brightest people he had been around. Golden is now a top level lawyer in the United States Department of Agriculture.

Golden saw Lee as a "moderate liberal" on the CAB. He said, "Lee was extremely popular and loved by the career people at the agency." One attribute that endeared Lee to the professionals at the CAB was his willingness to learn from the experts. He paid attention to the men and women who had spent much of their adult lives studying American aviation.[24]

Help for the embattled CAB was on its way. In appointing Lee as Acting Chairman, the White House had made it clear that Lee would be a caretaker until a new chairman could be nominated and confirmed. It was rumored that Carter would appoint Alfred "Fred" Kahn, an economist and chairman of the New York State Public Service Commission.

Lee, left, Civil Aeronautics Board Chairman Alfred Kahn, center, and Frank
Borman, president of Eastern Airlines, at a meeting of air carriers in 1978.

Lee became friends with Kahn who had been Dean of the
School of Economics at Cornell University. Kahn was open, candid, and totally straightforward in his personal relationships. While
Lee did not always agree with Kahn on some issues, both were in
favor of increased competition and lower fares.

Now, two New Yorkers and an outspoken Okie were in the
majority and the CAB operated smoothly.

Later, in 1977, Lee planned a trip to Belgium, Germany, the
Netherlands, England, France, and Ireland. Because Kim had gone
to Russia with Lee, and, to balance his parental duty to his other
daughter, Jennifer, Lee took her on the trip to Europe. He and
Mary Ann expanded the group to include his sister, Deloyce, and
Pat Meaders, the wife of Lee's good friend, Turner Meaders. Turner
was invited but apparently could not stand to be away from
Hughes County for that long.

Looking back, Lee says the trip was the worst nightmare of his
life and caused him to mutter, "Never take a trip with four
women!"[25] Lee not only labored bravely for long hours in airline

negotiations with foreign governments but also was the driver of the van with four backseat drivers. While he negotiated, they shopped and shipped their purchases home to America.

At the Intercontinental Hotel in Paris, Lee questioned a charge on his hotel bill for several hundred dollars for liquor from the bar in the room occupied by Jennifer, Dee, and Pat Meaders. Lee assured the cashier that there was some mistake. Lee suspected he, as an American tourist, was being cheated and he protested heatedly.

The hotel clerk was nice but insisted the bill was correct. In a rage, Lee went up to the room to tell Mary Ann. As he vociferously complained, Lee noticed Jennifer hiding in a corner. She had thought all the little bottles of liquor in the bar were complimentary, just like the wine and cheese basket. She had packed all the tiny bottles in her suitcase to hand out to her friends at home.[26] An extremely embarrassed Lee apologized to the cashier and replenished the bar. Everyone, except Lee, thought it was funny.

Lee concluded that he did not want to be a bureaucrat forever. He agreed with John Golden who said the bureaucracy was "an anvil that had worn out many a hammer."[27]

Looking for options, Lee applied for the dean's job at the OU Law School. His former classmate, Bill Paul, the chairman of the selection committee, was able to arrange for Lee to interview for the post but it was given to another applicant with no previous connection to OU.

Nevertheless, Lee was inclined to resign and return to Oklahoma. He had lunch with Senator Bellmon and asked if he would be disappointed if Lee left before his term expired. Bellmon said, "No, I'm a little surprised you have stood it this long." Lee did not know that Bellmon also was planning to leave the Senate very soon.

Lee confided in Bellmon that he someday wanted to be a federal judge. Bellmon suggested that Lee talk to David Boren, a Democrat, who was completing his term as Governor of

Oklahoma and was the odds on favorite to be elected to the United States Senate to succeed Senator Dewey Bartlett who was retiring because of poor health. Because Jimmy Carter, a Democrat, was in the White House, the senior Democratic senator from a state traditionally chose federal judges, or at least suggested nominations to the White House.

Lee's last year on the CAB involved many hours of debate over deregulation. The theme of his testimony before several congressional committees was that deregulation would result in lower fares and greater competition initially. However, if not properly monitored, Lee believed that total deregulation would result in larger, wealthier airlines that would drive the smaller carriers out of business. Lee also said that within 20 years, there would be few airlines left and fares would be raised at will because of the lack of competition. Looking back, it was a rare opportunity for Lee to say, "I told you so," because his prediction was painfully accurate.

> *I don't know anything about judging, but for two years in southeast Oklahoma, Lee and I hunted rabbits on the halves with a borrowed dog—and he ain't cheated me yet.*
>
> E L L I S F R E E N Y

Back *to* Oklahoma

IN THE FALL OF 1977, LEE RETURNED TO OKLAHOMA to attend the Grand National Quail Hunt at Enid. While in the Sooner State, he and Turner Meaders hunted quail with Joe Williams, president of The Williams Companies of Tulsa, on Meaders' ranch near Wetumka. During the hunt, Williams asked Lee about his plans for the future, knowing that his term at CAB would expire within a year. Lee told Williams that he wanted to come back to Oklahoma—but had no idea to where and in what capacity.

Shortly after Lee returned home to Virginia, he received a call from Fred Nelson in Tulsa. Nelson was a partner in the Tulsa law firm of Hall, Estill, Hardwick, Gable, Collingsworth, and Nelson (Hall-Estill). The firm did most of the legal work for The Williams Companies. Nelson asked if Lee would consider joining the firm after his CAB term ended. Lee told Nelson that he was interested but that his long-term goal was securing a federal judgeship. That fact did not change Nelson's invitation for Lee to join Hall-Estill.

Mary Ann and Lee flew to Tulsa to interview with the principals of Hall-Estill. They joined daughter, Kim, a student at OU, and the Hall-Estill partners for dinner. Kim had transferred to OU after a year at Randolph Macon College in Richmond, Virginia. The Tulsa lawyers were cordial and Lee was impressed with their firm.

When Lee returned to Washington, D.C., he began working out details of his association with Hall-Estill. On April 5, 1978, Lee made official his decision to leave the CAB six months early and join Hall-Estill in Tulsa. One of the reasons Lee gave for his timing was so that Jennifer, still in high school, could make the transition to a new school at the end of the summer, rather than in mid-semester if Lee stayed for his complete term at the CAB.

Lee wrote President Carter, "So that you will have as much advance notice as possible, I am hereby submitting my resignation as a Member of the Civil Aeronautics Board, effective June 30."[1] In the letter to the President, Lee said he believed that air travelers had already greatly benefited from increased competition and new low-fare offerings. Lee also said, "I am also pleased to note that, under our present approach, the airlines we regulate are enjoying their best profits in several years." President Carter was generous in accepting Lee's resignation.[2]

CAB Chairman Kahn called Lee's departure from the board "a great loss." Kahn said he and other members would miss Lee's "good humor, good sense, dedication to the consumer interest, and the mixture of toughness and shrewdness."[3] Vice Chairman Minetti, said Lee's resignation was a personal loss to him. Minetti himself would soon leave the board because of the mandatory retirement age of 70. Minetti had served on the CAB for 22 years.

Before Mary Ann and Lee left the nation's capital, they were honored at a reception hosted by Ed and Sheila Weidenfeld. Ed was associated with Hall-Estill's Washington, D.C. office. Sheila had been First Lady Betty Ford's press secretary during the Ford administration.

The lavish reception was attended by many of Lee's colleagues and friends, including CAB Chairman Kahn, Oklahoma Congressmen Wes Watkins and James Jones, United States Attorney General Griffin Bell, and John Harmon, the head of the Office of Legal Counsel in the Justice Department.

Lee and Harmon had become friends through bird dog field trial competition, first meeting at Summerduck, Virginia. It was another example of how seemingly insignificant relationships prove to be otherwise. Harmon would later play a key role in Lee's appointment to a federal judgeship and, more importantly, became Lee's foremost adult friend and companion for the next 30 years.[4]

Hall-Estill was generous in moving the Wests from Virginia to a home near Claremore, overlooking the Verdigris River. Lee purchased an additional ten acres and built a four-stall barn for his horses and a kennel for his bird dogs. He and Mary Ann were again full-fledged Okies.

The neighbors in the country neighborhood called Keetonville Hill were helpful and friendly. Jan and Bob Land became close friends immediately. Bob was a retired Army colonel and Jan was a free-lance writer. Jan and Mary Ann shared an interest in writing. Jan introduced Mary Ann to Millie Ladner, the book editor for the *Tulsa World*. Mary Ann was asked to write book reviews for the newspaper's Sunday edition. She also taught a creative writing class in the adult education department at Claremore Junior College. Mary Ann loved writing. Her story of the Locke-Jones War in southeast Oklahoma was later published in *Real West* magazine.

For the Wests' first Christmas at Claremore, Kim gave her mother a box of note cards with the name "Professor and Mr. West" embossed on the cover of each card.

Lee's work at Hall-Estill was interesting and rewarding. He was immediately thrown into litigation involving civil antitrust charges against Agrico, a wholly-owned subsidiary of The Williams Companies. Lee was accustomed to entering situations without knowing much about the subject beforehand and this time was no different. He spent long hours learning about antitrust actions. A great help to Lee was Mack Braly, the son of one of Lee's good friends in Ada. Braly was bright and an expert in antitrust litigation. Lee worked with other lawyers at Hall-Estill to negotiate satisfactory settlements or successfully defend several cases filed against The Williams Companies and its subsidiaries. He formed close friendships with several in the firm, including Thomas Golden, Frank Hagedorn, J. Patrick Cremin, Fred Cornish, and Claire Egan, who was later appointed to the federal bench.[5]

Lee's chances of becoming a federal judge were greatly enhanced by a series of events in 1978 and 1979. During the 19 months he practiced law at Hall-Estill, Judge Joseph Morris left the federal bench in Muskogee and United States District Judge Allen Barrow of Tulsa died. In addition, Congress passed legislation to authorize an additional Oklahoma slot on the United States Court of Appeals for the Tenth Circuit and two new federal district judgeships in Oklahoma. The events meant that, for the first time ever, there were five federal vacancies.

Most United States senators are fortunate to ever have the privilege to designate one or two federal judges during their service in the Senate. Certain conditions must fall right. The senator must be of the same party as the president and must, by tradition, be the senior senator of the president's political party from the state where the judicial vacancies exist.

The stars aligned magnificently for Senator David Boren who took office in January, 1979. Boren, even though a rookie in the Senate, was immediately the senior Democratic Senator from Oklahoma in the administration of Democratic President Carter. Oklahoma's other United States Senator was Republican Henry Bellmon, Lee's good friend. Boren was thus handed the opportunity to name four federal district judges at one time, a rare chance at leaving an extended legacy by the appointment of federal judges to lifetime positions.

Two nominating committees were created to screen applicants for the five vacancies. The Tenth Circuit position nominating committee was chaired by Alfred M. Pence of Laramie, Wyoming. The panel consisted of 12 members from the 6 states, Oklahoma, Colorado, Kansas, New Mexico, Wyoming, and Utah, that make up the Tenth Judicial Circuit.

Lee let it be known that he would like to be considered for appointment to both the Tenth Circuit and as a United States District Court Judge in one of the three Oklahoma federal judicial districts—the Western District, headquartered in Oklahoma City; the Northern District, based in Tulsa; and the Eastern District, located in Muskogee.

After interviews with applicants, the Tenth Circuit nominating panel sent four names to the White House for President Carter to select from. The four were Lee, Tulsa lawyer Stephanie Seymour, United States District Judge Dale Cook, and Oklahoma Supreme Court Justice Pat Irwin.

Lee also was interviewed by the nominating committee put together at Boren's request to screen potential applicants for the four federal district court positions that were vacant. Lee's old friend, Vernon Roberts of Ada, was named chairman of the panel that was officially called the U.S. District Judge Selection Advisory Commission of Oklahoma.

Friends and colleagues of Lee flocked to support his application to the federal bench. His former role model, Joe Stamper of Antlers, wrote, "Lee's accomplishments have been largely due to his own efforts, abetted by a wonderful wife whom I've also known since she was a little girl."[6] University of Tulsa Law School Dean Frank T. Read said of Lee, "He exudes warmth, he understands human frailties and is still able to project a sincere and abiding compassion for others."[7] Read's letter went to Attorney General Griffin Bell who was the President's point man for the Tenth

During the 1979 quest for a federal judgeship, Lee, center, was the guest at a reception in Ada. At left is Ralph "Fireball" Evans. At right is Ada lawyer Vernon Roberts who was the chairman of a 13-man commission appointed by United States Senator David Boren to screen applicants for four vacant federal judge posts in Oklahoma. The sign around Roberts' neck reads, "We Want West."

Circuit vacancy. Interestingly, John Harmon, a Bell staff member at the Justice Department, was one of Read's former law students.

From all points of Oklahoma came letters on behalf of Lee. Loyd Benefield of the Oklahoma City law firm of Benefield, Travis, Russell & Freede, wrote, "As a country lawyer, I still think of Judge West as a country judge…notwithstanding his sophisticated legal education and judicial experience. I think it will be a pleasure for lawyers…to appear before him."[8]

One of the most unusual letters received by Senator Boren in support of Lee came from Ellis Freeny, who like Lee, grew up in Little Dixie. Freeny, executive director of the Oklahoma

Lee is sworn in as United States District Judge for the Western District of Oklahoma, November 5, 1979. He was appointed to the post by President Jimmy Carter upon the recommendation of United States Senator David L. Boren of Oklahoma. *Courtesy Oklahoma Publishing Company.*

Cattlemens Association, wrote, "I don't know anything about judges or judging. But, Lee and I for two years hunted rabbits on the halves with a borrowed dog and he ain't ever cheated me yet."[9]

Bert McElroy of Tulsa wrote Lee on a Big Chief tablet, "As the son of one horse trader to the son of another, I say it's a wonderful country which gave you and me the chance to be somebody in our profession."[10] Other support letters and calls came from former

After being sworn in as a federal judge, Lee was honored at a federal courthouse reception. Left to right, Mary Ann, Lee, and daughter, Kim. *Courtesy Oklahoma Publishing Company.*

House Speaker Carl Albert, OU Law School Dean Earl Sneed, and United States Senator James Exon of Nebraska.

Lee's dear friend Duke Logan, master of colorful letters from his law office in Vinita, added his chapter of cheer during the deliberations. On behalf of his wife, Dorothy, Logan wrote, "We both hope you get the job. You need the work, your bride needs a permanent home, and the Western District of Oklahoma can get along with anybody that will grant a continuance on a bird day."[11]

Of the stack of letters of support, two of them were very special to Lee. Oldest daughter, Kim, wrote, "Every once in a while events enable us to tell someone special how really terrific they are. And being a member of a family of speechmakers, I decided to take

BELOW Lee greatly respected the senior members of the federal bench in Oklahoma City. In this photograph, he sits alongside veteran Judge Luther Bohanon. *Courtesy Oklahoma Publishing Company.*

advantage of the situation. Regardless of the outcome of this judgeship, I wanted you to know how very proud I am of you."[12]

"You're the most brilliant, nicest, and most of all, loveable man around," wrote youngest daughter, Jennifer. She said, "I'm so proud to have you as my dad, anyone would be proud to have you as their dad 'cause you've worked so hard all your life…You've given the family a lot more than a great home and lots to eat, you've given us a lot of time and love and understanding."[13]

Senator Boren's friendship with President Jimmy Carter was a plus for Lee. President Carter later recalled, "Judge West was enthusiastically recommended to me for appointment by Senator Boren, who was an important and influential friend in the Senate."[14]

Carter also heeded a good report from Attorney General Griffin Bell and Lee's hunting companion, John Harmon. President Carter said, "Griffin told me that Lee had a most commendable record on the Oklahoma state court bench and that, perhaps as significant, was the fact that he was an avid quail hunter."[15]

In early May, 1979, President Carter nominated Stephanie Seymour for the Tenth Circuit position. The White House also announced the selection of Lee; Thomas R. Brett, a Tulsa lawyer and a former Oklahoma Bar Association president; Tulsa attorney James O. Ellison; and District Judge Frank Seay of Seminole, for the four federal district judgeships. Lee and Mary Ann were elated.

Lee, age 49 at the time, and the other appointees underwent extensive Federal Bureau of Investigation (FBI) background checks, a process that took several months. Confirmation hearings before the United States Senate Judiciary Committee, chaired by Massachusetts United States Senator Edward Kennedy, were scheduled for October.

Before the confirmation hearings, the four federal district judge appointees traveled to Washington, D.C., to pay their respects to key senators. Lee shared a room with Seay at the Madison Hotel. Lee, Ellison, and Brett conspired to terrify Seay with horror stories of what he could expect in the confirmation hearing before Senator

Kennedy's committee. Seay spent several nights unnecessarily reviewing his old constitutional law notes in preparation for the hearing.

The only problem that the four district court nominees encountered was with a member of Senator Kennedy's staff who was upset that Ellison and Brett were members of the Summit Club or Southern Hills Country Club in Tulsa. It was rumored that the exclusive clubs had discriminatory membership practices. The possible delay in a smooth confirmation hearing was resolved when Ellison resigned and Brett was allowed to transfer his membership to his wife.

The confirmation hearing was short and without controversy. All four nominations for federal district judge in Oklahoma were approved unanimously by the Senate Judiciary Committee on October 31.

After the confirmation, in typical "Lee West style," Lee said, "While some of my relatives are proud, they would have been much happier if I had been named to the Pardon and Parole Board."[16]

Lee, Ellison, Brett, and Seay were sworn in on November 5, 1979. Fred Kahn, who had been elevated by President Carter to be Advisor to the President on Inflation, wrote Lee, "It couldn't have happened to a better guy. Congratulations!"[17]

> *Federal judges should be clothed in robes, not only that those who witness the administration of justice should be properly advised that the function performed is higher than that which a man discharges as a citizen in the ordinary walks of life, but also, in order to impress the judge himself with constant consciousness that he is a high priest in the temple of justice.*
>
> CHIEF JUSTICE
> WILLIAM HOWARD TAFT

tHe feDeRaL BeNCH

AN "INDEPENDENT JUDICIARY" WAS THE GOAL of delegates to the American Constitutional Convention in Philadelphia. Drafters of Article III of the new constitution intended to relieve federal judges of the normal pressures of politics by making their appointment for life--avoiding a periodic rendezvous with voters.

The debate over the tenure of federal judges was lively at the Constitutional Convention. Some wanted judges to be subject to removal by the president. But it was delegate Edmund Randolph of Virginia, reminding his fellow countrymen of their uncomfortable experience with British judges appointed by King George III, who proposed an independent judiciary to serve during "good behavior."

Article III has produced an elite corps of powerful jurists, an exclusive brotherhood bound by common problems and similar backgrounds. Winning appointment to a federal judgeship often highlights a lawyer's legal career. When a vacancy occurs, it is not unusual that dozens of names immediately are bantered about as a successor. President Harry S. Truman received a telegram in 1948 that said, "Judge _____ died yesterday at his farm...Judge _____ would be an excellent man to fill the vacancy."[1]

Judicial historian Donald Dale Jackson wrote of the importance of federal judges:

> Through their rulings, district judges establish policy on a vast range of legal and social issues. They operate in the zone of tension between traditional legal standards and changing public values. Legislatures can wait, but judges must react to the issue before them. A federal judge may fashion and sustain the moral principles of the community...His character and personal distinction, open to daily inspection in the courtroom, constitute the guarantees of due process.[2]

Eventually, vital questions facing America always find their way to a federal court. In the last quarter of the 20th century, it was the federal judiciary that forged ahead on social and governmental issues such as school busing and integration, the environment and pollution, and rights of minorities and prisoners.

A federal judge is without question a powerful person. He stands above his brethren and sisters on the state bench in professional prestige, in salary, and often, in the importance of the cases heard. For the two centuries of the American experience, it has been generally assumed that a party gets a more impartial hearing in federal court. A congressman in the 1870s said, "The United States courts are further above mere local influence than the county courts; their judges can act with more independence; cannot be put under terror, as local judges can; their sympathies are not so nearly identified with those of the vicinage."[3]

For Lee, being a United States District Judge for the Western District of Oklahoma was the fulfillment of a dream he had nurtured since his second year of law school. One of the first differences between state and federal court that Lee noticed was the massive difference in the trappings--the chambers, the courtroom, the staff. Lee was awed by the solemnity of the surroundings in his office, the United States District Courthouse at Northwest Fourth Street and Robinson Avenue in downtown Oklahoma City.

Author Joseph C. Goulden, in his book about federal judges, The Benchwarmers, discussed the atmosphere in which a federal judge labors. Goulden wrote, "The formal trappings of the judiciary remind the judge daily of his importance. The stage-setting of a federal courtroom is intended to give an aura of high dignity to whatever happens there. As a symbol of his prestige, the judge wears a black robe, a hand-me-down from the English monarchy that American public opinion does not permit to be draped across the carcass of any political official."[4]

Lee joined an esteemed group of active federal judges in the Western District.

Fred Daugherty had served on the court since his appointment by President John F. Kennedy in 1961, adding prestige to an already distinguished military and legal career. An Oklahoma City native, Daugherty began practicing law in 1937 after legal training at Cumberland University in Tennessee, Oklahoma City University, and the University of Oklahoma. Daugherty enlisted as a private in the Oklahoma National Guard in 1934 and moved through the ranks to become Commanding General of the famed 45th Infantry Division, retiring with the rank of major general.

Luther B. Eubanks had been a judge of the Western District since 1965—appointed by President Lyndon Johnson after 20 years as a county prosecutor and state district judge. He was born in New Mexico but his family moved to Atoka County, Oklahoma, when he was five months old. He graduated from the OU School of Law in 1942 and became county attorney in Cotton County,

Oklahoma, after three years in the United States Army during World War II. He also later served in the Oklahoma House of Representatives.

The third active member of the Court was Ralph G. Thompson, the nation's fifth youngest judge when he was appointed by President Gerald Ford in 1975. Thompson, a native of Oklahoma City and Phi Beta Kappa graduate of the OU School of Law, served in the Oklahoma House of Representatives and was the Republican nominee for lieutenant governor in 1970. He was in private practice from his admission to the bar in 1961 until his appointment to the federal bench. Thompson also rose to the rank of colonel in the United States Air Force Reserve.

Two former active judges, Luther Bohanon and Stephen Chandler, had taken senior status and did not carry a full caseload. Lee considered Judge Bohanon a role model in judicial courage.

For the first few months of Lee's tenure as a federal judge, his and Mary Ann's living conditions were complicated. They still owned a house and 10 acres near Claremore, property they were trying to sell. Mary Ann's aunt, Allen, was 94 years old and Lee thought she should sell her property in Antlers and move to Oklahoma City where he and Mary Ann could look after her.

Soon Lee and Mary Ann were able to sell the Claremore and Antlers properties and move Aunt Allen into their new home in the Old Farm Addition of Edmond, Oklahoma. Lee moved his bird dogs into a newly installed kennel behind the house. He did not have room to park his horse trailer and pasture his horses at the new home so he turned to his friend, Delmar Smith, a professional dog trainer. Smith allowed Lee to park the trailer and pasture his horses at his kennel.

Shortly after Lee and Mary Ann moved into their new home, his dogs, unaccustomed to their new surroundings, began barking incessantly one night. Lee opened the back door and shouted to the dogs in language the neighbors had never heard before. The dogs quit barking but in a few minutes a siren sounded and the doorbell rang. A policeman was at the door—summoned by a neighbor who had reported a domestic disturbance. Lee, consistent with his constant good humor, advised the officer, "I've convinced Mary Ann to leave me alone and all is well."[5]

When Lee arrived in the Western District, there was no time for a lengthy learning process. The district included basically the western half of Oklahoma and the caseload was among the heaviest in the nation.

The workload was daunting. Lee hired two law clerks, Barbara Bado and Dorothy Amis, and went to work. He and his staff worked about 16 hours a day—and lost ground. Most of the other judges were having similar problems. To help out, Lee's fellow new federal judge in Oklahoma, Tom Brett, agreed to take one-fourth of a regular caseload in the Western District even though it required him to travel from his post in the Northern District, in Tulsa, to Oklahoma City each week.[6]

Lee hired Jeannie Prather as his secretary. She had served in the same capacity while Lee was at the CAB. With tongue-in-cheek, Lee wrote a job description for Jeannie. In addition to secretarial and managerial skills, the position required an "interest in bird dogs and field trials and the ability to type pedigrees." The description also mandated that the applicant "be able to hang pictures and plaques at a moment's notice…and be willing to spend countless hours over a copy machine cutting and pasting laudatory articles regarding the Judge."[7]

Jeannie again served brilliantly until 1985 when she left to become a Certified Public Accountant. She now practices in Ada.

To catch up, Lee began trying two cases each day. He started one jury trial at 7:00 a.m. and recessed by noon. At 1:00 p.m., he tried another case to another jury until often 6:00 or 7:00 p.m. For almost a year, he put his staff and himself through the incredible pace—reaching the point of near exhaustion.

With his caseload almost unmanageable, Lee began looking for a better method of dealing with his docket. He looked at statistics and found that only 84 percent of the civil cases in the Western District were settling before trial—while the settlement rate was 91 percent in the rest of the country. He called the fact to the attention of Chief Judge Eubanks who naturally assigned Lee the responsibility of finding a solution to the problem.

Lee and Tom Brett devised a procedure where a judge not assigned to a particular case would conduct a settlement conference, in hopes that the parties would find middle ground and settle the case. The nonassigned judge could lend his experience to the procedure with a neutral evaluation—pointing out the strengths and weaknesses of the parties' positions.[8]

The experiment did not meet with universal acceptance. Lawyers and some judges grumbled at first. However, settlement conferences proved to be an immediate success. Not only did the Western District's settlement percentage go up, it passed the national average within a year.

Lee had hoped that the senior federal judges could conduct settlement conferences and use their vast experience as trial judges. However, Chandler and Bohanon were not interested. Instead, the Western District hired Pat Irwin, the retiring Chief Justice of the Oklahoma Supreme Court, as a full time Magistrate Judge to hold settlement conferences. Irwin was brilliant at his job and the settlement percentage of civil cases jumped to near 97 percent. Lee remembered, "In other words, we were trying about 13 percent fewer cases than previously and our relief was spelled P-A-T."[9]

One of Lee's first complicated cases was an antitrust action, *Daiflon Inc. v. Allied Chemical Corp.* The case had an agonizing history. Judge Luther Bohanon presided over the original trial, disagreed with the jury verdict for the plaintiff, and ordered a new trial. The Tenth Circuit Court of Appeals reversed Bohanon's decision and sent the case back to the Western District for trial on damages only. An appeal to the United States Supreme Court resulted in another reversal and the order for a new trial on both liability and damages.

Bohanon asked Lee to re-try the case—and Lee agreed to do so. In June, 1981, Lee began to look for ways to settle the complicated case without a full trial. He was aware of a procedure, called a summary jury trial, used by Tom Lambros, a federal judge in Ohio. The technique allowed the parties to get a better idea of what a jury would do in a given case. It involved letting the attorneys for the parties summarize the evidence they had to support their respective positions. The judge then instructed the jury on the appropriate law to apply to the specific fact situation. The jury rendered an advisory verdict—not binding, but certainly an indication of how jurors might react to the full presentation of the evidence in a long, time-consuming trial.

Lee called Judge Lambros who generously agreed to come to Oklahoma to guide Lee through the experimental procedure. To everyone's astonishment, a brief summary trial resulted in a quick settlement that garnered national attention. Judge Lambros and Lee were interviewed extensively by the *National Law Journal* and other legal publications who believed that judges everywhere were looking for methods to cut down on jury trial time. Lambros and Lee traveled around the country lecturing on the new procedure. The summary jury trial has continued to be helpful in settling complex and protracted lawsuits.[10]

Lee and fellow members of the court adopted other alternate dispute resolution (ADR) techniques, mandatory and non-binding arbitration, neutral evaluation, and mediation techniques. All have served the court well. The Western District became a court of distinction because of its success in alternate dispute resolution methods.

Lee and Magistrate Irwin, along with ADR clerk Ann Marshall, traveled to other federal courts to help set up ADR systems. The success in Oklahoma City led to congressional legislation and funding of ADR components of the present-day federal court procedures.

Because Lee was a pioneer in ADR, he was frequently called upon to help settle complex cases. The highest profile case was *Texas*

Utilities Co. v. Santa Fe Industries, Inc., litigation that had tarried in federal court in Santa Fe, New Mexico, for nine years. Two huge law firms, one in New York City and the other in Los Angeles, California, had been preparing for trial with 25 lawyers working on the case on each side. The parties had spent more than $60 million in costs and attorneys' fees just preparing for trial. Observers expected a full trial would cost another $140 million.[11]

Federal Judge Santiago Campos of Santa Fe called Lee to seek help to avoid a trial that he estimated would last eight months. Law clerk, Cindy Smith, accompanied Lee on a trip to Santa Fe on a Tuesday afternoon to try to settle the case with an advisory jury trial.

The next morning, Lee had breakfast with the executives of the four companies involved in the litigation. He posed a question—do you want to negotiate with or without your 50 attorneys present? The executives unanimously agreed to negotiate without their attorneys. Lee took part in almost non-stop negotiations through Thursday—when settlement was reached. The 50 attorneys were simply told that there was an agreement and to cease preparation for trial.

New and different attorneys were employed by the parties to formalize the agreement, prepare the necessary court documents, and make changes in the existing contract. This was done in great secrecy for fear that someone would sabotage the settlement. The quick resolution of the case resulted in massive publicity for both Lee and the summary jury trial procedure.[12]

Alternatives, a magazine published in New York City by the Center for Public Resources, proclaimed, "$100 Million + Saved by SJT." The publication applauded Lee's efforts to save millions of dollars with a two-day ADR procedure and a "handshake deal."

Judge Campos appreciated Lee's intervention so much that when it came time to formally approve the settlement in the case, he invited Lee to preside alongside him on the bench. Campos eloquently outlined the history of the dispute and read from a letter he had written to all counsel in the case. The letter was a glowing tribute to Lee's prowess as a peacemaker:

Dear Counsel:

To whatever other thoughts may occupy your minds this Ash Wednesday, I wish to add two of my own. Firstly, blessed are the peacemakers; secondly, in the hall of the peacemakers, with other peacemakers about him, sits one of them; he sits alone, the Honorable Lee R. West occupies the dais which today is raised and reserved for him, since he has earned and deserves special honor.

Sincerely yours,
Santiago Campos

Lee's work on the case even drew praise from one of the combatants in the *Texas Utilities Co.* case. The president of one of the companies wrote Lee, "Your insightful and personable manner clearly brought us to the essence of the issues, and your skill in maintaining the dialogue permitted us to reach a satisfactory compromise."[13]

Lee's abilities as a settlement judge give rise to many stories. Lawyer Stratton Taylor, President Pro Tempore of the Oklahoma State Senate, tells the tale of how he approached a settlement conference with Lee. Taylor brought in a mild-mannered corporate representative from the northeastern United States. Taylor and a Chicago lawyer impressed upon the corporate man that they wanted to make a modest offer and then be able to raise the offer to the amount of final authority given to settle the case.[14]

Taylor explained Lee's rural Oklahoma background and his legendary ability to get cases settled. Taylor, the Chicago counsel, and the corporate representative strode confidently into Lee's conference room for the settlement conference. After five minutes of verbal arm twisting, the corporate man forgot his instructions and offered his entire limit of authority. The Chicago lawyer was ashen in color and announced he was ready to jump out the courthouse window because the opportunity to settle the case reasonably was gone. The lawyer thought surely his legal career was over.[15]

Needless to say, the case ultimately settled for more than the authority given. Taylor said, "It was due in large part to Judge West's ability to not only get top dollar offered quickly--rather than drag on the proceedings—but also because he knew that there was more money to be offered."[16] Taylor saw Lee as courteous and firm—in complete control of the settlement conference.

On another occasion, Oklahoma City attorney Don Manners represented a New York insurance company in a severe injury case that was scheduled for a week-long trial on Lee's docket. Lee asked Manners why the company had not paid its $1 million limit policy. When Manners said he had been unable to convince the company to pay the $1 million, Lee took matters into his own hands.[17]

Lee called the switchboard of the insurance company in New York City and said, "This is Lee West, a federal judge in Oklahoma. I want to talk to the head man. He can either talk me on the telephone or I can have the U.S. Marshal bring him to Oklahoma City to talk about this case." Within seconds, the claims manager was on the phone. When Lee said, "I think you better pay this million dollars or a jury could stick you with a bunch more," the claims manager said, "Judge, where shall we send this million dollar check?" Lee had done in five minutes what lawyers on both sides of the case had not been able to do in 18 months.[18]

Young lawyers were made to feel welcome in Lee's courtroom. Cherri Farrar, now a judge on the Oklahoma Workers' Compensation Court, tried her first jury trial before Lee. It was a daunting task for a green lawyer—representing one of five plaintiffs who were suing a fried chicken franchise for sexual harassment. Farrar remembered, "Judge West made it easy for me—by making it hard." She explained, "I didn't want him to coddle me just because he was a friend of my father [Robert G. "Bob" Grove]. Instead, he held me to the same standard as the more experienced lawyers in the case. He treated me like a real lawyer. I got rid of my 'baby lawyer' jitters quickly."[19]

Lee presided over the 1981 trial of Ronnie D. Redbear who was convicted of murdering a fellow prison inmate by sticking a 12-inch shiv completely through the man's heart. Three years later, Redbear wrote Lee a lengthy letter praising Lee's fairness and impartiality. Redbear, who did not take the stand in the trial, wrote that he had spent three years in virtual isolation, but had done his best to educate himself in the English language and read profoundly, seeking to broaden his horizons and relocate his homeless and lonely Spirit.[20]

Redbear had been studying law while in prison, especially the rights guaranteed him as American citizen. "The laws themselves appear simple enough," Redbear said, "but the laws' application is a strange speckled bird."[21]

Redbear admitted he took a man's life, musing, "I took all his rights, his dreams, and his aspirations. I am deeply regretful. The deed can't be undone and neither can the tears be stopped or forgotten. That deed, Sir, is buried deeper than my memory." Redbear did not blame Lee, but blamed himself for not testifying in his own behalf. He wrote, "I can now see where the Court was hobbled by my silence."[22]

Lee wrote back to Redbear, remembering that Redbear's life had been scarred by one struggle after another, referring to himself as "another stomped down Indian." Lee was proud of Redbear spending his time behind bars studying law and trying to turn his life around. Lee said, "It appears the Great Spirit is answering your prayer for wisdom and I expect you will also find the strength you seek." Lee applauded Redbear's remorse for killing a fellow human. Lee wrote, "Regrettably, it makes little difference who is responsible for the fate that is ours—it is still ours. We, as individuals, must deal with the problems. We can overcome them—or succumb to them."[23]

Redbear is still incarcerated at the Federal Correctional Facility in Lompoc, California. His expected release date is March 31, 2037.

SUPPORT ACROSS PARTY LINES

*I am very proud of the fact that I have received strong
bipartisan support despite being a lifelong Democrat. All of
such support has been voluntary in the sense that no one ever
owed me any political debt or favor. Henry Bellmon first
crossed party lines to appoint me to the state court bench. He
also arranged my appointment by Republican President Nixon
to the Civil Aeronautics Board, with assistance from Senator
Dewey Bartlett and Carl Albert, then the Democratic Speaker
of the House. Later, with strong support of then Democratic
Senator David Boren, and concurrence of Bellmon, Democratic
President Jimmy Carter appointed me to the federal bench.*

*In appreciation for this bipartisan support, I have attempted
to prevent my political philosophy from influencing my
decisions down through the years. My colleagues, mostly
Republicans, who are among my best friends, repeatedly assure
me that I have frequently failed in my efforts.*

scandals galore

IN THE 1980S, FEDERAL JUDGES IN OKLAHOMA presided over cases resulting from two major scandals—one that rocked the foundations of Oklahoma government—the other that resonated throughout the nation's banking industry.

Soon after Lee assumed his position on the federal bench, the FBI and federal prosecutors targeted county commissioners in Oklahoma in a massive investigation called CORCAM, which stood for "corrupt county commissioners."

For years, daily headlines reported indictments of commissioners and equipment suppliers in what became the largest public corruption scandal in American history. Before the scandal ended, 162 current and former county commissioners and 62 suppliers were either found guilty or pleaded guilty and were sentenced by federal judges in Oklahoma City, Tulsa, and Muskogee.

From accepting his first plea from a commissioner who had decided to take his chances with Lee, rather than face a jury trial, Lee learned about a kickback scheme that was unprecedented. Dorothy Griffin, a lumber company owner in Farris, Oklahoma, agreed to cooperate with the FBI in early 1980 and made 130 tape recordings of her conversations with suppliers and commissioners.

Griffin admitted submitting fake invoices to one, and sometimes all three, commissioners in a county for non-existent supplies. When Griffin cashed the county draft, she kept five or ten percent as a cash payoff and gave the rest to the supplier to pass along to the commissioner as a kickback. It was also a scheme to launder kickback money on legitimate equipment and supply purchases.[1]

Blaine County Commissioner Orval Pratt was the first commissioner to go on trial in mid-1981. He was convicted by a jury and sentenced to seven years in prison. Once it was apparent that juries would not be lenient, many commissioners decided to plead guilty.

It was not unusual for Lee's docket to include formal acceptance of guilty pleas from two or three commissioners or suppliers in a given day. On December 9, 1981, Lee sentenced one of the key figures in the county commissioner probe. After an affable and craggy-faced Eston Ruel Fisher, a former Stephens County commissioner, appeared before Lee and asked for leniency, Lee sentenced him to three years in federal prison for taking kickbacks. All Fisher could say was, "I'm sorry for this your honor."[2]

On one day in January, 1982, five former commissioners pleaded guilty in separate courtrooms in Oklahoma City. Two of the former officials, Jere Johnson of Garfield County and Ike Roberts of Jefferson County, appeared without legal counsel before Lee to enter their guilty verdicts. Both admitted accepting numerous kickbacks from 1976 to 1981.[3]

The county commissioner scandal was rampant in rural Oklahoma until a former steel and supply company owner pleaded guilty before Lee in April, 1982. Virgil Peery implicated two of the popular and veteran county commissioners in Oklahoma County for the first time. Peery said he paid large kickbacks to both Frank Lynch and Ralph Adair. Peery pleaded guilty just days before he was scheduled to appear for a jury trial on an 18-count federal indictment.[4] Adair was later acquitted by a federal court jury on kickback charges. Lynch's trial ended in a mistrial but he later pleaded guilty.

Lee sentenced two more commissioners on August 10, 1982, after they pleaded guilty to taking kickbacks. Former Woodward County Commissioner J.M. Loomis was given two years in prison and ordered to pay a $3,000 fine. Former Blaine County Commissioner Monte Dean Compton was sentenced by Lee to two years in jail and assessed a $5,000 fine. Lee suspended 18 months of Compton's sentence for cooperating with the FBI probe, including allowing himself to be wired to record conversations of illegal kickbacks.[5]

By 1983, the statewide probe moved "from the courthouse to the country club," a promise made by United States Attorney and later federal judge David Russell.

In June, 1983, Lee listened as five businessmen pleaded guilty to participating in the kickback-for-purchase-of-equipment scheme. The businessmen included the heads of two of the state's largest heavy road-building equipment dealerships. Later, Henry Edward Boecking, Jr., owner of Boecking Machinery Company in Oklahoma City, was sentenced by Lee to two years in prison and ordered to pay a $10,000 fine.

Lee was on the bench when the last active case in the county commissioners scandal came to the courtroom. The key prosecution figure Dorothy Griffin appeared before Lee to be sentenced. United States Attorney Bill Price told Lee that Griffin had participated in the conviction of practically all of the more than 200 cases. She spent five years as a witness helping federal prosecutors make cases against commissioners and suppliers in the kickback scheme that had reportedly existed since statehood. "She paid a substantial penalty in terms of what she had done," Price said. Griffin spent a year as an undercover witness, traveling around the state talking to suspects and taping conversations. After she received threats on her life, she hid some of the evidence in her barn because she feared her house would be burned.[6] Lee sentenced Griffin to two years' probation and fined her $2,000.

Good things actually came from the county commissioner scandal. Multi-county grand juries were authorized to investigate crimes that occur in more than one county in the state. The way that county commissioners purchased their equipment and supplies drastically changed, resulting in anticipated savings of hundreds of millions of dollars in the future.

Just as the Oklahoma county commissioner scandal was in full bloom, another blight upon the state's image arose when Penn Square Bank, a moderately sized bank in a shopping center in northwest Oklahoma City, failed. The bank, at the center of questionable loan practices during an oil boom in Oklahoma, excited bankers and investors across the nation. Penn Square was a back door for large banks to participate in the oil and gas producing frenzy.

A sudden drop in oil prices, with resulting bankruptcies in the petroleum and contract drilling industries, caused Penn Square to fail. In domino fashion, other larger banks in distant cities fell. Many of the nation's banks were injured by Penn Square's demise[7]

Lee and the other federal judges of the Western District were in the middle of the legal jungle that grew at a rapid pace after Penn Square Bank's failure. There was a tidal wave of civil lawsuits and criminal prosecutions. Anticipating the flood of litigation, Chief Judge Luther Eubanks assigned certain types of cases to individual federal district judges. Some predicted it would take a decade for the cases to filter through the system.[8]

In May, 1984, Lee summoned former Penn Square Bank officials to his chambers to meet privately about the chances to settle 75 lawsuits involving Longhorn Oil and Gas and Penn Square Bank. Eighty lawyers were Lee's "guests of honor" and former bank chairman William "Bill" Jennings and members of the bank's board of directors sat through Lee's terse questioning of why these dozens of lawsuits could not be settled.

Conspicuously absent from the special meeting was Penn Square Bank executive vice president William G. Patterson, the oil and gas lender whose free-wheeling style was blamed for many of the bad loans that led to the 1982 failure of the bank. Lee had excused Patterson from the meeting.[9]

Lee, because of his past successes of settling large and complicated cases, was chosen by Chief Judge Eubanks to hold the settlement discussions. Lee's iron-fisted admonitions and sorting of the claims and counterclaims worked. Most of the civil litigation was settled or tried by 1986.

Also in July, a federal grand jury in Oklahoma City handed down a 33-count indictment against Patterson, charging him with misapplication of funds and wire fraud.

The high profile case was assigned to Lee who presided over a short two-hour session on September 10, 1984, to select a jury to hear the case.

Most of the charges against Patterson accused him of making loans to bank customers without their knowledge, then using the proceeds to pay the bad debts of other borrowers. Former bank chairman Bill Jennings called Patterson a "monster" he had turned loose on the world.[10]

From the beginning of the trial, defense lawyer Burck Bailey made inroads into the government's case. Bailey believed his best strategy was to make the trial a modern form of the medieval morality play— highlight what Bailey called "the rapacious greed of Penn Square Bank's borrowers," and the actions of the bank's officers and directors who had "hung Patterson out to dry."[11] It was a basic contest, in Bailey's view, between good and evil. The veteran lawyer tried to show his client, Patterson, was more of a scapegoat than a perpetrator.[12]

During the trial, Lee gave two of the three prosecutors a tongue-lashing for their courtroom maneuvers. He sharply admonished United States Attorney Bill Price for continually leading witnesses with lengthy questions requiring only a yes or no answer. Lee told Price, "If you keep testifying, I'll put you under oath."[13]

At one point during the testimony of former bank officer Russell Bainbridge, Lee warned Assistant United States Attorney Susie Pritchett that he would excuse Bainbridge as a witness unless she stopped asking him about events at the bank that were unrelated to the 25 remaining counts against Patterson. Frequently, Lee sustained defense motions before Bailey ever had a chance to rise from his chair and formally object. Once, Lee muttered, "Quadruple hearsay," before Bailey could object to testimony from Bainbridge.[14]

Bailey succeeded in portraying Patterson as a victim, rather than an ogre. The jury was apparently persuaded that Patterson did not intentionally defraud Penn Square Bank because he was such a large stakeholder in the bank.[15]

After the two-week trial, Patterson was acquitted on all counts of the indictment. He sobbed for 40 minutes in the courtroom after the jury's decision was announced. However, just before the jury began its deliberations, Lee received word from federal prosecutors in Chicago that Patterson had been indicted by a federal grand jury there for wire fraud and misapplication of bank funds in connection with the near-failure of the huge Continental Illinois National Bank, a bank to which Patterson had been selling participating loans to the tune of nearly a billion dollars. Lee kept the news from the jury, fearing their decision in the Oklahoma City case might be tainted by the latest developments in Chicago.[16] Later, after a mistrial in Chicago federal court, Patterson pleaded guilty to one count and was sentenced to a minimum time in prison.

In August, 1985, the first former officer of the Penn Square Bank was sentenced to prison. Lee gave Clark A. Long a three-year and two-year term after he was convicted of obstructing justice and self-dealing. Long had been accused of loaning large sums of money to oil drilling ventures in which he owned a substantial interest. Long had been arrested after a chase through Nichols Hills.[17]

Meanwhile, Lee was assigned several cases in the flurry of lawsuits filed by the accounting firm, Peat Marwick Mitchell & Co., against two federal agencies over the collapse of Penn Square Bank. Peat Marwick, the last independent auditor of the bank before its doors were closed, alleged that the Federal Deposit Insurance Corporation (FDIC) and the federal Comptroller of the Currency were negligent and contributed to the failure of the bank. The government agencies counterclaimed—at one point suing Peat Marwick for $154 million.[18]

Lee dismissed some of the lawsuits and oversaw an August, 1986, effort to settle the remaining cases. After a lengthy pre-trial, Lee announced that most of the remaining claims, including the

FDIC's lawsuit against the former officers of Penn Square, had been settled.

During the next two months, Lee and fellow federal judges worked feverishly with the bands of lawyers for the litigants who had remaining claims resulting from the Penn Square Bank fiasco. In what *The Daily Oklahoman* called a "mammoth settlement conference" on October 10, a major portion of the remaining litigation in the consolidated federal trial of Penn Square Bank cases was settled.

Stephen Jones was hired by a Chicago law firm as local counsel in still another case that arose from the failure of Penn Square Bank. Dozens of lawyers appeared in Lee's chambers for a settlement conference in a case involving a bank in Del City, Oklahoma. There were lawyers everywhere—sitting, standing, leaning against the wall. Jones remembered, "I never saw so many lawyers in one meeting. One well placed hand grenade would have knocked out three quarters of the commercial and bankruptcy bar of Oklahoma City."[19]

When Lee was advised that Chicago counsel had hired Jones, Lee quoted the Russian poet and writer Dostoevski, "a conversation with a clever man is always worthwhile," intending the quote as a compliment to Jones. Jones in turn quoted Tolstoy from *War and Peace*. Someone in the back of the room asked, "Are Dostoevski and Tolstoy with the FDIC?" Everyone had a good laugh even though Lee believed the question was asked seriously.[20]

In addition to delving deeply into the cases of Oklahoma's two major scandals of the 1980s, Lee was called upon in other cases to interpret laws that would affect the state's economic future.

In 1985, he declared as unconstitutional an Oklahoma law purportedly designed to insure the state's oil and gas resources were not squandered as a result of major corporate takeovers. The case involved Mesa Partners II, an investment group headed by billionaire take-over specialist and Oklahoma native T. Boone Pickens, Jr., that was trying to take over a California company for $3.5 billion.[21]

In his order, Lee found the Oklahoma law was so riddled with exemptions and exceptions for smaller takeovers, it did not realistically seem to be structured with conservation of Oklahoma's oil and gas as its main goal. Instead, Lee wrote, "This leads the court to believe the real target of the act is not the protection of energy resource assets but the potential slow-down and chilling effect on takeover bids in a way which unconstitutionally impinges on the power of the Congress" to govern interstate commerce. Lee said if all energy-producing states had laws like Oklahoma, "interstate tender offers for shares of corporate stock could grind to a whining halt."[22]

In the late 1980s, Lee heard several cases involving the collection of state cigarette and sales taxes on Indian lands within Oklahoma's borders. When the Oklahoma Tax Commission billed the Citizen Band Potawatomi Indian Tribe nearly $3 million for taxes on sales at the tribal grocery near Shawnee, the tribe sued, claiming that taxing sales on Indian land violated the sovereignty granted by previous federal treaties and laws.[23]

Lee partially agreed with the tribe's position, ruling that the Oklahoma Tax Commission could collect state taxes only on items purchased by non-tribal members at the Gallery Trading Post.[24]

Ultimately, the United States Supreme Court upheld Lee's ruling but shocked all parties by saying the Oklahoma Tax Commission could not sue Indian tribes if they failed to collect the taxes allowed by Lee's sweeping order. The highest federal court of the land agreed with the theory that an Indian tribe, as a sovereign nation, could not be sued without its consent.

In all cases that ended up going to trial, Lee met with lawyers representing all parties in a detailed pre-trial—intended to make the trial move quickly and smoothly.

However, a good pre-trail did not always result in an efficient trial. Lee's law clerk and later United States Attorney Dan Webber remembered an occasion when two competing lawyers failed to remember issues they were told not to mention. On his way back to chambers during a break, Lee muttered, "It's like watching two puppies try to hump a football."

feuding
with the FBI

IT WAS AN UNDERSTATEMENT that Lee had a long simmering feud with law enforcement agencies, particularly the Federal Bureau of Investigation. Early in his experience as a federal judge, Lee says he learned that the executive branch of the federal government, including the Department of Justice, and especially the FBI, misled not only opponents, but the court as well. He found support for his opinion years later in the blistering comments by Judge James Parker, chief judge of the federal court in New Mexico, in the Wen Ho Lee case that involved accusations of espionage against a Taiwanese-born American scientist.[1] Lee quickly formed the opinion that the criminal division of the United States Attorney's office in Oklahoma City, at least during his first years on the bench, was under the control of the FBI, rather than vice versa.[2]

On several occasions, Lee either dismissed a case or threatened to do so, based on his view that the U.S. Attorney's office or the

FBI, or both, failed to live up to their legal obligation to criminal defendants and to the court, either negligently or intentionally.

In one case, Lee granted a new trial because the government failed to turn over exculpatory materials to the defendant. At the retrial, an informant testified for the government but the assistant United States Attorney failed to reveal that the informant was being paid by the FBI. Initially, the assistant prosecutor denied knowing the witness was paid. But an FBI agent testified the assistant was aware of it since the first trial. The attorney eventually conceded she probably had "forgotten."[3]

Another time, Lee expelled an FBI agent from the courtroom because he believed the agent was signaling a prosecution witness how to testify.

In the trial of longtime Oklahoma City gambler Tracy Coy "Pody" Poe, an FBI agent testified that no strip searches had been performed in the course of the search of Poe's home. After being confronted with his report, the agent conceded that two teenage girls had been strip searched, albeit by a female agent. After leaving the witness stand, the agent discussed his testimony with other witnesses in violation of Lee's order. Based on the violation, Lee dismissed the case.

Ultimately, the Tenth Circuit Court of Appeals reversed Lee's dismissal and held that although the agent's conduct was careless, it did not merit dismissal of the case. In any event, Lee believed he had made his point.[4]

Lee also encountered problems with the criminal prosecution system in Oklahoma County. As a federal judge, he oversaw the habeas corpus review of the conviction of Rita Silk Nauni, a Native American woman convicted of first-degree murder of an Oklahoma City police officer.

The woman's defense at trial had been insanity. She had shot the male officer as he was attempting to put her son in a police cruiser after she had taken the gun from another female officer who was attempting to arrest her. Nauni first shot the woman officer with whom she was struggling. After getting the woman officer's gun, she ran to the police car and killed the male officer who was struggling with her son.

The wounded female officer testified at trial that Nauni had killed the male officer first and then shot her, saying, "Now, it is your turn, bitch." That statement had effectively removed an insanity defense and Nauni was convicted and sentenced to prison for 150 years.

The problem was that in an interview by a newspaper reporter immediately after the shooting, the wounded female officer reported another order of the shooting—her wounding first and then the murder of her male partner. That information was in the files of the prosecution but was illegally withheld from defense counsel who therefore could not cross-examine the officer on the pivotal testimony.

Nauni's conviction had previously been upheld by the Oklahoma Court of Criminal Appeals and she had served several years in prison while her habeas corpus petition was processed. Upon his review, it was obvious to Lee that Nauni had received nothing that resembled a fair trial. When confronted with the evidence, the wounded officer blamed the events on an assistant Oklahoma County district attorney who, the officer said, encouraged her to make up the inciteful words, "Now, it is your turn, bitch."

Lee ordered a new trial in state court. However, Nauni was released from prison and prosecutors made the decision not to retry her.

Lee believes that federal judges are in a unique position and have an obligation to prevent abuse by law enforcement, and in fact, faults himself for not being even more critical. He cites the FBI's handling of Ruby Ridge, the FBI laboratory scandal, the Wen Ho Lee case, the episodes of agents selling secrets to foreign governments, and the withholding of documents in the Oklahoma City bombing trial of Timothy McVeigh as examples of the government abusing its power.[5]

Lee refuses to cut the government any slack in regard to its obligation to give a defendant a fair trial. He finds the idea of what he calls "civic murder," the execution by a government of any person who is not guilty of the crime for which he or she is convicted, particularly disturbing.[6]

But, the government has won its share of cases in his court. In 1995, Lee upheld the conviction of one of Oklahoma's worst mass killers, Roger Dale Stafford, who had been sentenced to die for killing three members of a San Antonio, Texas, family along Interstate 35 in 1978. The murders of the Melvin Lorenz family were committed just three weeks before Stafford herded six employees of the Sirloin Stockade restaurant in south Oklahoma City into a walk-in freezer and executed them. Stafford was also under a death sentence for those six murders.

Lee's review of the death sentence given Stafford for the Lorenz family murders was one of a series of appeals efforts that lasted nearly two decades. On November 24, 1986, Lee upheld the death sentence handed Stafford for killing the Lorenz family. In his ruling, Lee rejected the claims of Stafford's court-appointed lawyer, Stephen Jones, that Stafford's wife at the time, Verna, should not have been allowed to testify because she had supposedly been hypnotized.[7]

Nine years later Lee was faced with still another appeal by Stafford's lawyers. Lee again rejected all legal arguments and denied Stafford's request for further review of his death sentence. Finally, after 17 years, Stafford was put to death at the Oklahoma state penitentiary for killing the Lorenz family.

Lee's tough stance in support of equal justice drew the praise of OU President David Boren, who wrote:

> I admire him most for his passionate commitment to the principle of equal rights for every single person. Lee West has fully understood that when the rights of any citizen are violated, the freedom and rights of all of us are endangered and eroded over time. He has been constantly on guard to assure that the rights of the powerless and unpopular are protected with the same zeal as those of the powerful and those whose views are mainstream.

It is because of the lifelong commitment to the rule of law by judges like Lee West that every citizen can have confidence in the fairness of our courts. In our large and diverse society, this faith in the impartiality of our system of justice is perhaps the most important element that holds us together as one people. Lee West, as a legal watchdog for citizens of all backgrounds, has made a lasting contribution to the strength of America.[8]

Reflections *of* Lee West

JUSTICE

I cannot begin to tell how honored I have been to serve as a judge on both the state and federal benches. While I do not believe for a minute that everyone is always treated fairly or equally in our court system, I do share Stanford University Law Dean Kathleen Sullivan's passionate statement:

> *What drives me is the conviction that the courts are the only place where people who are politically powerless can get a fair shake. You can never underestimate how important it is to have lawyers and courts defend people whom other people don't like.*

I am also honored by the statement of my daughter, Kim, now a United States Magistrate Judge in the Eastern District of Oklahoma, on the subject:

> *The core of my Dad's soul is that he is totally intolerant of anyone who attempts to utilize greater resources of any variety to the detriment of anyone less fortunate…He ensures that everyone comes into his courtroom on a level playing field.[9]*

> *Lee has lived with dogs way too long. If you whistle,*
> *he will come. When he is smiling, he's wagging his tail.*
> *He can't help either one. He's been around bird dogs*
> *so long, he's adopted bird dog ways.*
>
> J.   D U K E   L O G A N

for Love *o f* DOGS *a n d* HORSES

IT IS IMPOSSIBLE TO FULLY UNDERSTAND the true persona of Lee West without exploring his relationship with horses and dogs.

There is an old adage among bird dog men—Everyone during his lifetime is entitled to one good woman and one good dog. Lee always replies that he has two good dogs. Mary Ann fails to see the humor in that reply.

Lee grew up with dogs and horses. His father was a horse trader so there was always a pony to ride. Even when the West family hardly had sufficient food for the children, there was always a dog waiting his turn for the leftovers. Lee and his brother, Cal, Jr., became avid squirrel and rabbit hunters and provided a fair amount of meat for the family table. They also hunted for opossum, raccoon, and skunk and sold the hides.

Lee's addiction to quail hunting did not afflict his life until after law school. Once he began, he was hooked. After Governor Henry

Bellmon crossed party lines and appointed Lee to the state bench in 1965, they became friends and bird hunted together, along with their mutual friend, Turner Meaders of Wetumka, Oklahoma.

Other hunting companions were Jack Weiss, Leroy Mapp, Vernon Luke, George Gurley, Austin Deaton, and Buddy Keesee. In 1966, Governor Bellmon and Dr. E. Evan Chambers organized the Grand National Quail Hunt, patterned after the Wyoming One Shot Antelope Celebrity Hunt. The Grand National invited celebrities to come to Oklahoma to pair up with veteran quail hunters.

BELOW: At the 1969 Grand National Quail Hunt, Joe Foss, right, won the "Top Gun" Award with the most points. Lee, as Grand National president that year, presented a handsome trophy and a Remington Model 1100 shotgun to Foss, a World War II hero and former governor of South Dakota. As a fighter pilot, Foss was the first American ace in World War II to tie Eddie Rickenbacker's World War I record of shooting down 26 enemy planes.

ABOVE: As Kim, left, and Jennifer became old enough to ride horses, Lee made certain there was a friendly mount always available.

At the first Grand National, held on the Bollenbach Ranch near Kingfisher, Bellmon invited Lee to bring his dogs. The hunt was a huge success and captured nationwide attention. Within a few years, it became the most hospitable celebrity hunt in the country. Visitors went back to their homes praising both their friendly Oklahoma hosts and a healthy bird population.

ABOVE: Mary Ann, left, has endured Lee's endearment of hundreds of bird dogs for 49 years.

RIGHT: A South Dakota pheasant hunt in 1973. Left to right, Lee; Donna Foss; Joe Foss; Al Feldman, president of Frontier Airlines; Hoadley Dean, broadcasting executive; and Turner Meaders.

Lee served as president of the third Grand National Quail Hunt in 1969. Hunters from across the nation gathered. There were many celebrities present. Apollo astronauts Tom Stafford, Gene Cernan, and Ron Evans formed one of the 24 teams that competed for prizes. Governor Dewey Bartlett headed up the Oklahoma team. The White House team consisted of United States Postmaster General Winton Blount, presidential aide Fred LaRue, and Chuck Meachum, Commissioner of the Fish and Wildlife division of the Department of Interior.

Over the years, the Grand National sustained its high success of attracting celebrities to Oklahoma. Lee hunted with astronaut Wally Schirra; Governors Bellmon and Bartlett; singer Tennessee Ernie Ford; actor Max Baer who played Jethro in the "Beverly Hillbillies;" and congressmen Ed Edmondson of Oklahoma, Silvio Conte of Massachusetts, and John Dingell of Michigan.

Once Lee began spending his leisure time pursuing quail, he had to have his own bird dogs. He sought the best puppies to raise into champions. He spent a lot of each week caring for and training the dogs.

Texas lawyer and hunting companion John Harmon had compassion for Mary Ann who had to put up with Lee's hobby. Harmon wrote, "Can you imagine living with somebody who can't go anywhere, I mean anywhere, without eight or ten bird dogs in the back of his truck? Lee's idea of an August vacation at the beach for Mary Ann is a weekend in a trailer house in the middle of a dog training camp—lots of sand, no water, and plenty of sun."[1]

Patty Meaders tried to console Mary Ann one day when she said, "At least he's off chasing bird dogs instead of women." Mary Ann thought about the comment a moment and replied, "Women would be cheaper!"[2]

Lee raised both dogs and horses on the West family farm outside Ada. In 1958, he and Mary Ann purchased a Pontotoc County acreage, building it to 360 acres. Lee incorporated his horse ranch as the Barshoe Ranch and Kennel and started raising and racing quarter horses. Dr. Leon Self, a young veterinarian, and Lee became partners in the venture. Leon White, a horse trainer and jockey, trained some of the horses on the track that Lee and Dr. Self built on the Barshoe Ranch. John Criswell and Fireball Evans also cast some of their money into the pot to buy and train racing stock.

In 1961, Criswell and Lee established what they believed to be the first two-horse "syndicates" in Oklahoma. The Full Speed Syndicate and the Coldstream Guard Syndicate combined owners to finance the purchase, training, and maintenance of two yearling quarter horse stallions. Lee was teaching at the OU Law School at the time and convinced Dean Earl Sneed, Leo Whinery, and Lieutenant Governor Leo Winters to participate in the syndicates. Shareholders in the two horses were scattered among friends and family in several states.

Looking back, Lee probably violated about every securities law on the books when he formed the syndicates. He remembered, "It was from my pure ignorance. What I learned about securities law all came after that time, but fortunately no one ever complained."[3] Cold Stream Guard was a good horse. He became a Triple A rated race horse. Jerry Wells and Lee showed him until he acquired sufficient points to be an American Quarter Horse Association (AQHA) champion. He was later a "Supreme" AQHA champion, the highest honor available.

Austin Deaton, Jr., partnered with Lee in owning several horses. Many were successful—some were not. Deaton remembered a young colt he and Lee bought. Deaton said, "It grew up to be a midget and could outrun anything at 300 yards, but then it faded. Unfortunately, we couldn't find anybody to race at 300 yards."[4] Of other unsuccessful horse ventures, Deaton said, "One turned up dead in the ditch and another was cut badly on a wire. We considered it a successful year if one of our colts made enough money racing to pay his insurance premium."[5]

Lee's horse operation—he called it a "poor boy" operation—lasted until Lee left for his CAB post in Washington, D.C., in 1973. During the years of the horse operation, Lee's niece, Sandra Mantooth, lived with Lee, Mary Ann, and the girls. Sandra continued her interest in horses with some success. Her filly, Nita Boone, held the world's record at 220 yards for several years. The horse descended from a mare that Lee had given Sandra as a college graduation present.

Lee had one opportunity to get rich in the horse business. He turned down a chance to buy a mare named F.L. Ladybug for $1,250 from Marvin Barnes of Ada. Lee knew nothing about the horse's breeding and passed up the purchase. Later, F.L. Ladybug's colts won hundreds of thousands of dollars in prize money in the 1960s and 1970s.

> *A great dog will make a star—and a slave—*
> *out of an owner or trainer.*
>
> LEE WEST

fieLD tRiaLS

LEE ATTENDED HIS FIRST BIRD DOG FIELD TRIAL near
Ada in 1965 and became immediately addicted. The sport involved
both of the animals he loved most—horses and dogs. It also
required the ability to train both horses and dogs—an area where
he thought he had some talent. In addition, field trials provided Lee
an opportunity to compete—something he had liked to do since he
was a teenager.

Nationally known outdoor and wildlife writer and tax lawyer
Thomas S. "Tom" Word, Jr., of Richmond, Virginia, author of
None Held Back, explained field trials:

> They are a cult sport, pursued by a small fraternity of
> fanatics. They started in England in 1850. The first American
> one was at Memphis in 1874…
>
> A field trial is a contest for pointing dogs seeking upland
> game birds by scent—quail in the South, pheasants in the
> Midwest, prairie chicken, sharptail grouse, Hungarian par-
> tridge on the prairies…The sport is bloodless, for the
> pointed birds are not shot. Field trialers are ardent conser-
> vationists.

A field trial is also a show—a trial dog is a performer, and so is its handler…

Field-trial dogs guide the genetics of all working bird dogs. As with racehorses, a few great sires dominate pointer and setter bloodlines. The lineage of all bird dogs goes back through field trial winners to a handful of foundation sires from the turn of the last century.

A boy can save enough from a paper route to buy a weanling son or daughter of a National Champion—that makes the sport democratic, at least at the start. Campaigning on the major circuit is beyond the paper boy's reach, but many a great champion has been started by a farm boy.[1]

As in baseball, there are levels of competition in field trials. The top contests are called the major circuit. About 30 trials are held at the same times each year, starting in August on the northern prairies, then moving south, with quail trials in December and January in the Deep South.[2]

Tom Word explained why bird dogs are sometimes referred to as "pointers." "Bird dogs instinctively freeze—become a statue—when they detect the scent of game birds," Word said. The instinctive reaction is called a "point."[3]

Dogs compete two at a time, drawn by lot as "bracemates." They hunt for a prescribed time over a prescribed course. It takes a large piece of ground to host a field trial because bird dogs can hunt through five miles of country in one hour.

The judging is entirely subjective. According to Tom Word, "The dog that points the most birds is not necessarily the winner. The dog's hunting technique, rather than the quantity of its points, is key. The dog's performance is called his 'race'—a race to find and point birds."[4]

Word explained field trial dogs, "The adult dogs…are called all-age dogs. Like major-league baseball players, they are world-class athletes. Handled and watched from horseback, they can take your breath away with the speed and grace of their running—the statuesque majesty of their points.[5]

"Like race cars," Word continued, "all-age dogs perform on the edge—a hair's breadth from out of control, driven by a consuming instinct to find game. And like race cars, trial dogs suffer 'wrecks' when, in their exuberance, they forget their manners or get away from their handlers."[6]

How does a dog win in a field trial? Word said, "It must hunt at extreme range with extreme speed, making bold, independent casts for far-off objectives or along edges on the course likely to hold game birds. When the dog scents birds, it points with lofty style and awaits discovery by its handler or his assistant, called the scout. The handler then flushes the quarry under scrutiny of mounted judges. As the birds fly to safety, the handler fires a blank. The dog must remain a statue. If the dog will do all this with aplomb, it is called 'broke.' Being 'broke' is a great compliment to a dog—the big distinction between the field trial dog and the ordinary hunting dog."[7]

Field trial fans follow the sport through a weekly journal, the *American Field*, founded in 1874, the oldest sporting magazine in America. The magazine maintains the registry of working bird dogs and reports on activities of the Amateur Field Trial Clubs of America, the umbrella organization that loosely regulates the sport. Basic rules of competition, set by tradition, have remained unchanged for 120 years.[8] All field trials lead toward an annual National Championship.

Field trials provided an opportunity for eldest daughter, Kim, to spend time with her father. From the age of six, she bonded with him during the often long drives where Lee was her "captive audience." The trips afforded Kim the chance to discuss life, debate issues, and get to know someone that she always believed to be "an extraordinary human being."[9]

In Kim's eyes, Lee owed her time in the pickup truck on field trial weekends because he sometimes failed to pick her up at swimming practice and bargained his way out of attending school plays and Camp Fire Girls father-daughter banquets. He once forgot she was standing in a horse trailer and drove off without her.[10]

When Lee and Kim arrived at a field trial, Lee made a mad dash to locate an extra horse for her to ride and something for her to wear. Many times, Kim ended up riding "an old nag" and wearing her father's clothing, "at least 14 sizes too big." Lee once sacrificed one of the reins on the bridle on Kim's horse because he needed the leather for a dog lead. On another occasion, a saddle cinch broke and Kim landed, out of breath, on her back on the ground. She never forgot the feeling when Lee rode up and asked that she repeat

the "trick" so that everyone could have the opportunity to critique her dismount.[11]

When Lee went east to the nation's capital, he took his bird dogs and his good humor with him. Field trials in Virginia had waned in popularity and quality until Lee arrived. Even amateur handlers like Dr. Aubrey Morgan recognized the difference that Lee made in the atmosphere of field trials in Virginia. Morgan said, "People had a better time and they had fun. There was a great deal of kidding, a rough, good-natured type of kidding. Too pompous, too serious, and too self important people had to change around Lee."[12]

In Virginia, Lee participated in field trials with Parke Brinkley, Verle Farrow, Keith Severin, Stuart Lewis, Aubrey Morgan, Pat

Morgan, and John Harmon. Brinkley, the dean of Virginia field trialers and longtime judge of the National Championship, struck up a conversation with Lee about dogs the first time they met. Soon after Lee was appointed to the CAB, Brinkley was invited to a welcome dinner for Mary Ann and Lee. The two bird dog aficionados had never met except through the pages of American Field. However, upon being introduced, Lee said, "Find a table and save a seat for me and I will join you." The night was filled with bird dog talk.[13]

Harmon first met Lee in 1977 at a Virginia field trial. Harmon was on the staff of United States Attorney General Griffin Bell. Lee helped Harmon with his dog that won third-place. Lee called Harmon's wife, Joyce, and apologized for

Quail hunting in South Texas on Ben Vaughan's ranch. John Harmon got stuck in the sand at this site so many times, they named the corner after him. Left to right, P. Haas, John McFarland, John Harmon, Lee, Ben Vaughan, and John Treadwell.

the yellow third-place ribbon that Lee predicted "will cost untold thousands of dollars over the coming years." Lee was right. Harmon was hooked. He was one of hundreds of people who met Lee for the first time at a field trial.[14]

Attorney General Bell once accompanied Harmon and Lee on a quail hunting trip in south Texas. Bell remembered the climactic conclusion of the hunt, "On the last day, Judge West and John Harmon decided they would release all their dogs at the same time. There were 10 to 12 dogs—and they filled the air with quail. But unfortunately, not in the direction of the hunters."[15]

Harmon saw Lee's skills as a diplomat exhibited during a bird dog training day in northern Virginia. One of Lee's dogs ventured into the yard of a neighboring farm. There was wild commotion and chickens could be seen flying through the air. As Harmon and Lee rode closer, an irate farmer marched toward them with horrible stories of the carnage that had been inflicted by the dogs. Lee, distrustful of exaggerated claims, said, "I'll pay for the chickens but I am going to see the dead chickens first."[16]

The mad farmer kept walking toward Harmon and Lee. When he arrived just in front of the mounted hunters, he pulled Lee's dog out from behind him. The dog was covered from mouth to tail in blood and feathers. Harmon remembered, "That dog could not have been more covered in blood and feathers if he had been in a pillow fight with somebody throwing number 2 cans of tomato sauce."[17] Lee paid the farmer $35 and Lee never asked to see the chickens.

Lee also often took Jennifer to field trials with him. Just before the start of a 1973 "puppy stake," a trial for young bird dogs, Jennifer, age 12, walked up to one of the judges, Raymond Rucker, of Yukon, Oklahoma, and in a charming and pleasing voice said, "Mr. Rucker, may I see your judge's book?"[18]

Rucker assumed that Jennifer wanted to know what time her father's dogs were running. But Jennifer took the book and wrote something in it. She proudly handed the book back to Rucker and said, "Those are the three winners." Jennifer had chosen three pointers owned by her father. She batted .333 for the day, correctly picking one of Lee's dogs to finish first.[19]

Jennifer described growing up with her father as "trying to hold hands with the Tasmanian devil."[20] She said, "This is a man who woke up every morning going full throttle, long before sunrise, with absolute glee to see another day."[21]

One of Jennifer's first memories was when she got bucked off Skeeter, her paint pony, and how her father laughed because she had to catch her breath before she could cry. She recalled crossing Sandy Creek after a rain on the back of a horse. She knew she was "going to die" while Lee encouraged her from the other side. "You can make it, you can make it!" Lee yelled. And she did.[22]

Jennifer remembered the first time she saw her father indignantly outraged. A man was beating a horse when Lee intervened. She said, "In that Marine Corps tenor and with language to match, Dad made it clear that he would not tolerate behavior of that kind." Lee never touched the man but the man immediately stopped hitting the horse.[23]

One of the most significant side effects of being afflicted with the "disease" of loving bird dogs is the huge cadre of personal relationships Lee has established with his fellow trialers and hunters. J.B. Beall, a McAlester, Oklahoma, plumber nicknamed "Slow Leak," is a good example. The two have spent countless days working dogs and trying to outsmart pups. Beall said, "Lee West is as good a friend as you will let him be."[24]

Preston Trimble, the former longtime district attorney and district judge in Cleveland County, Oklahoma, believes Lee is the best known and admired amateur in the national field trial fraternity of fanatics. Trimble said, "His principal contribution to society is that he has raised some excellent dogs and has addicted countless people to the sport of riding horses after bird dogs in field trials, some

ABOVE: Lee rouses the troops early
each morning at Dog Camp. His cry is,
"Let's saddle the horses before daylight."

John Harmon, left, and Lee at the West Dog Camp.
Harmon was a star football player at the University
of North Carolina and attended Duke University
Law School. He clerked for Circuit Judge, and later
United States Attorney General Griffin Bell, Supreme
Court Justice Hugo
Black, and Supreme
Court Chief Justice
Warren Burger.
Harmon now
practices law
in Austin,
Texas.

The West dog camp near Arnett in northwest Oklahoma was home to trailer houses, dog pens, and a horse corral.

J.B. "Slow Leak" Beall, left, and Lee at the West Dog Camp. Beall, a McAlester plumber, is the head camp cook.

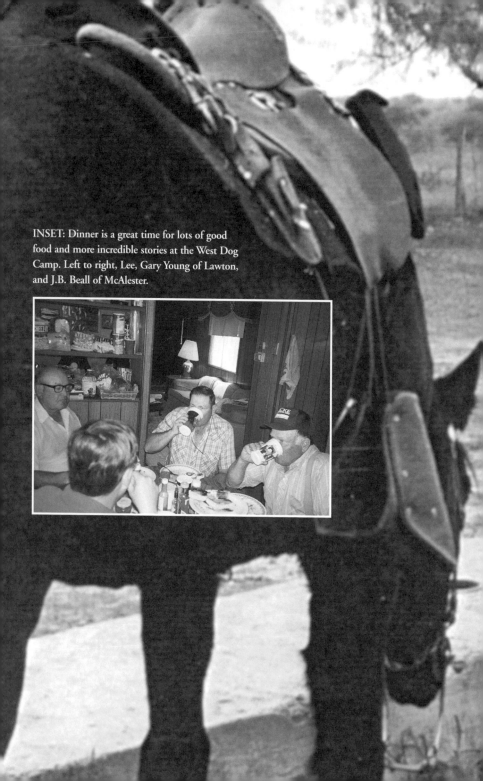

INSET: Dinner is a great time for lots of good food and more incredible stories at the West Dog Camp. Left to right, Lee, Gary Young of Lawton, and J.B. Beall of McAlester.

Lee and one of his prize dogs rest after a tough morning in the field.

of whom are now on their third wife. He gives puppies, saddles, lots of advice, loans, horses, tack, and supplies to young people or anyone who asks."[25]

Trimble calls Lee a true sportsman—the object of the game is to find the game. Trimble says, "Training with West is a true experience. That means you get to do everything because you need the experience. That includes opening gates, correcting his dogs, flushing them a bird, etc. The excuse he uses to not have to get off his horse is that he carries an antenna which is used to locate the dogs. It's a fake, but no one knows that but me."[26]

"West is a hell of a rider," Trimble commented. "He blasts across the prairie without fear or trepidation. He shows no mercy for those less able. He calls his horse that has gotten out from under me twice, his kid pony."[27] However, with his chiding of Lee, Trimble admitted one serious flaw in his own character. He said, "I love old West."[28]

Lee had an uncanny knack for training bird dogs. Dr. Aubrey Morgan observed Lee's compassionate handling of his dogs. Morgan said, "He could pick a puppy better than anyone I knew. The best in the litter was drawn to him. The list of dogs that Lee has bred and developed reads like a *Who's Who* in field trials."[29]

After Lee became a federal judge and settled down for good back in Oklahoma, he established a dog training camp, called the West Dog Camp. A clever description of the camp follows, written by Rex "The Little Cowboy" Tackett, a Texan who managed radio stations in several parts of the country, including a stint at KTOK-Radio in Oklahoma City where Lee and he became good bird dog buddies.

tHe west DOG camp

BY REX TACKETT

Hunkered down in the shinnery between the sand blow-
outs, just a couple hundred yards west of the memorialized
highest point in Ellis County, Oklahoma, (nothing more
than the tallest sand hill) resides the West Dog Camp. It's
just a little south of Arnett, Oklahoma, north of the
Canadian River and close to hugging the Panhandle of Texas
to the west. Established in 1981 by Judge Lee R. West and
another famous dog man, cousin, Bill West, it's a place hard
on women and horses but heaven for dog trainers and bird
dogs. Dog Camp's home is courtesy of Charles Nichols and
the Davidson Ranch.

The Dog Camp lease commands over 15,000 acres of
prime bobwhite quail habitat. The sand and oak shinnery
land rolls on and on with few fences, punctuated with fewer
windmill water holes, and views that will let you see dogs at
a mile or more when they appear to be only a white dot on
the horizon. When the dogs are at that range they are said to
be in there "deep, deeeep."

Dog Camp is made up of three house trailers, sand-run
kennels, barrels with chains, wired together horse pens and a
three-side horse shed.

The sand is deep and it drags on you with every step,
pulling on the horses and dogs alike. You are as likely to get
your rig stuck in the sand in front of the trailers as any place
on earth.

The whole place looks like a tornado lure. The only
explanation as to why a tornado hasn't dipped down and
snatched the camp up by its' roots, according to the regulars,
is that tornadoes don't strike the same place twice and Dog
Camp looks like it has already been hit, at least, once. This

camp is a whole lot like an ugly child, someone, somewhere sees the beauty. For the dog man, if bird dogs were a religion, the West Dog Camp would be a cathedral.

How many hundreds of puppies got their first taste of real freedom here? They run'em in a pack just before sunset. They open the gate to the puppy pen and thirty or forty pups roll and tumble out destroying everything in their path. More than one camp "new comer" has sought to capture the loosing of the horde on film, positioning themselves in front of the gate, only to be tumbled and left in the dirt as Lee rides to the west bellowing "here pup here." Oh, how the sight of that herd of pups is burned into your mind. Just to see them spread across the prairie. They run this way and that. Neither fur nor feather is safe from the onslaught. What youthful joy!

Running the pups is serious business because from that pack come the picks that go on to derby wins and often start capturing championships before they reach their adult form.

How many champions got their start here? How many championships have they won? More than 70, Lee West and the boys could tell you. There's Lee's dogs like champions Barshoe Curmudgeon, Barshoe Buzzsaw, Barshoe Suddenly, et al. The "Gang" has also done their share of winning Championships. Remembered are J.B. Beall's, Beall's Rose, Preston Trimble's Barshoe Bang, Bill Weaver's Barshoe Bushwhacker, et al. These dogs are the product of the patient and skilled hands of Lee West and all the gang that convene regularly in western Oklahoma.

The camp rules are simple. "There is no host and there are no guests. It is every S.O.B. for himself." The pompous drop like flies and the meek stand no chance at all. The dog *training might be the religion, eating is the passion. Lee warns all that chief camp cook J.B. Beall is also the plumber. Even Lee seems a little uncomfortable with this dual role. Faulty plumbing can shut the camp down just about as fast as air conditioner failure or the sighting of a tornado. While cleanliness is not a requisite for the camp, plenty of food (no tofu) and air conditioning for the noon naps are a must. Whatever the table fare, members are careful to not complain. That could lead to a new cook and even semi- qualified cooks are hard to come by in Ellis County. Should something foreign be spotted in the food it is either ignored or swallowed politely. What the meals lack in quality they make up for in quantity.*

Most striking and absolutely unchanging is the interior odor. It's a mixture of sweat, horse, dog, fried food, gravy, pinto beans, cabbage, and other odors unknown to men and certainly to women.

Some of the women known to have walked into this boar's nest (not often and not for long) include Mary Ann West, Joyce Harmon, Patti Trimble, Glenda Haag, and a few others who found just how fragile a marriage could be. They have come, seen and scampered.

Inside the trailer, the furniture looks like it came from a hard luck garage sale. The walls are covered with dog pictures and pages from the American Field *recounting the victories and losses in the field trial game. There is even a shrapnel scarred dog painting salvaged from Lee's office following the Oklahoma City bombing.*

Within the confines of the trailer and across the ranch, field trials have been re-run countless times, judgments questioned, marriages counseled, elections recounted, horses ridden and not ridden and stories told again and again.

tHe west DOG camp

Occasionally, someone will make the mistake of trying to say something serious. Preston Trimble was the brunt of one of these faux pas *when waxing elegant while extolling the virtues of being at camp. He was going on and on about the camaraderie of man and just being in the out-of-doors with horses, dogs and good friends. The judge had heard about all of this dribble he could stand when he admonished Preston with, "you stupid S.O.B, let me tell you what its all about, its about who has the best bird dog and a good horse." End of conversation! The boys may get sentimental about the passing of a good dog, a good horse or a good friend. It doesn't get much deeper than that.*

Human frailties are often forgiven but never overlooked. They stand bare naked to the wit of all. Flaws are picked at until they are inflamed. And, friendships never die.

> *Lee has more talent with young dogs than anyone I know. He
> can pick a future champion out of a crowd of puppies.*
>
> DR. AUBREY MORGAN

a STRING of CHAMPIONS

LEE HIMSELF DOES NOT UNDERSTAND why he has been
so successful with training bird dogs. Maybe it is because of his theory that you cannot teach dogs—but can only help them discover
what they were born knowing because of a thousand years of selective breeding. Perhaps, his success is because of how much he genuinely loves his dogs, has confidence in them, and has high
expectations for the prized animals. Somehow, the dogs seem to
know all this.

For whatever reason, field trial success for dogs raised and
trained at the Barshoe kennels was not long in coming. Lee began
winning shortly after he began to compete in local trials in 1966,
first with Barshoe Twiggy and Barshoe Kook. Barshoe Lemon was
named Oklahoma Dog of the Year in 1969. Barshoe dogs won 14
Oklahoma Dog of the Year Awards even though Lee was in
Washington, D.C., from 1973 to 1978.

In 1973, the Barshoe dogs began to distinguish themselves on
the national scene. Barshoe Suddenly was the winner of the 69th

American Field Quail Futurity in competition with 102 other derbies. She was co-owned with Bob Duncan of Blanchard, Oklahoma, and handled by professional trainer Hugh "Bud" Daugherty. At the time of Barshoe Suddenly's win, Lee was in Washington in confirmation hearings for his seat on the Civil Aeronautics Board.

Barshoe Suddenly was named the top derby in the nation in 1973. After Lee and Duncan sold her to Hoyt Henley of Montgomery, Alabama, the dog won the National Amateur Quail Championship, the National Open Free for All Championship, and several other titles.

Barshoe Rebel won an important placement in an open derby stake in Canada in 1973 and Lee sold him to Dr. Dorwin Hawthorne about the time that Lee moved to the nation's capital.

Champion Buckboard, originally named Barshoe Rebel, was the first of Lee's bird dogs to be named to the Field Trial Hall of Fame.

Lee was honored when Champion Buckboard was awarded the Purina Award as the top field trial bird dog in America in 1977.

Barshoe Rebel was re-registered under the name of Buckboard and later won seven prestigious championships. He was named the top dog in the nation, the Purina Dog of the Year in 1977 and was elected to the Field Trial Hall of Fame in 1983.

Barshoe Crossup was Lee's next good young dog. Out of a record breaking number of entries, she was named winner of the National Shooting Dog Futurity in Baldwinsville, New York, in 1976. The dog was handled by Bill Kuzer of Virginia while Lee was on a CAB trip in Argentina. Lee sold Barshoe Crossup to Dr. Dan Bateman of Albany, Georgia, and she went on to win the National Open Shooting Dog Championship, the Masters Open All Age Championship, and the Open Quail Championship at Paducah, Kentucky.[1]

Barshoe Buttonhook won the 1977 American Field Quail Futurity and the 1978 Continental Derby Championship.

In 1978, Barshoe Buzzsaw began a string of championships with the All American in Indiana. Lee sold him to Tom Faller. Barshoe

Silhouetted against the early morning sky, Lee prepared
to follow one of his champion bird dogs onto the
prairie, looking for upland birds.

Buzzsaw later won seven championships including the Open Invitational twice where he was pitted against the top 12 dogs on the continent. In the Open Invitational, he was called back for the finals a record six times.

When Barshoe Buzzsaw was nominated for membership in the Field Trial Hall of Fame in 1988, Andy Daugherty wrote, "He was happy every minute he was loose. He looked as good at 50 yards as at a half a mile. And he loved to be at either—as long as he was loose…He was ready every day. If you worked him five hours, the only thing tired was your horse and you."[2]

Daughtery told of the time Buzzsaw was called upon to run in ice and frozen conditions at the Invitational. He recalled, "The ground was frozen, the trees, everything. At the hour mark, his feet and legs were bleeding, and his tail had ice all the way around. I gathered him, started across the road, and could track every foot with blood. He wasn't quitting or tired. But I told myself, 'Old man, you have already done enough for me.' There would be no

Barshoe Buzzsaw was elected to the Field Trial Hall of Fame in 1988. Lee called him the best of many great bird dogs he owned and trained. Buzzsaw lived to the age of 12.

torture. I picked him up, put him in the truck, and headed for the kennels."[3]

Endurance was nothing that Lee or Daugherty ever had to worry about with Barshoe Buzzsaw. After the dog was 10 years old, he knocked a covey of prairie chickens, ran them a half mile to a bluff, and was pointing when his handlers arrived. Buzzsaw loved birds and he loved running.[4] Barshoe Buzzsaw was elected to the Hall of Fame on the first ballot.

Barshoe Brute provided a lot of bragging rights for Lee. He won early and often and Lee sold three-fourths interest in the dog to Bob Webber. After the sale he won several championships while being handled by professional Andy Daugherty. Barshoe Brute was the third of Lee's dogs to be honored as a member of the Field Trial Hall of Fame.

Barshoe Vintage and Barshoe Ingenue, two outstanding female bird dogs, won for Lee and for their subsequent owners, Tom Faller and Brad Calkins of Denver, Colorado.

Barshoe Czar was an exciting young dog. He was whelped by John Criswell who became partners with Lee in the dog's

Lee training dogs on the prairies of Saskatchewan, Canada. The story of his trip was reported in a special article in *Field Trial.*

ABOVE: John Harmon carries Barshoe Czar after the dog completed three hours of hunting required in the 90th National Bird Dog Championship at Ames Plantation in 1991. Barshoe Czar was a potent sire of champion bird dogs

training and competition. Before he was three years old, Barshoe Czar won four championships and a runner-up prize. Lee and Criswell sold the dog to Bill Heard of Oxford, Mississippi. Barshoe Czar's offspring, Barshoe Culprit and Barshoe Barracuda, won first and third in the 85th American Field Quail Futurity in 1989. Lee sold both dogs to Heard. Barshoe Barracuda later became an outstanding producer of champion bird dogs in the kennel of Lee's good friend, Cecil Rester.[5]

In August, 1991, Lee underwent surgery for colon cancer which had unfortunately affected several lymph nodes in his body. Doctors aggressively treated the cancer with a full, irreversible colostomy, followed by intense chemotherapy and radiation treatments. Lee went to the Mayo Clinic in Rochester, Minnesota, for a thorough review to make certain there was no other treatment he needed.

In 1991, Lee was invited to be the Master of Ceremonies at the 25th anniversary Grand National Quail Hunt. On the day's hunt, Lee guided General Norman Schwarzkopf, the recent hero of Desert Storm. Lee poked fun at the general's prowess as a shooter and applauded the Pentagon for promoting him to general and getting him off the front lines where, Lee said, "He might well have lost the war we had just won." Left to right, Lee, Mary Ann, General Schwarzkopf, and Pat Meaders.

While standing in line at the Oklahoma City airport to purchase his airline ticket, Lee's longtime friend, Leo Winters, walked up and informed Lee that he just wanted to go along on the Mayo Clinic "fun trip" with Lee. And with Leo along, it was a fun trip.

Some of Lee's friends were so convinced that he was about to die that they threw farewell parties for him. Some of his field trial competitors openly rejoiced at the prospect of the apparent end of Lee's field trial career. Little did they know that the best was yet to come.[6]

Lee's cousin and great professional dog trainer, Bill West, temporarily took over the training of Lee's dogs. Within two weeks of his major surgery, Lee was able to operate a four-wheeler to work dogs. A week later, Lee was back in the saddle again. With great help from Bill West, the training of the Barshoe dogs never slowed.

Lee won his first national championship with Barshoe Curmudgeon in 1993. The competition at the National Amateur Quail Championship at the sprawling 14,000-acre McFarlin-Ingersoll Ranch south of Claremore, Oklahoma, may have provided Lee with his greatest bird dog thrill ever. The National Amateur is the flagship competition of the Amateur Field Trial Clubs of America. The first championship was held in 1917.

In the 1993 championship, Lee was handling Barshoe Curmudgeon, braced against Miller's Silver Ending, a celebrated national champion. Silver Ending was being handled by Ferrell Miller, whom Lee considered the best amateur in the country.

Both dogs had a divided covey find early in the competition. When Ferrell later found Barshoe Curmudgeon pointing, in an act of true sportsmanship, he called point for Lee. Later, as Lee was leaving the Herb Stout Ranch and moving onto the McFarland Ranch, he could see Silver Ending standing proud and beautiful in the valley far below. Lee rode with a sinking heart because it

Grandaughter, Mary Ellis, left and her mother, Jennifer, astride one of Lee's favorite mounts, Monkey.

RIGHT: Barshoe
Curmudgeon, Lee's
first dog to win the
National Amateur
Quail Championship.
The dog performed
majestically in the
1993 competition.

BELOW: Lee poses
with a shotgun and
trophies he won
with Barshoe
Curmudgeon in the
1993 National
Amateur Quail
Championship.

RIGHT: Barshoe Esquire got his start, like so many other good dogs, at the Lee West Dog Camp in northwest Oklahoma. Tom Word described him, "He was a big, gangling pup and an escape artist. When Judge West and pals rode from camp with derbies to work, the pup would show up uninvited, having climbed the puppy-lot fence."[10] In the photograph, Barshoe Esquire appears with Sharleen Daugherty, wife of trainer Andy Daugherty, standing left, and Dale Busch, a judge in the Continental Championship.

BELOW: Lee, third from left, poses with Barshoe Benign who won the 75th National Amateur Quail Championship.

appeared to be such a spectacular find that surely Miller would win the national championship.

However, as the huge gallery got closer, they found a previously obscure Barshoe Curmudgeon standing majestically on point about 50 yards ahead of his competitor. Silver Ending was simply honoring Curmudgeon's point. When Lee flushed that covey of quail and fired the blank round in his shotgun, he was confident that he was about to win his first national crown. He was so excited he could hardly remount his horse to complete the competition.[7]

Lee won his second national championship in 1996 with Barshoe Curmudgeon's daughter, Barshoe Benign. A year later, it was a "three-peat" for Lee as he won the National Amateur Shooting Dog Championship with Barshoe Hard Twist. Other Barshoe champions produced in the 1990s were Barshoe Quickly, Barshoe Belligerent, Barshoe Bolshevik, Barshoe Bang, Barshoe Bushwhacker, Barshoe Barkeep, Barshoe Cossack, Barshoe Shoeshiner, Barshoe Gotcha, Barshoe Panacea, Barshoe Esquire, and Barshoe Sting.

In January, 1997, Lee won both Championship and Runner-Up honors in the Region 17 Amateur All Age Championships with Barshoe Quickly and Barshoe Sting—a rare double win in field trials. Barshoe Sting was only a derby at the time and later won the Continental Derby Championship and Runner-Up in the National Derby Championship that year. In 1999, Sting also won the Oklahoma Open Championship.

In one season alone, 1997-1998, Barshoe dogs were named champion 11 times and were named runner-up champions 7 times. Seldom, if ever, has any kennel in the country exceeded that record.

Barshoe Hardtwist won the Texas Open Shooting Dog Championship in 2000 and again in 2002. The latter was his 14th championship placement. Barshoe Panacea won the 2001 All American Open Shooting Dog Championship against 70 other dogs in South Dakota—her sixth championship placement.

In February, 2002, Barshoe Esquire won the 107th running of the Continental Championship at the Dixie Plantation in Georgia. There were 121 dogs competing in the one-hour qualifying heats and 16 of them were called back for one hour-50 minute final heats. The win came in the largest entry of dogs ever in the Continental Championship, the country's most prestigious field trial. Buckboard and Barshoe Quickly had previously won the Continental, making this the third win of the prestigious trial by Barshoe dogs.

Tom Word reported, "With a reaching race and five letter-perfect finds (one of a woodcock), Barshoe Esquire cleanly claimed the Continental All-Age crown for handler Andy Daugherty and owners Tom Faller and Lee West. Earning his sixth all-age championship, the athletic, tall eight-year-old liver-ticked pointer with solid liver head, was at the peak of his powers…His race was high drama, unfolding scene by scene."[8]

"He exudes excitement," Word wrote about Barshoe Esquire, "eating up the country with his reaching, high-headed stride. He's all-age to the bone. His performance at Dixie was masterful, a thrill memorable for Tom Faller, on hand to watch, and Lee West, who got the word by phone back home in Oklahoma."[9]

In all, the Barshoe Kennel has played a major role in breeding and developing more than 30 champions who have won more than 70 championships in the toughest competition, both amateur and professional. There is no doubt that Barshoe Kennel has had a substantial impact upon the breed and will for many years to come.

Champions Buckboard, Barshoe Buzzsaw, Barshoe Brute, and Barshoe Curmudgeon have distinguished records as sires. Barshoe Envoy was the mother of nine different champions—a feat that stood as the world record until 2002. Barshoe Cuz, Barshoe Fly, and Barshoe Barracuda also have excellent records of producing dams. The Barshoe Kennel enjoys national and international respect.[11]

Some of Lee's best friends are bird dog enthusiasts. The hours and days spent in dog camps and on the prairies of America have bonded friendships with men like John Harmon, Bud and Andy Daugherty, Bill West, Dean Lord, J.B. Beall, Bob Singleton, Pat Morgan, Mac Smith, Pat McInteer, Gary Young, Denton Sharp, Bob Shelton, Bill Weaver, Jere Korthanke, Dean Findley, Parke Brinkley, Aubrey Morgan, Verle Farrow, Tom Brigman, and Keith Severin.

Lee's uncanny abilities as a storyteller were described by Harmon:

> Lee is a story machine. He is a wonderful storyteller with both the memory and the imagination to make the true ones the best ones. More important, however, is that Lee generates stories from material on a wholesale basis. The stories about Lee are even funnier than the stories he tells, and like the stories he tells, the best ones are the true ones. Lee would say that his life, for the most part, is like one of his good stories—for the most part true.[12]

Lee carries the conversation at dog trials or on weekend hunting expeditions. Harmon marveled at how Lee never tempers or changes his message—no matter the political conviction of his audience. Harmon said, "How can he sit down with Republican friends and others who do not agree with him about anything, tell them everything that is wrong with their President, candidate, policy, or party, and leave everybody laughing and still friends?"[13]

Harmon's conclusion is that "Lee talks politics like a political cartoonist. He finds the soft underbelly of the other side's position or his own. Then, instead of stabbing with a knife, he makes everybody realize just how ridiculous your candidate or his candidate, your President or his President looks with his britches down and his underbelly showing."[14]

Lee honors a few of his friends with special titles. He calls Rex Tackett, Fred Davis, and Preston Trimble "among the flakiest of my bird dog friends." Lee believes that John Harmon may be the best amateur dog trainer he has been around in terms of talent and temperament. Lee said, "If Harmon had not let Supreme Court clerkships and the demands of an international law practice distract him, he might have been the best."[15] Harmon frequently takes Lee's "culls" and improves them enough to beat him in competition.

Harmon has been with Lee on dog trips that resulted in some of Lee's most embarrassing moments. Once, he and Lee went to the Abilene, Texas, airport to pick up a friend who was joining them for the weekend. Lee was dressed in his hunting best—his overalls (Oklahoma tuxedo), which were very dirty because he and Harmon had cleaned their birds in the parking lot of the airport.

When their friend's flight was delayed for several hours, Harmon and Lee decided to lay down on the floor in the vacant waiting area and take a nap. The next thing Lee knew, he was being rudely awakened by a police officer who was clearing the airport of vagrants. The officer said, "Now be quiet and come along with me fellow, you can't sleep here." Harmon was enjoying the sight of Lee trying to tell the officer he was a federal judge without any identification until the officer looked at Harmon and said, "Hey, you too, buddy, on your feet."[16]

On another occasion in Pierre, South Dakota, Harmon and Lee were staying in an old schoolhouse in a rural area. The abandoned building was watertight but had no furniture. Harmon and Lee drove 50 miles to Pierre to the Salvation Army to buy some used furniture for their home away from home. They were in their usual dress after a long day in the saddle—Lee in his overalls over a threadbare shirt. Harmon was dressed about the same. They drove up to the Salvation Army in Lee's green Ford truck that was "dented beyond its years."[17]

The two hunters selected a couple of beds, two chairs, a table, and a lamp. When they asked the lady who ran the Salvation Army store how much they owed for the furniture, she said, "Oh, we don't charge people like you, we are only too glad to help." Harmon and Lee thought about it for a moment and then convinced the lady to let them make a contribution.[18]

Lee is often asked, "Why does any dog want to become a great dog which requires him to strive so hard and so long under all kinds of weather conditions?" Lee says nobody knows, but his best answer is, "They can't help themselves." The same question applies to owners. People ask, "Why will one spend untold amounts of money, energy, and effort just to own a great dog?" Lee answers, "They can't help themselves."[19]

If there are no dogs in heaven, then when I die I want to go where they went.

WILL ROGERS

WINE ADS *and* COURTROOM ANTICS

THE DECADES-OLD ARGUMENT of whether or not alcoholic beverages could be advertised in Oklahoma landed in Lee's courtroom in 1981. Attorneys representing 4 cable television companies and 13 television stations filed suit against the Oklahoma Alcoholic Beverage Control Board (ABC), asking that a state statute forbidding advertising of alcoholic beverages be declared unconstitutional.

The litigants expanded when the Oklahoma Press Association joined the television stations' effort and Sooner Alcohol and Narcotics Education, Inc., (SANE), a perennial anti-drinking force in the state, sided with the state agency which enforced the ban on advertising.

Saying that "information is better than ignorance," Lee ruled the state ban on television advertising of alcoholic beverages was in violation of free speech under the First Amendment to the federal constitution and also denied equal protection under the law. Lee pointed out that consumption of alcoholic beverages had risen substantially in the previous 20 years despite the ban. The state had argued that the purpose of the advertising ban was to reduce alcoholic consumption in Oklahoma. Lee specifically ruled that no evidence was presented to him that the advertising ban directly protected the health and welfare of Oklahomans.[1]

Lee drew immediate criticism from SANE director Ross McLennan who charged that Lee's statistics on the increase of drinking in Oklahoma were wrong. Even though McLennan could not provide specific statistics on how much Oklahomans drank, he said Oklahomans had a low consumption rate and very few alcoholics. McLennan was convinced that Lee's ruling would increase the number of people turning from beer to wine and hard whiskey.[2]

Shortly after his decision, Lee left for a Texas quail hunting trip with John Harmon. Lee called back to the office where his secretary, Jeannie Prather, had been deluged with phone calls. Jeannie said, "The church people are eating me alive." However, one nice church lady at least called back to apologize for calling Lee an extremely bad name.[3]

Mary Ann received a call at home from an irate male caller. The man asked, "Doesn't your husband know that drunkenness leads to nakedness?" Mary Ann responded, "Oh, yes, he's known that for years. One of his favorite quotes is Ogden Nash's "Candy is dandy, but likker is quicker."[4]

Eventually, after five years of protracted appeals and additional lawsuits, Lee's original ruling was expanded by the United States Supreme Court to allow Oklahoma newspapers to accept wine and liquor advertisements. Radio and television stations, under a voluntary agreement with the National Association of Broadcasters, aired only ads for wine and beer.

During one lawsuit concerning the ban on liquor advertising, Lee's mixing of judging and dog handling caused great concern for an assistant attorney general, Lynn Barnett. She and attorney—and later federal judge—Stephen Friot, were waiting outside Lee's chambers for a ruling on the extent to which Friot could depose a state official in the defense of his client that had run afoul of the liquor advertising ban.

Lee's voice carried outside his office and was clearly heard by the waiting lawyers. He told the person on the other end of the telephone conversation, "That old bitch has not been getting anything done for the last two or three years and I intend to get rid of her."

Barnett's eyes grew to the size of saucers. Friot remembered, "She turned white as a sheet because she thought Judge West was talking about his wife." Barnett recovered after Friot, through tears of laughter, explained that Lee was talking about his bird dogs.[5]

Lee and three members of his staff. Left to right, Wilma House, Lee, Cindy Smith, and Beverly Grigsby. Wilma has worked for Lee more than 15 years. She graduated from Antlers High School with Lee and Mary Ann in 1948. Cindy, Lee's law clerk for more than 20 years, is known as Lee's "elbow law clerk." Of her work, Lee said, "Her legal research is flawless. When we have disagreed, she usually turns out to be right. No one ever had a better lawyer—or friend."

Lee's courtroom was never dull. In July, 1990, Lee began what he thought would be a normal trial for defendant Alfred James Prince, accused of robbing a Duncan, Oklahoma, savings and loan office. As the jury was sworn in, Prince, upset over Lee's refusal to replace his court-appointed lawyer, rose to his feet, exposed himself, and tried to urinate on his lawyer. He missed--but urinated all over the counsel table and courtroom floor.[6]

Lee immediately recessed court and sent the jury out to a waiting area. Prince moaned loudly as Lee admonished him that he must conduct himself in a manner consistent with order and decorum in the courtroom. Lee said, "If you refuse to do so, if you interrupt the proceedings, then the court will have no option but to remand you to the basement and allow you to observe the trial proceedings by way of video."[7]

Prince then began screaming and moaning loudly. Lee ordered Prince to a holding cell in the federal courthouse basement. Prince's attorney, Jerome T. Kearney, complained that surely his client could not get a fair trial because of what the jury had seen him do and because he had not been subjected to a psychological evaluation. Assistant United States Attorney Ted Richardson, asked for his response, only said, "Well, Judge, this is a first for me."[8]

Lee continued the trial until Prince's mental status could be evaluated. The defendant's disruptive tactics received considerable publicity. As a result, Lee received numerous gifts from his "sympathetic" colleagues in the form of hip boots, shower caps, raincoats, and other water repellant equipment. Even the rather droll United States Supreme Court Justice Byron "Whizzer" White observed, "Lee, I understand you have been springing a few leaks in your courtroom."[9]

Prince set fire to his hospital cell and tried to commit suicide while undergoing the mental competency examination. The examiner found Prince's behavior to be fabricated and declared Prince competent to stand trial.

Later, a second jury found Prince guilty even though he had a new lawyer, Bill Zuhdi. In affirming the conviction, the United States Court of Appeals for the Tenth Circuit released a humorous, tongue-in-cheek opinion written by Judge Wade Brorby.

Saying that parents should think twice about encouraging their children to enter law school, Brorby wrote, "The parent who happens to read this opinion may not be so quick to urge a loved child to become a lawyer after learning how the defendant in this case expressed his extreme personal dislike of his lawyer. Likewise, the would-be lawyer raised on the hit television series, "L.A. Law," to believe a law degree is that golden ticket to a glamorous career of big money, fast cars, and intimate relationships among the beautiful people may think twice before sending in his or her law school application when word of this case gets out."[10]

The Tenth Circuit applauded Lee and the lawyers for their actions in the Prince case, writing, "In conclusion, there is no rule of law equating intentional and public displays of incontinence with incompetence. The trial judge, court personnel, and lawyers who stuck with this case in spite of the unique hazards of working with this defendant are to be commended." In a word to prospective lawyers, Judge Brorby wrote, "As for the one-time budding lawyer whose hopes for a dazzling life have now been dashed by the facts of this case, we suggest an alternative career in screenwriting. Stories about lawyers are in wide demand, and this case—now that it is in the public domain—could be part of your first plot."[11]

A footnote in the Tenth Circuit opinion said, "Unusual stories like this one are apparently standard fare for the fictional television lawyers of "L.A. Law," who face many obstacles before cashing their paycheck and speeding off to another intimate dinner party."[12] Andy Coats later laughingly praised Prince for expressing his First Amendment rights—saying Prince's opinion of Lee's court was shared by most lawyers who appeared therein.

In another trial, an FBI agent became angry during discussions with defense counsel, William J. Skepnek. The agent, whose investigation had resulted in the indictment of the defendant, approached Skepnek after Lee had left the courtroom and said, "I ought to take off your tie and shove it up your ass." Skepnek related the conversation to Lee and said he thought it was intended to intimidate him and interfere with his client's right to representation. He admitted that he had never been intimidated.[13]

Lee humorously took care of the situation. He wrote an order citing the fact that Skepnek was a jovial personality who could be characterized as an "exuberant gladiator with a penchant for bow ties." Skepnek had played football at the University of Kansas and was 10 years younger and 40 pounds heavier than the FBI agent.[14]

Lee wrote, "The agent's unprovoked conduct in the courtroom raises questions not only as to his training and ability as an FBI agent but also as to his judgment and belief in his own physical capabilities." Lee said maybe the appropriate sanction would be to order the agent to carry out his threat. But, concluding that such a sanction might constitute cruel and unusual punishment to the agent in contravention of the Eighth Amendment of the federal constitution, Lee "happily" deemed the matter moot.[15]

Early in Lee's federal bench career, he was forced to remove an inmate from the courtroom during a trial on charges of stabbing a prison guard at the El Reno Federal Correctional Institute. Rickke Leon Green screamed every time his name was mentioned, and called his court-appointed lawyer, Kenneth Nance, a "snake," "humanoid," and a "puppet." When Green would not stop pounding the counsel table, Lee ordered him back to a holding cell and recessed the trial until maintenance workers could run cable from the courtroom to a portable speaker in the cell in the United States Marshal's office.[16]

It was the first time Lee tried a defendant who was not present in the courtroom. But it was not the first time Green had participated in courtroom disturbances. Years earlier, in a state trial for beating another inmate to death during a state penitentiary riot, Green and other defendants had to be shackled and gagged for the trial to continue.[17]

Lee did bring Green to the courtroom to hear the jury declare its verdict. Extra courtroom security was provided to the overflow crowd of spectators who had heard about the earlier displays by Green. This time, Green was calm as he listened to Lee announce the guilty verdict on a lesser charge of assault with a deadly weapon with intent to do bodily harm—somewhat of a victory because government prosecutors had charged him with assault with intent to kill, a much more serious crime. Green called his trial "frustrating" and demanded that he be removed from the courtroom without delay.[18]

In 1982, Lee was presented a case involving counterfeit E.T. dolls—stuffed versions of the lovable extraterrestrial in Steven Spielberg's movie. The problem was that counterfeit E.T.'s were showing up by the thousands as prizes on the midway of the Oklahoma State Fair. Universal City Studios filed suit in federal court in Oklahoma City to block the sale of the counterfeit dolls. Lee granted a temporary injunction and authorized United States Marshal Stuart Earnest and Oklahoma County Sheriffs Deputies Albert Johnson and Gordon Bulla to seize and impound all unauthorized E.T. paraphernalia. *The Daily Oklahoman* reported, "If E.T. phones home soon it might be because he's run into trouble with the law at the State Fair of Oklahoma."[19]

Whether Lee was assigned serious, monumental, or infamous cases, he loved being a judge. Despite growing up in poverty, he never had a strong desire to make huge amounts of money. On both occasions when he left private practice to become a judge, he took a 50 percent cut in pay. With his experience and acknowledged skill as a negotiator, mediator, and arbitrator, he could easily triple his judge's salary. But he has always placed a higher priority on the enjoyment and satisfaction he gets from the work he does.

John Harmon, who clerked for two United States Supreme Court Justices and a Circuit Judge, should know what makes a good judge. Harmon believes that for someone to be a good judge, that person must like being a judge. Once when Congress blocked a pay raise for federal judges and some left the bench to return to more lucrative private practice, Lee had no change of heart. When Harmon asked him if he was going to quit, Lee replied, "Quit? Hell no. I would pay them to have this job."[20]

However, Lee is quite sympathetic with other judges who, because of family obligations, are unable to continue doing the job that they like and feel they must leave the bench. Lee was one of 20 judges who brought suit against the federal government in *Williams v. U.S.*, contending that the government was

required to give judges a cost of living increase, even when Congress denied their own increase. The judges won in the lower court but the decision was reversed in the appellate court, two to one. The United States Supreme Court denied certiorari by a 6-3 vote.[21]

Lee's unique way with words and his Little Dixie delivery style bonds him to audiences. Listeners hardly stop laughing at one "Westism" until they are broadsided by another. Lee once debated United States Court of Appeals Judge Robert Henry, himself a wit of the highest order, about who was superior—a trial judge or an appellate judge. Lee quipped, "Trial judges must do twice as well as appellate judges to be thought half as good. Luckily, this is not very difficult."[22]

About appellate judges, Lee said, "If legal claptrap was a religion, the Circuit Court would be a cathedral."[23]

Lee's skills as a settlement judge

The judges of the United States District Court for the Western District of Oklahoma in 2002. Left to right, standing, Ralph G. Thompson, Wayne E. Alley, Joe Heaton, Lee R. West, and Vicki Miles-LaGrange. Seated, left to right, David L. Russell, Chief Judge Robin J. Cauthron, Tim Leonard, and Stephen P. Friot.

were tested in the spring of 2002 when he was asked to move the parties toward settlement in an emotional case involving the City of Tulsa.

In 1994, several black Tulsa police officers filed a class-action lawsuit against the city alleging systematic discrimination within the police department. The lawsuit grew more complicated through the years, with no resolution in sight.

However, Lee helped bring the parties together and, in meetings over a several month period, hammered out a settlement that ended the prolonged and divisive litigation.

> *I married the girl I fell in love with in the second grade—and for 49 years I have talked her into staying on for one more year—although it takes a little more talking each year.*
>
> LEE WEST

PURELY PERSONAL

NO ONE DOUBTS THE BRILLIANCE OF LEE WEST'S legal mind and his ability to "cut to the chase" in considering any complicated matter presented in his courtroom. However, it is Lee's candid and incredibly humorous outlook on almost every situation that arises in life that has made him an Oklahoma legend.

When he was chided for having Thanksgiving dinner in 1990 with the downtrodden at the Vici Café in Vici, Oklahoma, Lee rebuffed accusations that he had sneaked into the soup line on purpose. He admitted that he was dressed in his hunting overalls with an "older shirt" underneath and that he stopped by the café in his beat-up pickup truck.

After hearing the story, Ada attorney Michael G. Smith, a good friend, wrote Lee alleging that he represented the homeless of Vici. Smith said, "Our clients find despicable this act in the light of the fact that you are a federal judge and had just gotten a substantial pay raise. Besides, you ate too much and didn't need the meal."[1]

In a letter to Smith, Lee said he had been deprived of a traditional Thanksgiving dinner in the "bosom of his family" because his daughter Kim had convinced his "weak wife" to spend the holiday at the race track. Lee wrote, "I confess that I looked the part of all the other homeless partakers in the Vice Café because I was en route to a quail hunt and was dressed accordingly, plus I had the normal downtrodden look on my countenance of one who had just been abandoned by his family for the ponies."[2]

Lee justified his Thanksgiving dinner with the Vici homeless by writing, "Even though the managers/providers of the wonderful meal refused payment, I did contribute generously to a charity cup sitting by the cash register."[3]

At the June 10, 1994, swearing in of Tenth Circuit Court of Appeals Judge Robert Henry, Lee appeared on the printed program to give "defamatory remarks." As Chief Judge of the Western District, Lee had the responsibility to assign space in the federal courthouse. Reminding his audience, that included former United States Senator David Boren and Henry Bellmon, that appellate judges were always correcting the mistakes of trial judges, Lee said his first inclination was to put Judge Henry in a small closet without a telephone.[4]

On second thought, Lee said, and after cooler heads prevailed among his colleagues, he assigned Henry to a room with no windows and no bathroom. Lee said, "If he were deprived of bathroom facilities for several days, he would more quickly approach the attitude and outlook on life possessed by his more experienced brethren called appellate judges." Lee quipped, "He would, therefore, fit in more quickly to their way of thinking and doing business. As best I can tell, the plan is working perfectly."[5] The very first judge reversed by Judge Henry was, of course, Lee.

In 1994, when Lee's term as chief judge ended and he announced his move to senior status, his portrait was unveiled to hang in honor in the ceremonial courtroom in the Oklahoma City Federal Courthouse. Unknown to Lee, his old friend Bill Christian had superimposed a picture of a bird dog over Lee's portrait. When Lee and Mary Ann's granddaughter, Mary Ellis, unveiled the "bird dog portrait," everyone had a good laugh. When Lee's actual portrait was revealed, there were several cries of "put that dog back up!" The audience's reaction was, according to Christian, "like yelling to an ancient stripper, 'Put them on, put them on!'"[6]

At the portrait unveiling, Lee thanked Mary Ann, his sisters, his staff, his two daughters, and his "almost perfect" granddaughter, Mary Ellis. He paid homage to the three men—Henry Bellmon, David Boren, and Carl Albert—whom he said were most responsible for his career on the bench.

Noting that with senior status he would have less of a caseload and more leisure time, Lee said, "I have a couple of young bird dogs that I am uncommonly excited about—hopefully they are as good as their papa was. I intend to try to find out, starting this week." The young dogs were Barshoe Hard Twist and Barshoe Esquire who have since won 12 championships and eight runner-up crowns.

There is a serious and compassionate side that those close to Lee know about. He is a best friend to many people. His colleagues, both Republican and Democrat, have nothing but high praise for his skills as a judge. He would give the shirt off his back to his friend--and maybe his enemies.

One story of understanding and compassion involved Mary Ann's Aunt Allen Ellis who was like a mother to Mary Ann after Mary Ann lost her mother at age 12. Aunt Allen was an educated woman, attending business college in Paris, Texas, at the turn of the 20th century before moving north to Antlers. She worked her way up from a $25-a-month clerk at the First National Bank of Antlers to vice president. She worked at the bank until she was 82.

In 1980, at the age of 94, she came to live with Lee and Mary Ann. She was a delightful houseguest. Her mind was still sharp. Her only concern was that she would become a burden for Lee and Mary Ann. She often asked Mary Ann to look into a nursing home she might go to—just in case.[8]

MY COLLEAGUES

As I had on the state bench, I have formed close and lasting friendships with my colleagues on the federal bench.

Despite my celebrated—but exaggerated—irreverence for appellate judges, I have great respect for Judge Stephanie Seymour, former Chief Judge of the Tenth Circuit. Judge William J. Holloway, Senior Circuit Judge, is easily the kindest, most gentle friend I have. Robert Henry, with whom I joust often, is a truly brilliant man with unlimited ability as a jurist. He is easy to envy—and even easier to admire.

I have warm, long lasting friendships with Judges Jim Ellison and Tom Brett. I have long admired Judge Frank Seay because of his core of decency. Terry Kern, Sven Holmes, and Claire Egan are truly great judges in the Northern District, as are Judge Jim Payne and Dale Cook in the Eastern District. We lost two magnificent young judges when Mike Burrage and Layn Phillips resigned to return to the riches of private practice.

My colleagues in the Western District are, among other things, my closest friends. I have known Ralph G. Thompson since law school. He is a man of unusual talent and accomplishment. Wayne Alley has served as a general in the JAG, as the dean of the OU Law School, and as a federal judge—all with distinction. Tim Leonard served in the Oklahoma State Senate and was United States Attorney before bringing his common sense judgment to the federal bench. I lunch with them at least thrice weekly and, despite my efforts, they all remain somewhat confused in their political philosophy. Stephen Friot and Joe Heaton have quickly proven to be outstanding trial judges, capable of making lasting contributions.

Chief Judge Robin Cauthron and Judge Vicki Miles-LaGrange have already demonstrated the inevitability of a *world led and dominated by women—and almost certainly a better world for it. I say this despite their indignant refusal to accept my generous offer of a burka to sew on their robes.*

Lastly, I need to mention Judge David L. Russell, who is the co-author of this epic tale. Since he has the last word, I must be very careful in describing him.

Suffice it to say that I have long considered David Russell as my role model for judicial objectivity, just as I considered Judge Luther Bohanon my role model for judicial courage. In addition, I admire Judge Russell's enormous intellectual capability. Most importantly over the years, he has become one of my closest friends, who shares my deepest thoughts and literary and sporting interests more than any other man with the possible exception of John Harmon and Bill Paul. All of them are Just Friends *in the sense that Baxter Black means when he says in his poem of the same name, "You can't be more than just friends." I have an enormous amount of affection and respect for all of my comrades.*

As Aunt Allen became more frail, Lee had to help her out of her chair each evening as she prepared for bed. One time, as Lee took her hands to help her, she looked at him and said, "Lee, I've become a burden to you." Lee replied, "Oh, no, you're not a burden at all. In fact, I'm really glad you're here."[9]

Then, Aunt Allen disarmed Lee when she asked, "Why?" Lee said, "Well, with Mary Ann here and Kim and Jennifer in and out all the time, I sometimes think you're the best friend I have in this house." Aunt Allen looked at Lee and smiled, "Sometimes I think I'm the only friend you have in this house." Aunt Allen lived with Lee and Mary Ann until she suffered a massive stroke and died just weeks before her 98th birthday.[10]

Lee's softer side was remembered by daughter Jennifer, "On one of my parents' wedding anniversaries, Dad made a speech. He said that one of the greatest gifts a man can give his children is to love their mother." Jennifer and Kim both believe they are truly blessed by their father's love for their mother.[11]

Many awards have come Lee's way in his nearly four decades of public service. In 1981, the Oklahoma Trial Lawyers Association gave him the Outstanding Federal Trial Judge Award.

In February, 2000, Lee was presented the prestigious Humanitarian Award by the National Conference for Community and Justice (NCCJ), formerly known as the National Conference of Christians and Jews. Lee had been aware of the organization since his teenage years when young Christian minister Bill Pharr in Antlers had told him of the group's efforts to combat bias, racism, and bigotry. The NCCJ was formed in 1927 by forward thinking individuals such as Chief Justice Charles Evans Hughes and Justice Benjamin Cardozo.

In a rousing speech about protecting individual liberties, especially of the downtrodden and oppressed, Lee quoted two of his longtime friends. He said he once asked Tulsa oilman Julian Rothbaum how he managed to get along with everyone so well. Rothbaum had told Lee, "Judge, when you grow up as the only

Mary Ann, left, and Kim, on a 1995 boating trip.

Jewish boy in Hartshorne, Oklahoma, you have to learn to get along with everyone."12

Lee quoted Bill Christian, with whom Lee had recently ridden to House Speaker Carl Albert's funeral in McAlester. Lee asked Christian how he had been doing. Christian said, "I have just been trying to be the kind of man that my dog thinks I am." Lee thought that was not a bad definition of a humanitarian.13

In November, 2000, Lee was the recipient of the Judicial Excellence Award of the Oklahoma Bar Association. The *Oklahoma Bar Journal* called him a judge who possesses "a judicial

Jennifer, left, and Mary Ann in 1994.

University of Oklahoma President David Boren, left, presented Lee with the 2000 Humanitarian Award presented by the National Conference for Community and Justice. After receiving the award, Lee was chided by friend J. Duke Logan who said, "How can you be honored by the Christians and Jew—when you are neither?"

temperament that allows litigants and their lawyers to have a full and fair opportunity to present their case." Lee was only the second federal judge to win the award—the first was Judge Tom Brett.[14]

At a ceremony installing new federal judge Michael Burrage, Judge Frank Seay of the Oklahoma's Eastern District introduced Lee as "Oklahoma's most popular federal judge." Lee's quick response was, "That is somewhat akin to being called the tallest building in Antlers."[15]

As a senior United States District Judge, Lee continues to hear federal court cases and still serves as a settlement conference judge in especially complex cases. He also spends time with his dogs and horses. He said, "Although I am still competing and working dogs, I am slowing down considerably." He blamed old age, arthritis, and obesity.

Of his combat with fellow bird dog field trialers, he said, "The paucity of the game has a disheartening effect. I am not much of a threat to anyone. My young flat-bellied friends, some of whom might be considered protégés, are 'wearing me out' and let me win only infrequently now. It is a small consolation that they are sometimes beating me with my own bloodlines."[16] Even so, Lee's dogs have won four major championships in 2001 and 2002.

Lee still plans to compete on a regular basis, although he "may have to develop shorter horses and slower dogs." He is still looking for another great dog. But even if he never raises another champion pointer, he says, "I've already been blessed with more than my fair share."[17]

Lee continues to impart his vast knowledge of the federal court system to law students at OU. In 1999, he began a seminar on federal litigation practice and procedure for second and third year students. The seminar, now managed by Judge Tim Leonard, gives law students an opportunity to become acquainted with federal court practice and to meet and mingle with federal judges and prosecutors who appear as special lecturers.

Duke Logan compares Lee to the object of an old cowboy saying, "He's the kind of guy you want to ride the river with." Logan wrote, "It means when you go to cross a swollen river, pick someone to ride alongside so that, if you step off in a hole, he's the kind of guy who will turn back and help you across. Lee Roy has been riding back into deep water helping others all his life."[18]

OU Law School Dean Andy Coats and Lee have regularly exchanged insults and accolades over the years. In paying tribute to Lee, Coats said, "No one I have ever known is as universally loved and respected as Lee. Although he rose from humble beginnings to hold high public office for most of his adult life, he never lost his humility, his humanity, his essential kindness, his great and good humor, his generosity of spirit, or his love and respect for his fellow man."[19]

Left to right, Lee's nephew, Charles Snuggs, his wife Sharon, Lee, and niece, Sandra Mantooth.

Left to right, Jennifer, granddaughter Mary Ellis, and "Grandpa Lee" shortly after Mary Ellis's birth in 1986.

ABOVE: Mary Ann, left; Kim's husband, Greg Saunders; Kim; and Lee at Kim's swearing in as a judge on the Oklahoma Workers' Compensation Court. In June, 2000, Kim became a United States Magistrate Judge for the Eastern District of Oklahoma.

"The West girls" in 1999. Left to right, Jennifer, Mary Ellis, Kim, and Mary Ann.

Lee, right, and his "nearly perfect" granddaughter, Mary Ellis, who Lee calls "Mugwump."

Coats saved perhaps his greatest tribute to Lee for the unveiling of Lee's portrait in the federal courthouse in 1994. Coats said:

> You never, never see Lee West that you don't leave feeling a little bit better. Maybe the best thing you can do for your friends and the people around you is to raise their spirits.
>
> When you come in this courtroom in the future…your stomach is in knots, and you're getting ready to try a lawsuit…look up on this picture and think, "Brother, if Lee made it, so can I." Because when you look up there and think about Lee West, you will smile.[20]

epiLogue

ANY READER PERNICIOUS ENOUGH to proceed to this part of the book must have some contradictory conclusions about Judge Lee West. His often earthy humor, his expressed but not acted upon partisanship, his unbridled engagement with controversial subjects when not acting as a judge--all of these things are rather uncharacteristic of that unique and sometimes stiff society that constitutes the federal bench in America. But, as has been shown, Judge West also has other more traditional attributes of those who inhabit the judiciary. Lawyers of all ilks praise his fairness, his preparation, his active participation in settlement matters, and his not overly active interference with litigation matters. Indeed, the latter traditional strengths may even manage to overcome the former eccentricities. Truly, Lee's only great fault is his inadequate reverence for appellate judges.

This book has recounted Judge West's successful and remarkably varied career—perceptive student, accomplished Harvard law graduate, country lawyer, state trial judge, member of the Civil Aeronautics Board and finally its Chairman, urban private practitioner, and conclusively, we think, federal judge. Lee has both litigated and presided over his share of bizarre and important trials and proceedings.

Given such accomplishment, Lee could rest on his laurels, either by taking complete retirement or by simply not coming into the office particularly often. In his case, retirement would probably mean doing three things full time: (1) dog-trainin' and bird

huntin', (2) reading, and (3) presentation of political commentary-
-especially to those who'd prefer not to hear it. But, thankfully, that
is not going to happen. Lee's wonderful wife, Mary Ann, assures
me that Lee works as hard now as ever, although perhaps directing
himself a little differently, "As long as he is able to function and
move and go, he is going to do just what he is doing now." Such is
probably for the best, as one can easily imagine Lee getting in the
way at home. In any event, Lee is likely to stay out of the way, if
only because Mary Ann, who happens to agree with Lee's politics,
might fail to demonstrate adequate shock or offense at his pro-
nouncements.

Thus, Judge West will continue to be, and to do, what I most
like about him. He will continue to be a great, but selective,
teacher; an intellectual, with a voracious appetite for books--a
fighter and a referee after the style of the Marquis of Queensbury;
and, above all, a humanist and friend.

As a teacher, Lee will continue to take on a few clerks, often in
conjunction with one of the better talent scouts around, University
of Oklahoma President David Boren. Lee will also drop in, perhaps
more often, to those younger judges who have yet to obtain the
exalted status of "senior," to talk about, not just politics, but law
and human nature. Anil Gollahalli, after graduating from the
University of Chicago Law School, recently wrote me about his
mentor, "Serving as a law clerk for Judge Lee R. West was a wonderful introduction into the legal profession. While the exposure to
the court system was valuable, the true benefit of the clerkship
came from getting to know the Judge. Never have I met a man so
full of contradictions; he defies every stereotype and both
Oklahoma and the federal bench are better for it."

Gollahalli continued, "His southeastern Oklahoma roots are
clear. Even after having served as a federal judge for over twenty
years, Lee maintains a country wisdom and charm that allow him
to connect with people in ways that others cannot. At the same
time, the knowledge and experience gained from his years as a lec-

turer at OU and at Harvard, practicing attorney, state judge, member of the Civil Aeronautics Board, and federal judge allow him to quickly grasp complex issues and make informed decisions. The most valuable lessons I learned came from watching the Judge. Every case, regardless of the money or parties involved, garnered the same consideration. He has a deep sense of right and wrong and is courageous enough to stand up for what he believes. He knows the law and he knows what's fair. In sum, he is what a judge should be. It was an honor working for him."

As to Lee's status as an intellectual, that too will persist. I remember a seminar that the Federal Judicial Center arranged for judges in this district not long ago; we had a wonderful literature professor from Brandeis University. The professor posed a difficult question on *The Death of Ivan Ilyich*. Lee answered the question, picking up the theme in other Russian authors from Tolstoy to Turgenev. The manner in which Lee expounded, in his southeastern Oklahoma dipthongs, those somewhat dark and fatalistic Russian visions that were the subject before us was as amusing to us as it was astounding to our guest. Lee made us all look good. I bounced him out about this later, and he confessed, "One summer I just decided to read all the great classical Russian authors."

Lee's intellectualism is fairly private now, usually expressed in conversations with his colleagues or friends. But, occasionally, in an opinion or in an address such as his recent remarkable speech to the National Conference for Community and Justice, Lee will go public with unvarnished wisdom or intellect. Would that it could happen more.

And as to the "fighter and referee," all indications suggest that Judge West will continue to be available for heavy judicial lifting, taking a healthy share of cases, and continuing to excel at handling the difficult cases that just seem to seek him out. Whether the litigants be hate-mongering "reverends," pugilistic FBI agents, or religious mystics that converse with aliens, Lee West will provide unstintingly fair procedures and legal rulings.

Oklahoma's "poet lariat," Will Rogers, authored one of my favorite sayings, "It's great to be great, but it is greater to be human." Judge Lee West would certainly meet that observation. I have joked with him and publicly (and only in good fun, I would hasten to add) debated him on the topic of the relevant merits of trial and appellate judges. I have affirmed his cases, and reversed them--indeed, his was the first reversal I wrote. (He called me, advising, "Well, Henry, it didn't take you long!") Happenstance forces me to occasionally "grade his papers." But, when I write an article, it is choice that leads me often to run a draft by Lee.

Most of all, I enjoy the days when Lee calls up, announcing that he wants to drop by and show me something. It is always an interesting article, a new book, or most often, a perceptive article confirming a long-held West position, "When you're right so seldom, you can't help but say I told you so."

I am very grateful that Lee West's humanism is his humanity. We have every reason to believe that he will for many years continue to speak his mind. He, with Thomas Cahill, will argue that "without justice there is no God." He will speak out against the death penalty, noting the shocking truths revealed by corruption investigations or DNA evidence. He will rail against religious intolerance, bigotry, and bias. And yet, when he dons the judicial robe, even his passion will be bridled, channeling all his intellect and training into simply finding the law in the situation before him. In Henry Bellmon's long list of great accomplishments, the appointment of Lee West will be near the top.

Another part of Lee's humanity is his friendship. His life recalls Sam Houston's criticism of an adversary, "He has all of the characteristics of a dog except fidelity." Fidelity to his friends—loyalty—is simply not questioned with Lee. Not long ago a noted federal judge came into town to make a speech. Although most of our colleagues demurred, Lee and I went to the event, walking our colleague downtown to the meeting.

On the way back from the speech, the judge, demonstrating a certain obliviousness as to where he was, recounted that he had entertained Carl Albert, Speaker of the United States House of Representatives, some years earlier when the judge had occupied a State department position in Eastern Europe. The judge made a couple of highly critical remarks--remarks which Lee and I greeted with stony silence in hopes that the judge might recall where he was and with whom he was walking. Nonplussed, the judge rambled on in criticism of the highest ranking national leader Oklahoma has ever produced, and a leader who happened also to be a close personal friend of both of his hosts. Finally, the judge suggested that Speaker Albert liked to drink too much. Lee stopped walking, turning to cast our guest the sort of look usually reserved for a possum raiding the henhouse right before the shotgun goes off. "You don't pick up much on the subtleties, judge. But let me try to make it simple for you. Drunk or sober, Carl Albert was the best man you ever met." I doubt that the judge concurred, but if silence doesn't mean assent, it at least meant a more pleasant walk back to the courthouse. Now Carl Albert's accomplishments speak for themselves, but as to his consumptive habits, he only made it to 92 years of age--I wonder what he was drinking?

You know, after ruminating on Judge West for quite a while, thinking about his teaching, his intelligence, his superb legal work, his humanity and friendship--I must say that, just maybe now, Lee could have made a half-decent appellate judge.

Nah!

JUDGE ROBERT HENRY
*United States Court of Appeals
for the Tenth Circuit*

Notes

Hard Times in Little Dixie

1. Bob Burke and Von Russell Creel, *Lyle Boren: Rebel Congressman* (Oklahoma City: Western Heritage Books, 1991), p. 30-31.

2. Bob Burke, *Good Guys Wear White Hats: The Life of George Nigh* (Oklahoma City: Oklahoma Heritage Association, 2000), p. 21.

3. Robert S. Kerr, *Land, Wood and Water* (New York: Fleet Publishing Corporation, 1960) p. 14.

4. Interview with Robert E. Lee, January 9, 2002, Archives, Oklahoma Heritage Association, Oklahoma City, Oklahoma, hereafter referred to as Heritage Archives.

5. John Steinbeck, *The Grapes of Wrath* (New York: The Viking Press, 1939), p. 1.

6. Milton D. Rafferty and John C. Catau, *The Ouachita Mountains* (Norman: University of Oklahoma Press, 1991), p. 169-170.

7. Recollections of Lee Roy West, unpublished memoirs dictated in the summer and fall of 2001, Heritage Archives, hereafter referred to as Recollections of Lee Roy West.

8. Interview with Deloyce West Johnson, August 15, 2001, Heritage Archives.

9. Recollections of Lee Roy West.

10. Ibid.

11. Ibid.

12. Ibid.

13. Interview with Joe Stamper, October 15, 2001, Heritage Archives.

Settling Down in Antlers

1. Recollections of Lee Roy West.

2. Letter from Kimberly West to authors, March 5, 2002, Heritage Archives.

3. Letter from Joe Packnett to the authors, June 18, 2001, Heritage Archives.

4. George H. Shirk, *Oklahoma Place Names*, (Norman: University of Oklahoma Press, 1965), p. 9.

5. Recollections of Lee Roy West.

6. Ibid.

7. Ibid.

8. Ibid.

9. Ibid.

10. Ibid.

11. Ibid.

12. Ibid.

13. Francis L. and Roberta B. Fugate, *Roadside History of Oklahoma*, (Missoula, Montana: Mountain Press Publishing Company, 1991), p. 88.

14. Recollections of Lee Roy West.

15. Ibid.

16. Ibid.

17. Ibid.

18. Ibid.

19. Ibid.

20. Ibid.

21. Ibid.

22. Ibid.

23. Ibid.

Lightning Legs Leroy

1. Recollections of Lee Roy West.

2. Ibid.

3. Ibid.

4. Ibid.

5. Interview with Lee Roy West, September 10, 2001, hereafter referred to as Lee West interview.

6. Ibid.

7. Ibid.

8. Recollections of Lee Roy West.

9. Ibid.

10. Ibid.

11. *The Antlers* (Antlers, Oklahoma), February 27, 1947.

12. Ibid.

13. Recollections of Lee Roy West.

14. Ibid.

15. Letter from Joe Packnett to authors, June 28, 2001, Heritage Archives.

16. Ibid.

17. Ibid.

18. Ibid.

Off to College

1. Recollections of Lee Roy West.

2. Letter from Joe Packnett to authors, June 28, 2001, Heritage Archives.

3. Recollections of Lee Roy West.

4. Ibid.

5. Ibid.

6. Ibid.

7. Ibid.

8. Ibid.

9. Ibid.

10. Interview with Bernard "Bernie" Ille, August 14, 2001, Heritage Archives.

11. Recollections of Lee Roy West.

12. Interview with William G. "Bill" Paul, December 10, 2001, hereafter referred to as Bill Paul interview, Heritage Archives.

13. Bob Burke and Louise Painter, *Justice Served: The Life of Alma Bell Wilson,* (Oklahoma City: Oklahoma Heritage Association, 2001), p. 12.

14. John W. Dean. *Blind Ambition,* (New York: Simon and Schuster, 1976), p. 117.

15. Recollections of Lee Roy West.

16. Ibid.

17. Ibid.

Naval Cruises and More Classes

1. Recollections of Lee Roy West.

2. Ibid.

3. Letter from Duke Logan to authors, August 29, 2001, Heritage Archives.

4. Letter from Lee Jenkins to authors, September 20, 2001, Heritage Archives.

5. Recollections of Lee Roy West.

6. Letter from Lee Jenkins to authors, September 20, 2001, Heritage Archives.

7. Bill Paul interview.

8. Recollections of Lee Roy West.

9. Ibid.

10. Ibid.

11. Bill Paul interview.

12. Recollections of Lee Roy West.

13. Ibid.

14. Letter from Lee Jenkins to authors, September 20, 2001, Heritage Archives.

15. Ibid.

16. Recollections of Lee Roy West.

17. Ibid.

18. Bill Paul interview.

19. Recollections of Lee Roy West.

20. Ibid.

21. Ibid.

The Marines and Marriage

1. Edwin H. Simmons, *The United States Marine Corps,* (New York: The Viking Press, Inc., 1974), p. 1.

2. Recollections of Lee Roy West.

3. Ibid.

4. Ibid.

5. Ibid.

6. Letter from Lee Jenkins to authors, September 10, 2001, Heritage Archives.

7. Ibid.

8. Ibid.

9. Ibid.

10. Ibid.

11. Ibid.

12. Undated letter from Lee Roy West to Mary Ann West, Heritage Archives.

13. Ibid.

Clarence Darrow of the Second Battalion

1. Letter from Lee Roy West to Mary Ann West, August 24, 1953, Heritage Archives.

2. Recollections of Lee Roy West.

3. Ibid.

4. Ibid.

5. Interview with Bob Middlekauf, August 27, 2001, Heritage Archives.

6. Letter from Lee Roy West to Mary Ann West, December 5, 1953, Heritage Archives.

7. Ibid., December 7, 1953, Heritage Archives.

8. Ibid.

9. Ibid.

10. Ibid., March 11, 1954, Heritage Archives.

11. Ibid., March 11, 1954, Heritage Archives.

12. Ibid., March 23, 1954, Heritage Archives.

13. Recollections of Lee Roy West.

14. Ibid.

15. Ibid.

Hitting the Books
1. Bob Burke and Louise Painter, *Justice Served: The Life of Alma Bell Wilson*, (Oklahoma City: Oklahoma Heritage Association, 2001), p. 45.

2. Letter from David L. Fist to Lee West, October 5, 1954, Heritage Archives.

3. Letter from J. Duke Logan to authors, August 29, 2001, Heritage Archives.

4. Ibid.

5. Recollections of Lee Roy West.

6. Ibid.

7. Ibid.

8. Ibid.

9. Ibid.

10. Ibid.

11. Ibid.

12. Letter from John W. Hager to Lee West, July 25, 1955, Heritage Archives.

Practicing Law
1. Letter from Robert Nash to Lee West, May 4, 1956, Heritage Archives.

2. Francis L. and Roberta B. Fugate, *Roadside History of Oklahoma*, (Missoula, Montana: Mountain Press Publishing Company, 1991), p. 197.

3. Recollections of Lee Roy West.

4. Ibid.

5. Letter from Sam Crossland to Fred Mock, February 5, 1957, Heritage Archives.

6. Recollections of Lee Roy West.

7. Ibid.

8. Ibid.

9. Ibid.

10. Ibid.

11. Ibid.

12. Ibid.

13. Ibid.

14. Ibid.

Academia
1. Recollections of Lee Roy West.

2. Harvard College Website, www.harvard.edu

3. Recollections of Lee Roy West.

4. Ibid.

5. Ibid.

6. Ibid.

7. Ibid.

8. Ibid.

9. Ibid.

10. Ibid.

11. Ibid.

12. Ibid.

13. Ibid.

Appointment to the Bench
1. Interview with Jim Gassaway, August 5, 2001, Heritage Archives.

2. Interview with William "Bill" Christian, February 15, 2002, Heritage Archives.

3. Betty Crow and Bob Burke, *The House Oklahoma Built: The History of the Oklahoma Governor's Mansion*, (Oklahoma City: Oklahoma Heritage Association, 2001), p. 104-105.

4. Recollections of Lee Roy West.

5. Remarks of Henry Bellmon at the swearing in ceremony of United States Court of Appeals Judge Robert H. Henry, June 10, 1994, Heritage Archives.

6. Letter from Maurice Merrill to Lee West, August 20, 1965, Heritage Archives.

7. Interview with Bob E. Bennett, February 10, 2002, Heritage Archives.

8. Ibid.

9. Recollections of Lee Roy West.

10. Ibid.

11. Ibid.

12. Ibid.

Emmit Ray McCarthy
1. Recollections of Lee Roy West.

2. Ibid.

3. Ibid.

4. Ibid.

5. Ibid.

6. Ibid.

7. Ibid.

8. Ibid.

9. Ibid.

10. Ibid.

Familiarity Breeds Contempt
1. Recollections of Lee West.
2. Ibid.
3. Ibid.
4. Ibid.
5. Interview with Barney Ward, August 31, 2001, Heritage Archives.
6. Recollections of Lee Roy West.
7. Ibid.
8. Ibid.
9. Barney Ward interview.
10. Ibid.
11. Letter from Stephen Jones to authors, March 14, 2002, hereafter referred to as Stephen Jones letter, Heritage Archives.
12. Interview with Marian Opala, October 15, 2001, Heritage Archives.
13. Ibid.
14. Ibid.
15. Stephen Jones letter.
16. Stephen Jones letter.
17. Ibid.

Practical Jokes and Fate
1. Recollections of Lee Roy West.
2. Ibid.
3. Ibid.
4. Ibid.
5. Ibid.
6. Text of paper delivered by Lee West to the Oklahoma Judicial Conference, July 17, 1967, Heritage Archives.
7. Ibid.
8. Ibid.
9. Recollections of Lee Roy West.
10. Ibid.
11. Ibid.

The Civil Aeronautics Board
1. Recollections of Lee Roy West.
2. Ibid.
3. Ibid.
4. Robert Burkhardt, *The Federal Aviation Administration*, (New York: Frederick A. Praeger, Publishers, 1987), p. 26-27.
5. Recollections of Lee Roy West.
6. Bob Burke and Ralph Thompson, *Bryce Harlow: Mr. Integrity*, (Oklahoma City: Oklahoma Heritage Association, 2000), p. 231.
7. *The Wall Street Journal* (New York, New York), March 13, 1973.
8. *National Journal Reports* (Washington, D.C.), April 6, 1974.
9. Letter from Larry Derryberry to John M. Nelson, March 16, 1973, Heritage Archives.
10. *The Washington Post*, (Washington, D.C.), March 24, 1973.
11. Ibid.
12. *Aviation Week & Space Technology* (Washington, D.C.), April 2, 1973.
13. Ibid.
14. Ibid.
15. Letter from Denver N. Davison to Henry Bellmon, October 11, 1973, Heritage Archives.
16. Letter from Florence K. Murray to John Pastore, July 17, 1973, Heritage Archives.
17. Letter from Florence K. Murray to Lee West, July 23, 1973, Heritage Archives.
18. Letter from R.H. Coleman to Lee West, March 28, 1973, Heritage Archives.

19. Letter from Lavern Fishel to Lee West, July 16, 1973, Heritage Archives.
20. *National Journal Reports*, April 6, 1974.
21. *The Daily Oklahoman*, July 12, 1973.
22. Ibid.
23. Ibid.
24. *The Ada Evening News* (Ada, Oklahoma), July 13, 1973.
25. Ibid.
26. *Tulsa World* (Tulsa, Oklahoma), July 16, 1973.
27. Ibid.
28. Bob Burke and Ralph Thompson, *Bryce Harlow: Mr. Integrity*, p. 213.
29. Recollections of Lee Roy West.
30. Ibid.
31. Letter from Henry E. Peterson to Senator Warren Magnuson, October 13, 1973, Heritage Archives.
32. *National Journal Reports*, April 6, 1974.
33. Recollections of Lee Roy West.
34. Ibid.
35. Official transcript and report of the confirmation hearing of October 30, 1973, before the Subcommittee on Air Transportation, Committee on Commerce, United States Senate.
36. Ibid.
37. Ibid.
38. Ibid.

Airline Regulator
1. Recollections of Lee Roy West.
2. Ibid.
3. Ibid.

4. Interview with Juliana Winters, November 15, 2001, Heritage Archives.

5. Ibid.

6. Recollections of Lee Roy West.

7. Ibid.

8. Ibid.

9. Ibid.

10. Ibid.

11. Ibid.

12. Ibid.

13. Ibid.

14. *National Enquirer*, October 21, 1975.

15. Ibid.

16. Recollections of Lee Roy West.

17. Ibid.

18. Ibid.

19. Ibid.

20. Ibid.

21. Speech by Lee West to the Association of Local Transport Airlines, May 20, 1977, Heritage Archives.

22. Ibid.

23. Recollections of Lee Roy West.

24. Interview with John T. Golden, September 27, 2001, Heritage Archives.

25. Ibid.

26. Ibid.

27. Ibid.

Back to Oklahoma
1. Letter from Lee West to President Jimmy Carter, April 5, 1978, Heritage Archives.

2. Ibid.

3. *Tulsa Tribune* (Tulsa, Oklahoma), April 7, 1978.

4. Recollections of Lee Roy West.

5. Ibid.

6. Letter from Joe Stamper to Senator David Boren, January 31, 1979, Heritage Archives.

7. Letter from Frank T. Read to Griffin Bell, February 2, 1979, Heritage Archives.

8. Letter from Loyd Benefield to Alfred M. Pence, February 9, 1979, Heritage Archives.

9. Interview with Ellis Freeny, February 20, 2002, Heritage Archives.

10. Letter from Bert McElroy to Lee West, May 6, 1979, Heritage Archives.

11. Letter from J. Duke Logan to Lee West, May 4, 1979, Heritage Archives.

12. Undated letter from Kim West to Lee Roy West, Heritage Archives.

13. Undated letter from Jennifer West to Lee West, Heritage Archives.

14. Letter from President Jimmy Carter to authors, February 22, 2002, Heritage Archives.

15. Ibid.

16. Recollections of Lee Roy West.

17. Letter from Alfred E. Kahn, November 15, 1979, Heritage Archives.

The Federal Bench
1. Donald Dale Jackson, *Judges,* (New York: Atheneum, 1974), p. 248.

2. Ibid., p. 250.

3. Joseph C. Goulden, *The Benchwarmers: The Private World of the Powerful Federal Judges,* (New York: Weybright and Talley, 1982), p. 5.

4. Ibid., p. 8.

5. Ibid.

6. Ibid.

7. Ibid.

8. Ibid.

9. Ibid.

10. Ibid.

11. Ibid.

12. Ibid.

13. Ibid.

14. Letter from Stratton Taylor to authors, February 7, 2002, Heritage Archives.

15. Ibid.

16. Ibid.

17. Interview with Don Manners, February 1, 2002.

18. Ibid.

19. Interview with Cherri Farrar, March 20, 2002, Heritage Archives.

20. Letter from Ronnie D. Redbear to Lee West, January 25, 1984, Heritage Archives.

21. Ibid.

22. Ibid.

23. Letter from Lee West to Ronnie D. Redbear, July 2, 1984, Heritage Archives.

Scandals Galore
1. *The Daily Oklahoman,* January 12, 1986.

2. Ibid., December 10, 1981.

3. Ibid., January 28,1982.

4. Ibid., April 15, 1982.

5. Ibid., August 11, 1982.

6. Ibid., May 7, 1985.

7. Bob Burke, *Good Guys Wear White Hats,* (Oklahoma City: Oklahoma Heritage Association, 2000), p. 290.

8. *The Daily Oklahoman,* July 21, 1982.

9. Ibid., May 3, 1984.

10. Ibid., September 19, 1984.

11. Letter from Burck Bailey to authors, February 22, 2002.

12. Ibid.

13. *The Daily Oklahoman*, September 19, 1984.

14. Ibid.

15. Phillip L. Zweig, *Belly Up: The Collapse of the Penn Square Bank*, (New York: Crown Publishers, Inc., 1985), p. 420-421.

16. *The Daily Oklahoman*, September 28, 1984.

17. Ibid., August 17, 1985.

18. Ibid., August 22, 1985.

19. Stephen Jones letter.

20. Ibid.

21. *The Daily Oklahoman*, April 30, 1985.

22. Ibid.

23. Ibid., May 3, 1988.

24. Ibid.

Feuding with the FBI
1. Wen Ho Lee, *My Country Versus Me*, (New York: Hyperion, 2001), p. 7.

2. Recollections of Lee Roy West.

3. Ibid.

4. Ibid.

5. Ibid.

6. Ibid.

7. *The Daily Oklahoman*, June 25, 1995.

8. Letter from David L. Boren to authors, March 4, 2002, Heritage Archives.

9. Letter from Kimberly West to authors, March 5, 2002, Heritage Archives.

For Love of Dogs and Horses
1. Letter from John Harmon to Leo Winters, April 16, 1992, Heritage Archives.

2. Ibid.

3. Recollections of Lee Roy West.

4. Interview with Austin Deaton, Jr., November 1, 2001, Heritage Archives.

5. Ibid.

Field Trials
1. Letter from Thomas S. Word, Jr., to authors, July 17, 2001, Heritage Archives.

2. Ibid.

3. Ibid.

4. Ibid.

5. Ibid.

6. Ibid.

7. Ibid.

8. Ibid.

9. Letter from Kimberly West to authors, March 5, 2002, Heritage Archives.

10. Ibid.

11. Ibid.

12. Letter from Thomas Word, Jr., to authors, July 17, 2001, Heritage Archives.

13. Letter from Parke Brinkley to authors, August 22, 2001, Heritage Archives.

14. Letter from John Harmon to authors, February 5, 2002, Heritage Archives.

15. Letter from Griffin Bell to authors, February 26, 2002, Heritage Archives.

16. Letter from John Harmon to authors, February 5, 2002, Heritage Archives.

17. Ibid.

18. *The Daily Oklahoman*, April 8, 1973.

19. Ibid.

20. Letter from Jennifer West to authors, March 11, 2002, Heritage Archives.

21. Ibid.

22. Ibid.

23. Ibid.

24. Letter from J.B. Beall to authors, August 5, 2001, Heritage Archives.

25. Letter from Preston Trimble to authors, August 7, 2001, Heritage Archives.

26. Ibid.

27. Ibid.

28. Ibid.

29. Ibid.

A String of Champions
1. Recollections of Lee Roy West.

2. 1988 nomination for National Field Trial Hall of Fame, Heritage Archives.

3. Ibid.

4. Ibid.

5. Recollections of Lee Roy West.

6. Ibid.

7. Ibid.

8. Draft of magazine article submitted by Thomas Word, Jr., to authors, March 15, 2002, Heritage Archives.

9. Ibid.

10. Ibid.

11. Recollections of Lee Roy West.

12. Letter from John Harmon to authors, February 5, 2002.

13. Ibid.

14. Ibid.

15. Recollections of Lee Roy West.

16. Letter from John Harmon to authors, February 5, 2002.

17. Ibid.

18. Ibid.

19. Recollections of Lee Roy West.

Wine Ads and Courtroom Antics

1. *The Daily Oklahoman*, December 19, 1981.

2. Ibid., December 24, 1981.

3. Recollections of Lee Roy West.

4. Mary Ann West interview.

5. Interview with Stephen Friot, March 21, 2002, Heritage Archives.

6. The Daily Oklahoman, July 13, 1991.

7. Official transcript of *United States of America v. Alfred James Prince*, CR-90-96-W, Western District of Oklahoma, hereafter referred to as Prince transcript, Heritage Archives.

8. Ibid.

9. Recollections of Lee Roy West.

10. July 9, 1991 opinion of the United States Court of Appeals for the Tenth Circuit in *United States of America v. Alfred James Prince*, 90-6370, Heritage Archives.

11. Ibid.

12. Ibid.

13. May 5, 1989 order of Judge Lee West in *United States of America v. Donald Eugene Ryans dba Ryans*

Moving and Storage and Westside Movers, CR-89-12-W, Western District of Oklahoma, Heritage Archives.

14. Ibid.

15. Ibid.

16. *0*, April 27, 1982.

17. Ibid.

18. Ibid.

19. Ibid., September 25, 1982.

20. Letter from John Harmon to authors, February 5, 2002.

21. Recollections of Lee Roy West.

22. Transcript of Lee West-Robert Henry debate before a meeting of the Oklahoma City chapter of the Federal Bar Association, February 26, 2002, Heritage Archives.

23. Ibid.

Purely Personal

1. Letter from Michael G. Smith to Lee West, January 30, 1990, Heritage Archives.

2. Letter from Lee West to Michael G. Smith, February 2, 1990, Heritage Archives.

3. Ibid.

4. Transcript of the swearing in ceremony of Judge Robert H. Henry, June 10, 1994, Heritage Archives.

5. Ibid.

6. Interview with William "Bill" Christian, February 15, 2002, Heritage Archives.

7. Transcript of the Presentation of Portrait of Judge Lee R. West, November 29, 1994, Heritage Archives, hereafter referred to as Portrait Presentation.

8. Recollections of Lee West.

9. Ibid.

10. Ibid.

11. Ibid.

12. Transcript of February 24, 2000, speech of Lee West to the National Conference for Community and Justice, Heritage Archives.

13. Ibid.

14. *Oklahoma Bar Journal* (Oklahoma City, Oklahoma), September 26, 2000.

15. Recollections of Lee Roy West.

16. Ibid.

17. Ibid.

18. Letter from J. Duke Logan to authors, August 29, 2001, Heritage Archives.

19. Letter from Andy Coats to authors, January 15, 2002, Heritage Archives.

20. Portrait Presentation.

BIBLIOGRAPHY

NEWSPAPERS AND PERIODICALS

Ada Evening News
Ada, Oklahoma

Antlers American
Antlers, Oklahoma

Aviation Week and Space Technology
Washington, D.C.

National Enquirer
New York, New York

National Journal Reports
Washington, D.C.

New York Times
New York, New York

Oklahoma Bar Journal
Oklahoma City, Oklahoma

Oklahoma Journal
Midwest City, Oklahoma

The Antlers
Antlers, Oklahoma

The Daily Oklahoman
Oklahoma City, Oklahoma

The Washington Post
Washington, D.C.

Tulsa Tribune
Tulsa, Oklahoma

Tulsa World
Tulsa, Oklahoma

Wall Street Journal
New York, New York

BOOKS

Burke, Bob and Louise Painter. *Justice Served: The Life of Alma Bell Wilson*. Oklahoma City: Oklahoma Heritage Association, 2001.

Burke, Bob and Von Russell Creel. *Lyle Boren: Rebel Congressman*. Oklahoma City: Western Heritage Books, 1991.

Burke, Bob. *Good Guys Wear White Hats: The Life of George Nigh*. Oklahoma City: Oklahoma Heritage Association, 2000.

Burke, Bob and Ralph Thompson. *Bryce Harlow: Mr. Integrity*. Oklahoma City: Oklahoma Heritage Association, 2000.

Burkhardt, Robert. *The Federal Aviation Administration*. New York: Frederick A. Praeger, 1987.

Crow, Betty and Bob Burke. *The House Oklahoma Built: The History of the Oklahoma Governor's Mansion*. Oklahoma City: Oklahoma Heritage Association, 2001.

Dean, John W. *Blind Ambition*. New York: Simon and Schuster, 1976.

Fugate, Francis L. and Roberta B. *Roadside History of Oklahoma*, Missoula, Montana: Mountain Press Publishing Company, 1991.

Goulden, Joseph C. *The Benchwarmers: The Private World of the Powerful Federal Judges*. New York: Weybright and Talley, 1982.

Jackson, Donald Dale. *Judges*. New York: Atheneum, 1974.

Kerr, Robert S. *Land, Wood, and Water*. New York: Fleet Publishing Corporation, 1960.

Rafferty, Milton D. and John C. Catau, *The Ouachita Mountains*. Norman: University of Oklahoma Press, 1991.

Shirk, George H. *Oklahoma Place Names*. Norman: University of Oklahoma Press, 1965.

Simmons, Edwin H. *The United States Marine Corps*. New York: The Viking Press, Inc., 1974.

Steinbeck, John. *The Grapes of Wrath*. New York: The Viking Press, 1939.

Zweig, Phillip L. *Belly Up: The Collapse of the Penn Square Bank*. New York: Crown Publishers, Inc., 1985.

INDEX